The Bewildered Society

THE

BEWILDERED

SOCIETY

George Charles Roche III

Arlington House   *New Rochelle, N.Y.*

To Muriel and Al
I think they would like to be together on this one.

Library of Congress Catalog Card Number 76-183677

ISBN 0-87000-155-8

MANUFACTURED IN THE UNITED STATES OF AMERICA

CONTENTS

1. *THE AGE OF BEWILDERMENT*

2. THE POLITICS OF BEWILDERMENT

1
The Age of Bewilderment

PROLOGUE

We do not know what is happening to us, and that is precisely the thing that is happening to us — the fact of not knowing what is happening to us. Modern man begins by being disoriented with respect to himself, *de payse;* he is outside his own country, thrust into new circumstances which are like an unknown land. Such is always the vital sensation which besets man in periods of historical crisis.

José Ortega y Gasset,
Man and Crisis

The twentieth century has characteristically adopted a self-congratulatory tone. Modern society assures itself that we are all better fed, better housed, better educated, with more leisure time, more cultural opportunities, and more of all the features which make for the good life. Still, while many inhabitants of this promised land may be consuming more, they seem to be enjoying it less.

Meanwhile, the social philosophers of our age are characterized chiefly by a thoroughgoing pessimism. Judging from the great majority of their works, the whole affair is about to blow up in our faces. Oswald Spengler set the tone for this pessimism, though he was far from the first prophet of doom. The decline of Western civilization has been a favorite theme ever since. Soren Kierkegaard in the nineteenth century, Pitirim Sorokin, Arnold Toynbee, and any number of others in this century, have added their depressing chapters to the analysis of modern civilization. It would be comforting to dismiss all such commentators as cranks, but the nagging doubt remains — they may be right.

As the result, most of us are more than a little confused. We are constantly told that we've never had it so good, that the problem of material needs is now solved, that the high road to "Progress" opens before us. Yet something inside us seems to suggest that the pessimists may be right after all. Never have racial tensions been more sharply defined; never have our young people displayed more disdain for the institutions and values of society; never has it been more apparent that increased material prosperity is a sadly incomplete answer to the fulfillment of peoples' lives. Our cities are filthy, our wilderness is disappearing, our public entertainment reaches new lows in taste, our educational structure totters between regimentation and anarchy; worst of all, more and more of us seem unable to find a genuine identity in the sea of change which surrounds us.

In this age of bewilderment, we are all quick to point out the many problems we face, and even quicker to place the blame upon some element or another within society. While we are assigning that blame, we might properly assign a bit more of it to ourselves, for our acquiescence in a system which makes so little of individuals, and for our failure to realize what has been happening to America in the twentieth century.

It is an unfortunate fact that men are peculiarly adaptable to the environment in which they find themselves. We accept restraints quite readily, if those restraints are added piecemeal to our lives. Without intending to, we lose sight of the things which give our lives human purpose and direction. Soon we reach the point at which we urge our young men to give their lives for something called the American Way of Life — which proves upon examination to be an amazing injunction to *die* for a higher standard of *living*.

Once these systematic restraints and distortions of life are sufficiently far advanced, all reasonable discussion is replaced by sloganizing. Once people's emotions are sufficiently inflamed by the distortions stemming from an inhumane scale of existence, there develops what C. G. Jung has described as a "psychic epidemic." There are signs throughout our society, especially among our young people, that we are now reaching just such a point. In the process, the old landmarks of human existence are fast disappearing, the old loyalties seem to lack meaning. The promises of the social engineer and the state planner have come to sound hollow, but no more hollow than the clichés about "Free Enterprise" and the "Self-made Man."

The proper object of all social concerns should be men: Who are they? Who can they become? Such an inquiry involves far more than merely material concerns. When we neglect such nonmaterial values, we are left with the dead hand of economism as our only remaining guide. Economism may be able to tell us how to produce more goods, how to organize society more efficiently. It can tell us nothing about the men who must live in such a society.

Today we find ourselves increasingly concerned with attempts to secure a permanent material prosperity, to achieve "social stability." We no longer emphasize growth and individual diversity; instead, we prefer "security." We must make the child secure by limiting competition and achievement in the schools. We must protect the adult from the consequences of his actions. The businessman must not suffer competition; the thug must not suffer punishment.

While we thus increase a kind of "security," we do so by demanding increasing conformity from the individuals within the system. Socially imposed standards steadily reduce the individual's area of unique and personal development.

Today we are surrounded by warnings of the high price which such comformity demands of us. If men are to live as men, they must do so on a *human* scale which allows them to be truly men, not mere statistical cannon fodder. Men must have a higher purpose than to staff a mass industrial society.

Liberal and conservative both complain of the antihuman, depersonalized quality which has invaded American life. They both deplore the lack of taste, the lack of cohesion, the lack of direction which plagues our society. One blames "Big Business," the other "Big Government." Both might more accurately complain of "Big Society." Big Society passes under many names: collectivization, urbanization, proletarianism, enmassment. All of these terms and many more describe a society closely tied to massive organization and material goals.

In our rush to master nature, called "Progress" by some and "Industrial Development" by others, we seem to have loosed upon ourselves a process of enmassment which seems fated to continue until men's unique capacities and needs are swept aside in the rush to worship at the altar of giantism and material values.

Properly conceived, of course, the advances of science and industry could indeed help to provide man with a better life. But, unlimited and undirected by any concern for the individual, the process loses touch with the world of truly human scale. It may be argued that such criticism of "bigness" is out of touch with current realities. In point of fact, my criticism of enmassment and its effect on the individual is based on the assumption that enmassment itself, indeed, our entire present-day social order, is progressively further out of touch with reality — out of touch with a proper view of the individual and a proper understanding of his needs and shortcomings.

The Age of Bewilderment has many causes, only one of which is "Big Government," yet the critic of the government planning ideal has his finger upon an important point, perhaps *the* important point: Freedom *is* the highest goal. A man denied the chance to be a freely choosing moral agent is in effect being denied the exercise of precisely that quality of his nature which distinguishes him as a man. But so long as the advocate of freedom continues his defense of the present economistic, enmassed civilization, so long as we believe that "Big Government" is the only element in society which can threaten the full development of the individual, then we are seeing only part of the problem.

The ways in which enmassment has been produced in our society, creating an existence increasingly harmful to the individuals who live within it, are far more complex than we generally admit. The harm which enmassment perpetrates among us is also more pervasive than we realize. The problems of bureaucracy (both public and private), of urbanization, of technology — the ramifications for our psychological, moral, and cultural health — are all deeply involved in the question of enmassment. This book is an examination of such problems in present-day America.

> "Things reveal themselves passing away," someone remarked to William Butler Yeats, and it is an historical fact that every established order writes its great apologia only after it has been fatally stricken. When the forces of the old and the new come into crucial and dramatic conflict, then spokesmen appear to formulate the traditional assumptions and to defend what it had always been supposed could never be indicted.[1]

Life on the human scale is the cause which I would defend. Let us hope that such a cause need not "pass away" in order to rally its defenders.

[1]Richard M. Weaver, *The Southern Tradition at Bay* (New Rochelle, N.Y.: Arlington House, 1968), p. 112.

I

BUREAUCRACY

No civilization hitherto has been able to resist the destructive effect of urban and bureaucratic centralization. It has been well said that the great city is the grave of a culture, and in the same way the substitution of a centralized bureaucratic control for the spontaneous activity of normal social life involves a process of ossification and the senile decay of the whole social organism.

Christopher Dawson,
The Dynamics of World History

We live in the century of the Common Man. Presumably our political decisions and our social standards are determined by the Common Man's preferences. In reality, nothing could be further from the truth. As egalitarian politics has swept all before it, the individual citizen has found himself increasingly subservient to forces beyond his control. These social, political, institutional, and technological forces, acting in the name of the Common Man, have largely collectivized the lives of common men.

One of the key political assumptions of our age, deeply rooted in our technological progress, has been the ideal of *consumership*. Social progress is often measured in hedonistic terms. Presumably the more the Common Man consumes, the higher the state of our civilization. However uncivilized this measurement of "civilization" may be, such an appeal is always good democratic politics. It seems that there are no upper limits to the material appetites of us common men, and we like politicians who tell us we are "entitled" to the satisfaction of those appetites.

The gigantic political, social, and technological institutions which have sprung up in response to the politics of consumership have changed the traditional definitions of freedom. To define freedom as the chance to go your own way might have had meaning in a simpler age, but modern collectivized life — big business, big labor, big society, big education, big government — seems to make the practice of such freedom rather difficult for most individuals. How free to go their own way are most men today?

As a reaction against that loss of freedom, we have turned to government for protection of our interests. Thus we react to our loss of freedom by running ever further from freedom, straight into the arms of more collective control.

Unfortunately, those who would exercise that control are woefully unqualified to do so. After preaching the new doctrines of mass society, after rejecting the traditional moral foundations of our social order, much of today's intellectual leadership finds itself bankrupt when faced with the problems peculiar to our age. The effort to achieve "social justice" and "security" is doomed to failure unless a higher purpose than material concerns motivates our efforts. If the fullest development of the individual is our ultimate purpose, we must make the individual the referent for our institutions. The collectivization of the twentieth century has conspicuously failed to do this and has substituted mass and materialism as the dominant factors of modern life.

One of the factors fixing collectivism in all its forms most strongly upon the back of Western society is the idea, apparently shared by most of us, that big government, and the extensions of bigness which spread from government into the private sector, should be used as a problem-solving device in our lives. Not only do the "masses" demand such bigness, but even most of those alleged defenders of "free enterprise," the businessmen, are quick to appeal to government control to "stabilize" the marketplace, to regulate *their* competition. The limited government of the classical liberal has become the unlimited government of the modern liberal.

As a defender of individual freedom, the dominant liberal ethic of Western society is proving a conspicuous failure.

The Marxist State

While the liberal has found it increasingly difficult to define or defend a workable individual freedom in the twentieth century, the Marxist has followed a remarkably similar pattern. Like the present-day liberal, the Marxist favors using government to solve social problems. Like the present-day liberal, the Marxist tends to dismiss moral values as outworn remnants of bourgeois prejudices — relative at best, and usually negative in their total social impact. Like the present-day liberal, the Marxist has been primarily motivated by a vision of society in which man would achieve "freedom" from material concerns through the widespread application of technology. For both liberal and Marxist, utopia has been slow in arriving.

The 1930s witnessed a flirtation with Marxism by many liberal intellectuals. At last a rationale seemed available to explain the war, hunger, depressions, and fascism confronting the twentieth century. More important, Marxism seemed to offer a way out, a means by which "the people" might be truly "free" from the pressures and concerns plaguing modern life.

Marx, however, had misled his followers and their fellow-travelers with his assumption that class warfare would drive a wedge between the bourgeoisie and the proletariat. It would be a more accurate description of modern technological society to suggest that both bourgeoisie and proletariat are prisoners of the same system.

Mass-oriented technological society has demonstrated its capacity to build an enormous productive machine, but it apparently cannot recognize the necessity for maintaining a human dimension in its institutions — it has not provided room for the individual person. It might provide more material goods (although the Soviet regime has also been notably deficient on that score), but it does not seem to provide more freedom for the individual. Planning and bureaucracy seem to beget only more planning and bureaucracy. Whatever else may have happened with Karl Marx's prophesies, the Marxist state has certainly not withered away.

The Conservative Alternative

The rush to find security in big institutions, especially the institution of big government, is not peculiar to the modern world. The final disintegration of the Roman Empire brought such insecurity of person and property that the Roman freeholder rushed to sign over his holdings and his future to the nearest available noble powerful enough to promise security. "Better a serf than a corpse," seemed to be the motto of a society dissolving into anarchy. The modern world confronts the individual with a different sort of insecurity, based not upon anarchy, but upon enormous, impersonal forces apparently beyond the control of the individual. How does the individual order his life when faced with a society beyond his control?

The answer of the twentieth century has been the turn to government. We expect to be protected from massive impersonality by turning to the most massive impersonality of all: big government.

Some men, generally labeled conservatives, have perceived that big government is far more destructive than constructive in its results. But many of the opponents of big government have based their case too exclusively upon a narrowly economic base. When traditional American limited government, private property, and individual freedom are defended only by an appeal to material concerns, the case is given away to the liberal statist before the argument really begins, since a "conservatism" based upon material concerns is only the alter ego of the collective, secular, depersonalized, anticultural society which the liberal has already developed in America. The confused and distressed citizen already suspects that what is good for General Motors may not necessarily be good for him. He begins to perceive that it makes very little difference which definition of "bigness" and which standardized, sterotyped values are used, so long as the net effect is to render the individual obsolete.

Government Bureaucracy as the People's Friend

Liberal, egalitarian politics rolls over the American landscape almost without opposition. The shibboleth of democracy is invoked to convince people that popular sovereignty is king. One of our best kept secrets is that popular soverignty suffers constant abridgement. The key to maintaining political power in a democracy consists in successfully keeping that secret. The democratic politician rules the lives of the citizens only so long as he can pretend that he is not ruling their lives.

Sometimes the pretense wears a bit thin. The wielders of power begin to speak of "public apathy" and the "ignorant masses." The vanity of power convinces some men that society must be remade, whether or not the members of society understand the necessity for social overhaul. The long arm of mass communication reaches out to all of us and is used to describe how poorly society is operating — with poverty, exploitation, waste, and the rest of the sad picture which is constantly thrust before us. This picture, with problems seemingly so far beyond our limited individual competence, is then contrasted with the "positive action" which collective politics offers. Men with plans and power, men who "know what to do," announce themselves available to help us deal with these problems which are presumably so far beyond individual solution:

> The present disposition is to liquidate any distinction between State and Society, conceptually or institutionally. The State *is* Society; the social order is indeed an appendage of the political establishment, depending on it for sustenance, health, education, communications, and all things coming under the head of "the pursuit of happiness." In theory, taking college textbooks on economics and political science for authority, the integration is about as complete as words can make it. In the operation of human affairs, despite the fact that lip service is rendered the concept of inherent personal rights, the tendency to call upon the State for the solution of all the problems of life shows how far we have abandoned the doctrine of rights, with its correlative of self-reliance, and have accepted the State as the reality of Society. It is this actual integration, rather than the theory, that marks off the twentieth century from its predecessors.[1]

As all problems have been thrust into the political arena for their promised solution, we have forgotten that political action interferes with the processes of growth, because growth involves social interaction, and social interaction demands individual distinctions. Politics demand a degree of

[1]Frank Chodorov, *The Rise and Fall of Society* (New York: Devin–Adair, 1959), pp. xix–xx.

conformity which does not permit the individual an opportunity to make those distinctions.

Life lived on the collectivized political scale is life which to that extent has departed from the individual, human scale. When people are so stripped of human associations that government becomes their "state-appointed good friend," life on the human scale is drawing to a close.

The System Breaks Down

Unfortunately, the "state-appointed good friend" cannot deliver on his promises. Mr. Michael Harrington, author of *The Other America,* the 1962 book which presumably convinced the late President Kennedy that he should begin "The War on Poverty," now himself describes the condition of the poor *after* the development of the federal poverty program by saying: "Politically and morally it is worse than ever."

Mr. Harrington is not alone in his criticism of government projects motivated by humanitarian zeal and egalitarian politics. Such programs seem to produce generations of welfare recipients lacking both the means and the will to help themselves. What to do with such citizens? One is reminded of Aristotle's question: "Is 'democratic behavior' behavior democracies like, or behavior which will preserve a democracy?"

It seems that our materialistic emphasis, plus the democratic philosophy (as currently misconstrued) together produce corruption on an unprecedented scale. In Rome the leadership became corrupt and led the rest of society to destruction. In our more democratic and materially prosperous age, the means are available for corruption on all levels of society — now each of us can do the job for himself.

We are offered the choice of becoming manageable, of finding our place in a complex and standardized social order which treats people as objects. If we are willing to become objects, the rewards of the system are ours for the taking. Or, so the modern message goes.

The men who have thus lost faith in the individual have also lost any capacity to distinguish between education and manipulation. They are not evil men. In fact, they are so impatient to achieve good for society that they cannot wait upon the slow processes of education. Action *now.* The root assumption of that action is that men can be, *must* be, manipulated for their own good, for society's good. Thus the slogans, thus the depersonalized individual, thus life on a collective rather than a human scale.

Albert Einstein once described the crisis of our time:

> It concerns the relationship of the individual to society. The individual has become more conscious than ever of his dependence upon society. But he does not experience this dependence as a positive asset,

as an organic tie, as a protective force, but rather as a threat to his natural rights, or even to his economic existence.[2]

It is small wonder that many of us, especially the young, view bureaucracy's claims with such suspicion, when the inefficiences and failures of collective power pose such a threat to our continued existence as men. Not only does the system seem to work poorly — it also exacts a fearful psychological price.

Coercion

There is no shortage of reasons why the collective ideal proves so unpalatable. One of the most compelling reasons is the everlasting willingness to use compulsion. A crime wave? More policemen! Juvenile delinquency? Longer periods of compulsory education! No doubt there are occasions when society must use compulsion to protect itself — nearly all men of good will, conservative or liberal, would agree. Unfortunately, all too many of those same men, conservative and liberal, seem today to believe that most important advances in the human condition can be achieved only through compulsion. Too many of us believe that men can be forced to be good.

Every time we develop a blueprint to improve our society, some men rebel against our well-intended efforts. Someone is always asserting his uniqueness, acting in an incalculable manner, refusing to cooperate in our efforts to help. What can we do except regard such malcontents as sick men? What can we do but mistrust the individual? Thus reasons the social engineer of both "conservative" and "liberal" stripe. Thus we all reason when we are willing to use compulsion in the lives of others.

The central political fact of our time has been liberalism's capacity to sound like an embattled minority, when in reality its ideas are dominant and in fact constitute the "Establishment." The contemporary liberal thus makes political capital out of "revolt" against the elements of a superindustrial, technological, depersonalized, anticultural way of life, when in reality that society of which he complains is the logical result of the ideas he espouses. The secular state, a materialistic, mass-oriented culture, a proletarian population: These are the logical outgrowths of modern liberalism. When the pseudo-conservative contents himself with a defense of "business–civilization" against the rhetoric of contemporary liberalism, he finds himself defending the same antipersonal social organization which forms the core of the liberal Establishment. The individual citizen discovers himself to be without a spokesman. Surrounded by enmassment and its advocates at every turn, the individual is confronted with collective power reaching far beyond his capacities of control or direction.

[2]Adrienne Koch, ed., *Philosophy for a Time of Crisis* (New York: Dutton, 1960), p. 96.

All shades of the political spectrum talk of "freedom," but the individual finds that the freedom referred to is Robespierre's variety: Men are to be compelled to be free. Compulsion, direct and indirect, is the dominant characteristic of the age.

The popular and influential economist who wrote *The Affluent Society* believes that more middle-class income should be socialized since people spend their private funds foolishly. The middle class "ought" to have different values. Let us exercise compulsion to correct the situation! The poor, starved public sector deserves better treatment — so our Congress and President raise their salaries 50 to 100 percent while preaching to American citizens about the necessity for "holding the line on inflationary wage increases." And so it goes. Freedom is the most discussed word of our times, but the reality of our lives seems to be found in control and restraint, while the collective structure grows ever larger and more powerful. Thus do we demonstrate our love of "freedom."

We are all at fault. We wish to be free but are quick to urge that *our* professions require licensure, that *our* businesses need "stability," that *our* positions need tenure, that *our* retirement plans need government subsidy. Collectivism is in reality nothing more than the institution of group force to attain group goals. We all desire "freedom," but on the other hand, not so fast!

The Planning Ideal

In such a system, we all get exactly what we deserve. So long as we believe that mass technological society demands mass political solutions, we will find our lives ordered by the planning ideal and its grim results.

One of the modern analysts who perceived this most clearly was the Spaniard, José Ortega y Gasset:

> Society, that it may live better, creates the State as an instrument. Then the State gets the upper hand and society has to begin to live for the State. But for all that, the State is still composed of the members of that society. . . . This is what State intervention leads to: The people are converted into fuel to feed the mere machine which is the State. The skeleton eats up the flesh around it. The scaffolding becomes the owner and tenant of the house. . . .
>
> Society begins to be enslaved, to be unable to live except *in the service of the State.* The whole of life is bureaucratized. What results? The bureaucratization of life brings about its absolute decay in all orders.[3]

[3]José Ortega y Gasset, *The Revolt of the Masses* (New York: Norton, 1957), pp. 121–122.

It was Ortega's perception that bureaucratization brings with it men who have risen within the system precisely *because* they ignore the individual and allow no concern for personalities to block their exercise of power. In a mass-democratic age, such an attitude is dictated by the ruling passion of the masses. Soon it becomes the prime business of the bureaucrat to use the machinery at his disposal to crush any creative minority which disturbs the dull sameness of mass conformity, not merely in politics, but in industry, in education, even in matters of taste.

Those who believe that such bureaucratizaton is an exclusively modern phenomenon are dangerously mistaken. In times of crisis and rapid change, men have always turned to bureaucracy, to collective, coerced solutions for economic, political, and cultural problems. There is apparent security in bureaucracy and in bigness, public and private, political and social. Or so man hopes each time a new crisis confronts him.

The current crisis is largely technological in nature. As the power of technology has magnified men's impact upon their fellowmen, the consequences of our actions are more far-reaching than ever before. A man at the controls of a bulldozer has an impact far beyond that of a man with a shovel in his hands. The results of that technological change have become so frightening that we have flown to safety in bureaucracy, in a low-pressure, paternalistic, all-encompassing bigness which is extremely limiting to the individual, but which we hope will protect us from the full implications of technological change.

Individual Conformity

Today bigness presses upon the souls of men. Centralization demands simplicity. Bureaucracy cannot tolerate the diversity and complex interrelationships within which individual personalities thrive. The resultant simplification brings restraint and regimentation. The collective solution points the way toward a new anthropocentrism — a new faith in Man. A new technology and a new organizational principle demand a new social form, sacrificing the individual human being to the greatness of Man.

The primacy of the person over the machine has not been asserted by modern society. As a result, the apparent "efficiency" of technology has now been applied to human affairs:

> . . . confronted with the problem of organizing for a high technology, the response in both the East and the West has been to develop centralized bureaucratic, hierarchic organizations which are authoritarian and hence, stultifying in their effects on people. Technology, rather than being used to create a more humane society, has become the chief determinant of the forms and goals of human organization, and thus the societies of East and West wage battles around their GNP's, and respectively create mythologies around heroes of produc-

tion or consumption. In approaching the problem at this level, the distinctions between bureaucratic collectivism and corporate liberalism are seen as secondary to the fundamental similarities of style, structure, and value system. The fundamental authoritarianism exists in both cases, although expressed in different mixes of ideological appeal, bribed manipulation, and implicit or explicit coercion. But both systems diverge grossly from a libertarian ideal and fail to establish some of the basic conditions for a social order capable of maintaining the primacy of the person.[4]

The individual conformity thus demanded of man in the bureaucratic, technological society finally stultifies all growth. This is true because growth in knowledge has always come about when an individual has doubted some portion of the established concepts and tried to effect a change in them. It is this unpredictability about the individual and about established concepts that makes for growth. When the planning ideal interferes with that unpredictability, it kills the new ideas which make growth possible. Thus the planning ideal seems always doomed to failure in serving the interest of the men composing society.

War

In no area is that failure more readily apparent than in the tendency of the modern technological State to wage war and to reduce its individual citizens to cannon fodder.

Technical progress and conduct of war today are merging. We have reached a state of affairs where the technical potential of a state is the determining factor in the event of war. Superior technology means victory, inferior technology means defeat; that is the briefest possible formula to which a definite phase of technical progress can be reduced. This equation forces all modern states, with relentlessly increasing mechanical compulsion, to support, to speed up, and to push to the utmost the drive for technical perfection. For its own self-preservation, the modern state has to promote, and subject everything possible to, technical automatism. Since the technical potential is decisive in war, it is actually a form of armament. Technical progress now drops the economic mask it had been wearing in the early days of technical organization. Technically organized work becomes preparation for war; its connection with war becomes constantly more unmistakable.[5]

[4]"The Primacy of the Person," *Manas, XXI* (July 10, 1968), pp. 6–7.
[5]Friedrich Georg Juenger, *The Failure of Technology* (Hinsdale, Ill.: Regnery, 1949), p. 167.

The Cold War and its persistent tensions have generated a constant threat of mass destruction. Perpetual crisis has seemed to necessitate big government, the development of a highly advanced technological structure (in which men serve technology rather than technology serving men), and a close liaison between big government and big institutions in the private sector via defense contracts. The weapons industry, the space industry, the large research projects on our college campuses, all demonstrate the point.

Bureaucracy and Bureaucrats

Because we still have a largely pluralistic society, the full effects of our bureaucratization have been disguised from us. But the private sector today suffers from the same disease which afflicts the public sector. In one sense, bureaucracy is nothing more than an institutional form which evolved in response to the complexities of our society. But bureaucracy has also come to signify an empire-building leadership in charge of a conforming and timid rank and file. It has come to signify bigness for its own sake. Hierarchy and organization have become so stratified that the men working within the system simply cease to function as individuals. Bureaucracy has become the organizational form of modern life — life on an increasingly nonhuman scale.

However bureaucracy may originate, it seems to grow. In Parkinson's caustic phrase, "Those who hold that this growth is essential to gain full employment are fully entitled to their opinion. Those who doubt the stability of an economy based upon reading each other's minutes are equally entitled to theirs." It is reasonable to inquire whether or not those who foist superbigness on American society as the wave of the future stand to gain personally or professionally in the process. How many outspoken advocates of bureaucratic bigness stand to profit by such empire building? Advertising, mass communications, and education are among those areas which immediately come to mind as protagonists of the new society who frankly expect to play a hand in running the new order.

And thus bureaucracy and bigness feed and grow:

> It is much to be suspected that the oppressive weight of bureaucracy in our time (and in some other times) should be blamed in part upon the formal status that bureaucracy takes unto itself. Everyone who has tried to reform bureaucratic organizations has testified to the difficulty of touching them, to say nothing of cutting them down. The bureaucracy begins to assume an inner justification. Its size, its vertical height with the various strata of authority, and its many offices and channels add up to a form toward which one is invited, if not impelled, to take an attitude of aesthetic reverence. With so many people working together reinforcing each other's effort, and presenting a common

front to the world, there arises the image of a great creation. How can anyone strike at a thing so ostensibly designed to serve the needs of the community! To threaten it seems like threatening the very principle that underlies community and culture. The bureaucracy having acquired this status as another means of survival, endures, even when there is a crying need for its alteration or abolishment. A new entity has come into being to protect it: its formal structure as a thing in itself. By the time the critic has gotten past this, he may be too confused or too exhausted to continue.[6]

Bureaucracy thus becomes a contest for the pursuit and the maintenance of power. The modern "humanitarian" psychology promises us that such power, both public and private, will be used to "build a better society." But the exercise of that power always seems to involve compulsion. People must be molded into a certain behavior pattern — people must be restrained from other behavior patterns. Since more and more of us are members of one or more of these enormous institutions which manipulate society, we are peculiarly exposed to mass spiritual epidemics, to outside influences which act upon us as upon a mass, rather than as a collection of individuals.

The bureaucratic officeholder, the mass man who inhabits the gigantic institutional structure of our time, is discouraged by the very nature of the system from the exercise of any real responsibility. Institutional hierarchy and the mechanism of decision-by-committee guarantee that no genuinely responsible action can be taken. The individual finds himself divorced from the real world.

The technical official . . . who clerks in one of those numberless bureaus and lords it over some card file whose purpose — a purpose perhaps unknown to the official himself — is the rationalization on consumption: such a man might quite easily get the notion that all is well with the world because his files are in order. The scribe tends to confuse the world with a bureau, since his card file is his world, the center of his life. To conceive of the universe as a huge bureau would be an excellent idea if only nature had intended us to live on red tape.[7]

Modern American Tendencies

The bureaucratic tendency touches all aspects of our lives: law, government, business, labor, education, the tax-exempt foundations. Big organization is the distinguishing characteristic of the age. All social tasks of

---

[6]Richard M. Weaver, *Visions of Order* (New Rochelle, N. Y.: Conservative Book Club — Omnibus Volume #6, 1966), p. 237.
[7]Juenger, p. 142.

importance are today in the hands of large institutional structures. Yet the flaccid response of that organizational structure when it is directly challenged (as for example when the institution of big education is directly challenged by campus radicals) should lead us to wonder just how purposeful the whole structure really is.

All this may lead to the question: Well, who *really* runs things? What people fail to see is that, while it may take leadership to start things running, or to stop them, very little leadership is needed once things are under way — that, indeed, things can get terribly snarled up and still go on running. If one studies a factory, an army group, or other large organization, one wonders how things get done at all, with the lack of leadership and with all the feather-bedding. Perhaps they get done because we are still trading on our reserves of inner-direction, especially in the lower ranks. At any rate, the fact they do get done is no proof that there is someone in charge.[8]

Whether or not anyone is at the controls, the institutional juggernauts of our times continue to grow. Labor leaders have created their own inflexible hierarchy. Education has become an empire unto itself. Organized religion has its own version of institutional giantism. Much of the new managerial structure of business falls in the same category. Voluntary and charitable institutions have also grown enormously, as have the foundations. The Ford Foundation maintains larger staffs in many cities throughout the world than do most nation–states. Bigness is the central fact of our age.

The Committee

Accompanying this bigness has been the assumption that a group of people are better able to render decisions and solve problems than the individual. This attitude permeates current policy in business, education, religion, the military, and the professions. All decisions of consequence are now corporate. Leave it to the committee. The effect of this attitude is to relieve the participating individuals from personal responsibility.

Today the ideal committee member is the man who "adjusts," who works on the team. No creativity, no frankness, no individuality must interfere with that process. Today, method is king. It is in this fashion that bureaucracy robs men of their minds.

Bigness is not only the cause but the effect of the system. Endless boards and committees in our companies and foundations often make research funds available in terms of how large, how "safe" and how universally acceptable a proposed line of inquiry promises to be. Bureaucrats like

[8]David Riesman, et al., *The Lonely Crowd* (Garden City, N.Y.: Doubleday, 1953), p. 255.

bureaucratic projects; size lends respectability. Thus we institutionalize "no-think."

The Organization Man

It is easy to fight obvious tyranny; it is not easy to fight benevolence, and few things are more calculated to rob the individual of his defenses than the idea that his interests and those of society can be wholly compatible. The good society is the one in which they are most compatible, but they never can be completely so, and one who lets The Organization be the judge ultimately sacrifices himself. Like the good society, the good organization encourages individual expression, and many have done so. But there always remains some conflict between the individual and The Organization. Is The Organization to be the arbiter? The Organization will look to its own interests, but it will look to the individual's *only as The Organization interprets them.*[9]

That "organizational determination of interest" tends to dehumanize the individual, since he becomes limited to serving as a means of achieving institutional goals. To that extent, he ceases to be an individual. Such institutional life comes to be conducted without regard to persons. The activities of the individual within the institution are guided by a book of rules. The institutional structures which touch an individual's life come to dominate so large a portion of his capacities and attitudes that he takes his definition of life and personality from that collective experience. The road to success in such a system is through "adjustment," through losing one's self in the larger process, through learning to conform rather than create. Bureaucracy takes over when men are no longer willing to try or willing to think for themselves.

Just as the "Organization Man" has come to characterize much of modern business, so his counterpart is the commonplace in labor organization. More and more men, it seems, have a faith in the power of organization to assure their future.

If business and labor have both demanded of the individual that he find a place in "the system," our educational structure has made the same demand of the student and the teacher. No other aspect of our overinstitutionalized society has grown as fast as the university:

The old idea of the university as a loose association of individualists — if not outright eccentrics — each going his independent way has all but disappeared. Administrative office, once held in mild contempt

[9]William H. Whyte, Jr., *The Organization Man* (New York: Simon and Schuster, 1956), p. 397.

by the scholar, has gained in stature and power; and organization —
of course, of schools, or interdepartmental programs, and of research
— has become the order of the day. As administrators are taking over
and organization is coming to be valued above men, the dedicated
teacher–scholar is inevitably going out of fashion and being replaced
in favor by the academic bureaucrat. The latter is, in general outline,
hardly distinguishable from his brother in business or industry — less
prosperous by far, but almost equally subservient to the rules and
regulations of his professional office.[10]

Bureaucratic centralization, bigness for its own sake, institutional monstrosity repressing the individual into his place within the system, have
become the accepted standards of twentieth-century America. Our politics,
our economics and our social order all drive us in the same antipersonal
direction, with results which the following chapters should make abundantly clear.

[10]Richard LaPiere, *The Freudian Ethic* (New York: Duell, Sloan and Pearce, 1959), p. 234.

II

TECHNOLOGY

Today, as every day, I have heard of ugly congested cities, with polluted atmosphere; of planes . . . colliding in mid-air; of overpopulated continents and starving populations; of mechanized, regimented, dehumanized life; of brain-washing and nuclear warfare. As a member of the scientific community, I am awed by the thought that these social nightmares are to a large extent the products of industrial civilization — born out of science. . . . There is no longer any thoughtful person who believes that the conversion of science into more power, more wealth, or more drugs necessarily adds to health and happiness or improves the human condition. Indeed, haphazard scientific technology pursued without regard for its relevance to the meaning of life could spell the end of civilization.

René Dubos,
Horizon

Lately we hear a great deal about having "solved the problem of production." We are told that technological advance has rendered obsolete the old human problem of limited means vs. unlimited appetite. From here on in human history, we must school ourselves in consumership, now that "the problem of production has been permanently solved." While it is true that we are producing and consuming far more than ever before, is it possible that this whole process has come about because technology allows us to live beyond our means? Are we consuming the natural resources, the soil and water, which are the birthright of generations yet to come?

As technology "progresses," it enhances our capacity to exact a higher and higher price from the natural order. Any mechanical process consumes more energy than it produces. Thus the question: Is technology productive or consumptive in character? If we are increasing "production" by a technology which destroys the substance of the earth and befouls the remains, leaving junkyards, polluted air, and polluted water in the wake of its "progress," then we should reconsider whether such a process is truly a means of satisfying human wants.

The Problem of Human Wants

Meanwhile, the list of human wants also seems to be lengthening. Our whole economy is geared to an endlessly increasing appetite for material goods. Consumership has become the prime modern virtue, replacing any oldfangled notions of thrift or self-discipline. The present American population may be the most unabashedly materialistic people who ever existed. "The American Way of Life" has come to signify American technological triumph — has it also come to signify man's losing battle with the machine? Today's foreign visitor wants the higher standard of living which he sees in America; as he drinks his Coca-Cola, he believes with all his heart that, when better cars are built, Buick will build them. But he also sees in America an astonishing conformity. He sees the same advertisements, hears the same clichés, experiences at every hand a mass conformity engendered by mass production and mass consumption.

> . . . since modern man has not defined his way of life he initiates himself into an endless series when he enters the struggle for an "adequate" living. One of the strangest disparities of history lies between the sense of abundance felt by older and simpler societies and the sense of scarcity felt by the ostensibly richer societies of today. Charles Péguy has referred to modern man's feeling of "slow economic strangulation," his sense of never having enough to meet the requirements which his pattern of life imposes on him. Standards of consumption which he cannot meet, and which he does not need to meet, come virtually in the guise of duties.[1]

It seems that men's dissatisfactions are always greatest when we have much and want more. In Eric Hoffer's phrase, "We are less dissatisfied when we lack many things than when we seem to lack but one thing." Today men find themselves surrounded by so many technical advances, such a flood of material things, that they begin to assume that this is their due. "Progress" is now inevitable — technology will continually give us more and more for less and less. In such a faith, the existing state of affairs, however excellent, becomes deficient when compared with a supposedly endless series of better tomorrows.

It is also true that the more a man has with which to indulge himself, the less willing he is to submit to the discipline of work. Men and nations throughout history have proven that luxury and hard work are seldom companions. Soon the results of vastly increased production are evidenced in two ways: men seem to want more and more, and are less and less willing

[1]Richard M. Weaver, *Ideas Have Consequences* (Chicago: University of Chicago Press, 1948), pp. 14–15.

to work for it. Thus we become more dissatisfied with our lives — consumership proves a harder taskmaster than we first suspected. A "higher standard of living" proves more illusive than technology has promised us.

What Constitutes Civilization?

The endless production and consumption of more material goods may be an inadequate definition of "Progress."

> The problem of progress really coincides with what Windelband has called the problem of Civilization, which asks the question "whether and how far . . . the change in human impulses and in the relations of human life . . . has served to further the modern order and man's true happiness." The fact of change is unquestioned, but has there been *progress?*[2]

Do materialism and conformism insure progress? Do the advance of technology and a "higher standard of living" constitute civilization? While most of us are sure that more "conveniences" improve our lives, it is interesting to note that the inventors of these items have not agreed. Alexander Graham Bell would never allow a telephone in his home. The man said to be primarily responsible for the ideas which produced the TV set, Vladimir Zworykin, when asked to name his favorite program, replied, "None."

Men have labored for centuries to conquer nature and end the backbreaking struggle for survival. At the moment when we appear to have accomplished our goals, we find we have nothing to do but amuse ourselves, a task which seems harder and harder to accomplish. In desperation we turn to our other alternative, work — producing more of the "prosperity" which seems to bore us so terribly. It seems that we grow more powerful in our command of nature only to suffer a growing sense of confusion concerning the purpose for which all this new power should be exercised. As we master nature with technology, we sometimes forget that we ourselves are a part of nature. Are we thus mastering *ourselves* with technology? Is the machine working for man — or man for the machine?

There are many signs in our present consumption-conscious society that we have confused the accessories of civilization with its substance. A longer life-span, an abundance of newspapers, more television sets, a life less exposed to the dangers and hardships of nature: All these and many more of technology's fruits are potential tools to achieve a more civilized existence for men. But such items are not proof of civilization in themselves.

[2]Lyle H. Lanier, "A Critique of the Philosophy of Progress," *I'll Take My Stand* (New York: Harper and Row [Torchbook], 1962), p. 125.

Civilization is the achievement of a more humane scale of existence, the state of society in which the individual may develop his potential. To know whether or not our modern "necessities" and conveniences add to our civilization, we must ask: How does man utilize his longer life-span? What is the content of those many newspapers? What is the level of the programming broadcast on the electronic marvel of television? The answers to such questions in our time are not always reassuring.

Technological Values Insufficient in Themselves

It would be a serious mistake to repudiate technology and all its works. The production of more goods can do wonders for human existence. Technological progress is really man's response to the conditions of his environment. In this sense, technology has always been with us. The modern complaint that "man has advanced technologically but not morally," is also not as new as we might suspect. The author of the Book of Job leveled the same charge. It seems that when men devise ways of improving their material existence they sometimes grow careless of their moral concerns. If the rapid advance of technology is not closely allied with moral concerns, men may use their newfound power not to build, but to destroy.

The most important changes since 1900 may prove to have been philosophic rather than technological. We seem to have regressed from certainty to uncertainty, from faith to doubt. Nineteenth-century theories of evolution and scientific determinism have provided a legacy of confusion for the twentieth century which leaves us unsure of our bearings. Technological progress, yes . . . but: "For what shall it profit a man, if he shall gain the whole world, and lose his own soul?" The tiled bathroom may yet prove an insufficient basis for civilization:

> Science has seemingly achieved so much. We can travel with the speed of light, we shall soon be visiting the moon and exploring the Milky Way, we even have the means to blow ourselves and our earth to smithereens. We can send our words and even our smiles flying through the air to be picked up tens of thousands of miles away; we can turn back rivers, plant our deserts, and abundantly and effortlessly satisfy every human requirement, from potato crisps to skyscrapers, from royal jelly to giant computers. All this has happened in one lifetime. Is it surprising then that those who have brought it about should see themselves not as mere mortal men but as very gods? Or that they should take on the functions of a god, claiming the right to decide whose life is worth protracting and whose should be cut short, who is to be allowed to reproduce and who should be sterilized; reaching with their drugs and psychiatric techniques into the mind, the psyche, and shaping it to suit their purposes; re-sorting the genes,

replacing worn-out, derelict organs with new ones freshly taken from living flesh, fancying, perhaps, that in the end even mortality will be abolished — as an old vintage car can be kept on the road indefinitely by constantly putting in new spark plugs, dynamos, carburetors, as the old ones wear out; even redefining the moment of death to suit their convenience, so that we are to be considered dead when Dr. Christiaan Barnard says we are.[3]

Is the modern world falling into a new idolatry? If so, we need be reminded that the age-old cure for the "worship of things" remains the same: a recognition of human dignity which derives from our connection with something higher than the products of our own creation. A mere intoxication with material things, an infatuation with never-ending change, change for its own sake, makes too little of men. As the lyrics of a contemporary song have it:

> And the people knelt down and prayed
> To the neon god they had made.

The technological arrogance of modern men ("Man is the master of things") may prove to be the means of their technological subservience (Things are the master of Man).

Perhaps this is why our generation is beginning to have doubts about our ability to improve man's lot through technological advance alone. We may be rediscovering the old truth that self-mastery is more important than the mastery of nature. A technology which does not possess self-mastery can therefore become extremely dangerous. Indeed, it becomes progressively more dangerous as it becomes more effective in its control of nature — it becomes a Frankenstein's monster of power unlimited by ethical concerns. The proof of this surrounds us on every hand. We may well be living in the most brutal culture which has ever existed. Does that statement seem extreme? Consider the warfare which has characterized our century, warfare far more technically "efficient" than ever before. Consider the carnage which has accompanied the development of the automobile on American highways.

Our age's answer to such a question is, "That's all very well to talk, but how would you get along without the automobile?" Apparently we regard the thousands of deaths each year as not an exorbitant price to pay for our transportation and convenience. My criticism is not leveled at the automobile, but at a social order so callous in its values.

[3]Malcolm Muggeridge, "Men Like Gods," *The Christian Century*, February 5, 1969, pp. 176–177. (A sermon delivered at St. Aldate's Church, Oxford, on December 1, 1968).

Whatever may be true of the doctrine of progress in the abstract, it is likely, as held by the average American, to prove a dangerous infatuation. We reason that science must have created a new heaven because it has so plainly created a new earth. And so we are led to think lightly of the knowledge of human nature possessed by a past that was so palatably ignorant of the laws of electricity; and in the meanwhile we are blinded to the fact that we have men who are learned in the laws of electricity and ignorant of the laws of human nature. True, the most optimistic of us cannot help seeing some signs of moral degeneracy. But are we not spending seventy-five million dollars a year on automobiles, with a fair prospect of soon having successful airships? In view of these glorious achievements, why be disquieted by the increase in murders, in suicides, in insanity, in divorce, by all the multiplying symptoms of some serious and perhaps fatal one-sidedness in our civilization that is bringing down on us its appropriate nemesis? The doubts that beset our minds can all be conjured away by the very sound of the magic word Progress.[4]

We must be able to recognize human problems when we see them. When something goes wrong with an automobile, we fix it. Human problems are less easily repaired. To devote enormous energy to the solution of technical problems while pretending that such solutions constitute an advance in human understanding is a dangerous process indeed. Properly controlled, technology is a boon to man and a valuable servant; uncontrolled, technology becomes a dangerous taskmaster. For example, the whole world envies American technology and the wealth it provides, yet how successful have we been in exporting the secret of our "success?" We tend to export our society as well as our technology, often with disastrous results for so-called "underdeveloped" countries. Consider the tragedy of uneconomic steel mills in the Middle East or in Latin America. Showplaces of technology, these misguided attempts to further "development" are often an enormous drag on the country so "aided," costing far more in precious economic resources than the mills will ever produce in such a setting. One such mill in Venezuela, it has been calculated, could be abandoned — the capital investment written off and the mill given back to jungle growth — with every worker in the plant paid $30,000 a year not to work for the rest of his life — with Venezuela importing all of its steel at the going market price — and yet the Venezuelan economy would be money ahead. Wouldn't the people of such an "underdeveloped" country be better off to live their own lives than to do a failing job of living our lives? This remains true no

[4]Irving Babbitt, *Literature and the American College* (New York: Regnery, 1956), pp. 42–43.

matter how much "aid" we provide. Indeed, exporting our technology, even when we finance it, may be the worst thing we can do to people we are presumably helping.

Nevertheless, most of us continue to believe that increased production (no matter what we are producing; no matter at what cost to society) is the answer to every conceivable human problem. In 1966, twenty years after writing *The American Dilemma*, Gunnar Myrdal was asked whether or not he saw the problems he had earlier described now being solved. Myrdal replied, "Solution? There are solutions for technological problems but there are no solutions to human problems." This is a distinction that many moderns are not prepared to grant.

> The accepted hierarchy of values is fixed according to their usefulness, quite regardless of truth. Spiritual culture is suppressed. The question rises not only of values created by man, but of the value of man himself. The real aims of human life have been dimmed. Man has ceased to understand why he is living: He has not time to meditate on the meaning of life. Man's life is filled with means for living, which means have become ends in themselves.[5]

As the result, we have increasingly lost contact with the spiritual values of man. The tenuous spiritual insights of the Western world have suffered in the process. The result is a barbarization and dehumanization of those very qualities which distinguish us as men.

Today we are coming to fear technology, because we fear that we ourselves are scheduled to be "engineered." We are understandably ill at ease when "experts" inform us that, if we protect ourselves with the proper civil defense techniques, *only* 60 to 100 million people would die in this country in the event of nuclear attack. We begin to suspect that technology has indeed outrun humanity.

The Acceleration of Change

In America's race between technology and humanity, we have gained free time for ourselves beyond our wildest dreams — but never have we been so hurried, so lacking in genuine leisure as we are today. The pace of our society is furious; the rate of change is constantly accelerating. To visit an area where one was reared after an absence of a decade is to visit a completely changed community. Furthermore, the changes we see around us are only the beginning. We are only *entering* the period of radical technological change. Ninety percent of all the scientists who ever lived are alive today.

[5]Nicholas Berdyaev, *The Realm of Spirit and The Realm of Caesar* (New York: Harper and Brothers, 1952), p. 86.

Fifty percent of all the money ever spent on research and development in the United States has been spent in the last 10 years.

This radical alteration of our technological and social horizon has enormous consequences. Technology is no longer a separate entity outside our culture. Today it stands at the very center of our cultural and social organization. This rush to technological "progress" so dominates our thinking that we hurry on to the institution of changes which may threaten the happiness or even the existence of men. Change, never mind what change, is the order of the day. Things are moving so rapidly that today we have the "technological bends": We are altering the face of our society faster than we can assimilate that alteration.

Max Ways, one of the senior editors of *Fortune* has warned:

> Unless we change our thinking, we won't be able to cope with the change that is taking place. Change, of course, has always been a part of the human condition. What's different about it now is the pace of change, and the prospect that it will come faster and faster, affecting every part of life, including personal values, morality, and religions, which seem most remote from technology.
>
> So swift is the acceleration that trying to make sense of change will come to be our basic industry. Aesthetic and ethical values will be evolving along with the choices to which they'll be applied. The question about progress will be "how good?" rather than "how much?"

We are all involved in this race between quality and quantity. The unfounded fear that computers would replace clerks gives us an example of what we face. Businesses are discovering that computerized operations make it easier and easier to gather piles of unnecessary statistics, requiring *larger* and *larger* staffs to comprehend needless information. The quantity is there — how about the quality?

In the race we are running, society is chronically unstable and uncomfortable. Men as political, social, and moral agents are adjusting their lives to suit the needs of technology. Man is serving the machine, and even here he finds himself in the hands of a constantly changing master. Wear and tear, plus obsolescence, demand repairs and replacements which consume an enormous amount of human effort. The junkyard has become one of our national symbols.

The pressures of technology become greater each year. Modern society exacts a faster and faster pace. We find ourselves adapted to processes of "production" until we ourselves are valued primarily in utilitarian terms, in accord with our "productivity." Sadly enough, we have forgotten that man's principal productivity, his principal claim to humanity, has always rested in his spiritual and rational capacities, both of which require contemplation, time to think things through.If our flashy social order sometimes seems a bit shallow, if our well-dressed and "sophisticated" fellow-passenger on the airplane has thought processes on the comic-book level, we have a right to wonder what role the dehumanizing, anticontemplative pace of modern technological organization played in the sad estate to which we are falling.

The older status-rooted way of life passes from the scene under the pressure of rapid technological change. The social prestige of traditional skills and occupations is destroyed. Traditional values are swept aside. In the furious pace, there is no longer enough time for such things. The farmer must be a businessman, not a man of the soil; the worker must be an automaton, not a craftsman.

> It would be fatuous to deny the extraordinary progress towards an easier life and the increase in the material welfare of the masses which we owe to the economic revolution. . . . But this we may be permitted to say: Today we are aware of the high price that had to be paid for it and that we will continue to have to pay, and we are by no means still certain that the price is not too high. We distrust the optimistic assertion that technology and the machine are completely innocent of all this and that the blame rests squarely on man alone who is using them in the wrong way and will just have to learn the right one. We know that there are limits to mechanization both of men and work, to the emancipation from nature and the division of labor, limits which cannot be overstepped without grievously impairing man's happiness and the soundness of the social fabric. . . .[6]

The Natural Order

Winston Churchill's observation that "the Stone Age may return on the gleaming wings of science" serves as a grim reminder that technology has been used for destructive purposes, and can be again. It is also well to remember that the destructive effects of technology are not limited to warfare. There are signs that all life-forms will face great technologically induced obstacles to continued existence in our immediate future. Can we reach a point of unlivable atmosphere for animals and plants, a point at which life cannot continue in our water and our air?

Technology assures us that this cannot happen. The technological means to deal with such problems is just around the corner, we are told. But at one time we were also told that nuclear testing would not foul the atmos-

[6]Wilhelm Roepke, *The Social Crisis of Our Time* (Chicago: University of Chicago Press, 1950), p. 47.

phere, that detergents would not pollute our surface waters, that in-
secticides would not harm plants and birds and people. Now we know
better.

"Now we know better." But still the rapid pace of technological "advance" continues, almost totally unexplored in the vast changes which it
introduces into the ecological balance of life on earth. The very food we eat
can be laden with death. We have all heard of the experiments recently
conducted in which insecticide was sprayed on alfalfa; the alfalfa was fed
to cows; the normal dairy process was followed, converting milk to cream
to butter; the butter was fed to rats — and the insecticide, with its potent
cargo of death, was then found in the bodies of the rats. Nor do we pollute
only our food supply. Once the toxic substances from our factories and our
great urban centers reach a sufficiently potent level, the very animal and
vegetable life which inhabits our waterways ceases to exist. The polluted
water now passes over gravel so contaminated that it can no longer perform
its purifying function.

Who is the culprit in this assault upon our water and food? Surely
technology and applied science can protect us from such a threat. Surely
at least those centers of technology and scientific control, the cities, must
offer a haven:

> A modern skyscraper like the Pan Am Building in New York
> City is a marvel of applied science. It creates space for thousands
> of additional workers. But these workers must emerge onto streets
> that were narrow and crowded to begin with, fighting their weary
> trip home and back again the next morning. They must breathe
> air fouled with the exhaust of another marvel of applied science,
> the modern automobile. . . .[7]

If we have come to fear the present, what of the future? All the pol-
lutions previously mentioned pale by comparison with the pollution
stemming from technology's greatest "triumph," nuclear fission. The
pollutive capacities of nuclear bombs is already well demonstrated.
What of the "peaceful" uses of atomic energy? The insurance companies, professionals at the evaluation of risk, have proven singularly unwilling to insure nuclear power stations against third-party risk. It
seems that we do not know what effect such releases of nuclear energy
might have. Yet to argue that we proceed with nuclear fission only
when and if we can say we *know* what the long-range effects will be, to
argue that any other course is a reckless tampering with human existence, is to block "Progress." Or so we are told.

[7]Paul B. Sears, "Old Nature, Modern Man," *Audubon*, May–June 1968, p. 78.

Technology and Bigness

Today the little men, the protestors who don't want to go along, are often told they are holding up "Progress." Can society allow its great institutions to be blocked by cranks? So goes the argument. Sheer size and novelty must be our new criteria. It is worth noting the various forms in which that argument makes its appearance. Have you ever noticed that the promises of the Good Life are not unlike in the Communistic Soviet Union and the Economistic United States? Is not a higher material standard of living the be-all and end-all of both systems? If man is to be viewed as a product of society, if society's progress can be measured in material terms, then what right does the individual have to question a system obviously capable of producing more and more? Our attitude becomes quantitative, not qualitative.

As the result, the bureaucratic nature of the modern technical and political structure tends toward a certain mechanical impersonality, toward an "efficiency" which does not react sympathetically to dissenting views. We are dominated by the idea that the secret of "Progress" is an endlessly increasing production and consumption of goods. This has produced an economic and cultural tension so great that the individuals within society have tended to lose definition and, as a result, we have been steadily pressed toward a mass society.

The first symptom of such a society is a contempt for the individual human being. Men tend to assess themselves and their fellows by the technical standards of production — they become replaceable parts of a productive machine and are men no longer. From such a technological view of man and society, it is only a short step to acting in the name of "good for the whole society," which in practice often means manipulation of large blocks of men without concern for the individuals which compose those blocks. What such a society forgets is that happiness and dignity are human concerns, not mere technical problems.

The mechanization of material production and the mechanization of human organization go hand in hand. The worker specializes until he becomes as mechanized as his machine. Specialization afflicts all occupations in our society until we perfom increasingly narrow and stereotyped tasks. The production which results is equally stereotyped. Consider the standardization of sorting, packing, and labeling processes displayed by our food stores as technology has advanced. Consider the standardized automobiles which pour from Detroit, whatever the brand name may be. Mass production finally generates standardized consumers to use the standardized products.

The age of standardization has generated a new problem: people control. We have the tools, now we need men to staff the system. Thus the emphasis upon "industrial morale"; thus the preoccupation with communication and control techniques. Men in such a system lose the capacity to choose. They become more tightly tied to the organization. They are only fit to fill the narrowly specialized slot which technology has prepared for them. Thus, as the system becomes more widespread and complex, it exerts a greater and greater control over the individual. He must play the role assigned him since he is no longer suited to any other role.

This is true with worker and businessman alike:

> Indeed, a society increasingly dependent on manipulation of people is almost as destructive of the craft-oriented professional and businessman as a society in the earlier stages of industrialization is destructive of the handicraft-oriented peasant and artisan. The professional of the more recent period is pushed upstairs into the managerial class while the artisan of the earlier period was pushed into the proletariat; and this testifies to a profound difference in the two historic situations. Yet in both cases the industrial process advances by building into machines and into smooth-flowing organizations the skills that were once built, by a long characterological and apprenticeship process, into men.[8]

Still, one vital difference remains between the prisoner of the jail and the prisoner of the technological system. The technological prisoner has been fed the notion that the very bigness which engulfs him will provide his prosperity, will render him secure. Thus the social ideal, the beehive mentality, advances in lockstep with the technological organization of work and production. Technology generates the masses — the masses call for technological advance.

Today's ideology of "Progress" demands this faith in machinery and organization. The worker runs to the organization to "protect" himself in a mass society. The businessman runs to the organization of government to "protect" himself from a system grown too enormous to comprehend. The university runs from the older concept of individual research to the modern concept of "interdisciplinary groups" and "team research." The student runs to mass movements to discover his identity in a system where bigness has gone beyond all reason, a system where 3,000 students in a single class watch a television monitor in place of a professor. The farmer runs from the land as he becomes so mechanized and specialized that he cannot exist without becoming part of a larger and larger capital investment pool.

As we run from our individual occupations and identities, we form a mass society. We find ourselves prey to another technological "advance," the mass communication media. It seems one of the primary goals of those media to enumerate for our mass society all the various shortcomings under

[8]David Riesman, et al., *The Lonely Crowd* (Garden City, N.Y.: Doubleday, 1953), p. 156.

which we suffer, all the things which we do *not* have. Perhaps this is the basis of the appeal which big government has had. Technology promises man relief from all his obligations, relief from the frailties and obligations of the human condition. However false this promise, it has been widely accepted. As this promise must ever be broken, could it be that big government has become so attractive to modern men because it promises to manipulate the affairs of the world so as to achieve the promise of technology? So long as government announces itself as the foe of "the interests" who are blocking the technological cornucopia's flow, men seem to believe it is the fault of those "interests" that technology has not provided a utopia and that government can somehow rectify the situation. Government is of course powerless to improve the workings of technology for all men (though it *can* gain enormous technological triumphs at the considerable expense of the general public). So, too, is technology powerless to relieve the anxieties of men when it is itself the chief culprit in producing those anxieties. As more and more men slip from their role as individuals and assume their slot in mass society, as more and more people become directly dependent on the workings of an enormous system, bigness is furthered in all aspects of our lives: government, production, consumption, amusement — truly mass organization from the cradle to the grave.

By supplying the ruling oligarchy with more effective instruments of coercion and persuasion, applied science has contributed directly to the centralization of power in the hands of the few. But it has also made important indirect contributions to the same end. It has done this in two ways; first, by introducing over ever larger areas of the industrial and agricultural economy the methods of large-scale mass production and mass distribution; second, by creating, through its very progressiveness, an economic and social insecurity which drives all those concerned, owners and managers no less than workers, to seek the assistance of the national state.[9]

[9]Aldous Huxley, *Science, Liberty and Peace* (New York: Harper and Brothers, 1946), p. 12.

III

URBANIZATION

There remain some perfectly simple and elementary facts which are unanswerable. Can it be denied that, as Walter Lippmann once said, one can hanker after the rose-clad cottage of one's youth but not after a neon-lighted service station? Can it be disputed that a businessman who wants to sell Christmas cards having some sentimental, if elementary, appeal prints dreamy villages with gaily decorated horse-drawn sleighs or snowy landscapes and not automobiles or garages or a town of concrete blocks glittering with advertising? Is it imaginable that Segantini's well-known painting Plowing in *Oberhalbstein* in the Munich collection should have a tractor in the foreground instead of horses? Would it not be better to ponder such things, and others, instead of dismissing them with a supercilious smile?

Wilhelm Roepke,
A Humane Economy

It is a widely accepted assumption that true civilization demands large-scale urban centralization. Yet no single city of Western civilization reached a population of 1,000,000 before the nineteenth century. Does this mean that no civilization or cultural attainment existed before that time? A host of earlier literary, musical, and cultural figures of all sorts make such an assumption completely absurd. At the beginning of the nineteenth century, Vienna, then probably *the* cultural center of Europe, had a population of only 200,000. Whatever the reason which explains our rush to the city, cultural pursuits seem an inadequate excuse.

Still, two-thirds of the American people today crowd into less than one percent of our land area. Traditionally rural America has become urbanized. In 1870 farmers formed one-half our population; today they comprise only about six percent of our society. Within the past 25 years, the number of farms has been halved. Meanwhile, the average size of farm holdings has increased enormously.

As technology has advanced, machinery costs have kept pace, necessitating larger and larger aggregations of capital. At the same time, the farm subsidy program, originally designed to "save the family farm," has been so structured as to funnel the great bulk of its vast funds into the hands of large farm operators, thus saddling the small farmer with a vast bureaucracy whose largess he does not share. Bigness in technology, coupled with bigness in government bureaucracy, is making the family farm a thing of the past. Farming has become big business, and even what farmers remain are urban-oriented in their values and cultural attitudes.

When the city previously served as the cultural center for a predominantly rural society, that rural society gave strength and direction to the life of the city. Today urban life is completely dominant. More and more farm homes stand empty, their lands sold to farming corporations that control vast acreage. The small towns which served those farm homes also enjoy steadily less prosperity and influence. Store buildings are closing. Such businesses as remain are often nationally-franchised hardware stores, major brand gasoline stations, or chain-operated drive-in restaurants, all representatives of urban, mass society. There are fewer people on the Great Plains today than at any time since the homesteaders. There are steadily fewer passenger trains and buses running, with fewer scheduled stops in the little towns.

Those people who remain in the small towns are also in the grip of modern technology — the radio, TV, the automobile. Rural society draws its patterns from urban life. To all intents and purposes, rural society has ceased to exist as a separate entity, now deriving its identity as an underprivileged stepsister of urban society. Thus we adopt an exclusively urban culture.

"It's Good Business"

One of the primary reasons for this development of an *exclusively* urban culture is the unabashed economism which dominates our age. As economic growth and the ethic which makes production and consumption our sole aims have captured the modern imagination, the earlier American society, based upon a hierarchy of personal, local, individual loyalties and associations, has simply ceased to exist. That less centralized American life, life on a smaller, more human scale, life involving direct and tangible relationships with other people, has been exchanged for the elusive goal of a "higher standard of living," meaning more and more material goods in the hands of more and more consumers. Many urbanized Americans today no longer have neighbors, no longer feel themselves a part of a community uniquely their own. Today we are all too often mass-men, interchangeable links in an endless chain of producers and consumers. Even such family farmers as still exist do not farm to raise their food; they farm to produce a "cash crop," enabling them to buy "nationally advertised brands" at their grocery store.

The economistic, exclusively producer–consumer, viewpoint can destroy the quality of human life if the insistence upon sheer quantity becomes too great. It has already done so in rural and small-town America where all economic and cultural opportunities have been so downgraded that today the energy and creative talents of the young are funneled off to the urban centers. Our urban society offers the glitter of advanced technology, sold to young people everywhere by means of our mass media, plus high financial rewards for the creative talent it consumes. As the result, the young are leaving our farms and small towns never to return.

The city thus feeds upon the country to replenish and enlarge its population, not only in terms of creative talent, but in terms of proletarian laborers as well. Here again, in the case of the laborer, economism works its urbanizing influence:

> A score of years ago I visited a rich area which was just beginning to use cotton-picking machines. The workers' cabins stood in fields which were plowed and planted up to the buildings. There were no gardens, no chickens or cows; dependence upon field wages was absolute. I was told, literally, "We're getting machinery in here to do the work. We're getting thirty cents for cotton now, but we're fixing to make money if it goes down to twelve." When I asked what would happen to the workers and their families, I was told, "We'll let you worry about them up in Cleveland and Detroit."[1]

We have reached the point where Cleveland, Detroit, and the rest of America's urban center do indeed have much to worry about.

Overcrowding

As the city recruited talent from the country, there was an initial burst of creative activity in the urban centers. This creative activity stemmed from the new talent, the fresh individuals who sparked new life into the cultural accumulations already existing in the city. The "talented individual who flees small-town intellectual repression to achieve creative fulfillment in the big city" is a theme which has been commonplace to twentieth-century American literature. However true this may have been at one time, it would seem far from an accurate statement of the situation today.

The grandson of the talented individual who "achieved creative fulfillment in the big city" often finds the big city an anonymous, depersonalized place which suffers from a ruptured sense of community, a place so depersonalized as to thwart creative capacities. Such depersonalization always has that effect, since creative individuals must first be people, real people.

[1]Paul B. Sears, "Old Nature, Modern Man," *Audubon*, May–June 1968, p. 76.

Many people in today's urban society feel the difficulty involved in being a real person. Roger, a young service station attendant, seeing the Colorado license plates which I then had on my car, once asked if there *was* "still any room in Colorado — any ranch land." He said he had to get away. "This place [New York] used to be a nice place to live, but now there's no room!"

"Now there's no room." Studies with animals seem to indicate that overcrowding produces aggressive and finally unbalanced behavior. Does our rising urban crime rate suggest a parallel in human affairs?

It *is* true that we have a larger population today, but it is misleading to blame our overcrowding on the "population explosion." In fact, one-half the counties in the United States are *losing* population. Our problem is not a population explosion, but a population implosion. In short, we are not plagued with *more people* so much as we are with *urban centralization.* In one of his *American Scholar* columns written in the last years before his death, Joseph Wood Krutch described the result:

> To my mind, New York has become almost a horror; Arizona, vastly less attractive than it was fifteen years ago. The latter's willingness, its eagerness even, to cloud once pure air with smog, to expand two cities in a most helter-skelter way, to be greedy for money at the expense of most other contributions to the good life, is typical of the country as a whole, and public figures, who once seemed to set themselves against all this, yield to political necessity and come out in favor of it.

All the elaborate social statistics concerning wealth and consumption tell us nothing about the life of a New York commuter who spends several hours a day going to and from work under hectic and filthy conditions which would have been indignantly rejected by an American farmer a century ago (before technology and urbanization so "raised" our standard of living). The irony of the commuter's daily ordeal lies in the fact that the expense of his transportation is duly counted a part of the Gross National Product, and a measure of the "standard of living" enjoyed by the commuter. However such an item might appear in the economist's calculations, we never seem to ask how that portion of the commuter's existence should be considered on the balance sheet of his personal life.

Nor is the commuter alone in the urban assault upon the individual. Forget for a moment the plight of the poor who lack the mobility to escape from their urban hell, surrounded by filth and violence. Such people exist in large numbers, as any visit to one of our urban centers immediately makes clear. Forget these unfortunates for a moment — think instead of the urban middle class, the people who have the means to lead the *better* urban life:

Nor is it easy nowadays to escape from the crowdedness of life and
the flood of people in order to be alone for a while. In my experience,
a typical Sunday outing in New York means taking one's car and
driving out of town along an exactly prescribed traffic lane and in the
midst of other endless columns of motorcars, stopping at the edge of
a wooded area and parking the car in the space provided, paying one's
entrance fee and looking, with thousands of others, for a free square
yard to sit down on, stretching one's legs by walking up and down a
few paces, and then returning, in the same manner as was used in
coming out, to one's flat on the fifteenth floor of an apartment building. After that, one is supposed to be refreshed and ready to face the
week's subway trips and office work somewhere up on the fiftieth
floor, and perhaps might even be energetic enough to spend an evening at the movies in Rockefeller Center, in company with ten thousand others, having first, as part of an endless human serpent, shuffled
through a cafeteria in order to stoke up with the necessary calories
and vitamins.[2]

Mass society has come to mean not merely a crowded and filthy condition, but also a *managed* condition. The mass-man is increasingly managed
in his work, his amusements, his upbringing, his attitudes. He is taught in
his enormous schools (appropriately referred to as "plants") to adjust to
society. Find your place — conform. Thus we are depersonalized.

Psychological Effects

No matter how well housed and clothed a man might be, he also needs
time for solitude, time to be apart from the crowd. Solitude and the chance
to think things through are absolute prerequisites for the development of
personal character. One of the crying needs for urban man today is just such
a chance to find *himself.* Instead he often only *exists* while riding or driving
to work in a horde of people, eating lunch at midday inches away from other
diners all around him, returning home through another welter of traffic,
only to attempt to relax or sleep in the face of the everpresent noises from
the apartment next door.

The invasion of our privacy occurs on an unprecedented level in urban
society. A medical doctor in one of our large urban centers became so
distressed with an air hammer's brutal assault on the silence near his home
that he stepped into the street and began to converse in polite, "civilized"
tones with the workmen. He waited his chance and, suddenly produced an
ax from behind his back, attacked the air hose which gave life to the

[2]Wilhelm Roepke, *A Humane Economy* (Chicago: Regnery, 1960), pp. 39–40.

hammer. While his assault upon private property is not defensible, we all have our moments when there is a certain appeal to the good doctor's direct approach to the invasion of privacy.

As privacy becomes harder to maintain and as introspection is more difficult to attain, the number of Americans suffering from chronic illness continues to rise. Today nearly one out of two residents of the United States suffer from a chronic health condition. As we distort our environment, we begin to distort ourselves. Consider noise as an example of what we do to ourselves. We assault our ears with a cataract of noise in our urban, technological society, thus distorting and destroying the normal sound levels of human environment. The result? Dr. Charles Lebo of the University of California tells us that the young people who spend hours listening to "hard rock" music, if it can be called music, are condemning themselves to permanent hearing loss.

We adults should be slow to criticize. We have built a civilization, if it can be called civilized, where the sounds of the internal cumbustion engine, the subway, the jet, the pneumatic hammer, the siren, TV, garbage disposals, air conditioners, vacuum cleaners, and countless other technological "advances" have taken the privacy of silence from us all. At New York's Mt. Sinai Hospital, a connection has been established between noise and the failure of human nervous, circulatory, and digestive systems. More is in store for our abused systems: The increased noise of the jumbo jet and the supersonic jet; the snowmobile, a motorized, ski-mounted vehicle designed to provide winter recreation transportation and presumably guaranteed to destroy the white silence and isolation of our snow-covered forests; more, in fact, of all the technological "Progress" and mass accumulations of people that already plague us.

Study after study has revealed that human efficiency and health, both mental and physical, decline sharply as the sound level rises. Meanwhile, the noise of urban, technological life is matched by its pollution, by its overcrowding, by all the environmental disasters we produce for ourselves in such enormous quantities. Death rates from heart disease are approximately 40 percent higher in urban areas. Death rates for lung cancer (among nonsmokers) is 10 times higher in urban areas. A Cornell University team examining white, middle-class adults in New York City found the number of psychiatric disorders to be two-and-a-half times as great as the national average. Physically or mentally, men do not seem to prosper in their urban environment.

The Desire to Escape

More and more the new mass-men who fill our cities look for relief and escape from their urban environment. They look back nostalgically to the family ties, the local culture and the natural surroundings of an earlier day. Such young city dwellers are tied to the urban culture by economic bonds and have few if any roots in their new life:

> They are very much aware of the fact; surprisingly often they will bring up the home town, and though they have no intention whatsoever of going back, they dwell on what they left behind. Interestingly, the minor note that recurs most frequently is trees. "You know, the birds don't sing here yet," one [woman] explained to me, waving disgustedly at the little sapling outside the picture window. "The trees are so small. When I was a child in Jeffersonville I remember so well the great big trees outside the house. There were squirrels and birds around all the time. I think that's what I miss most of all."[3]

In this age of a higher and higher standard of living, have we become so "prosperous" that we can no longer afford natural surroundings, beauty, cleanliness, and repose?

Sometimes our daydreams of escape take other forms. History is enormously popular today. We want to know about the American past, especially the Western past. We open antique stores and pioneer museums. We hold Founders' Days. Our television, movies, and fiction offer escape to an earlier and simpler day.

Perhaps one reason we are so quick to turn from the present to the past, from reality to fantasy, is our eagerness to establish our own identity as individuals. A man who is little more than a cog in a vast, impersonal machine completely beyond his control or comprehension may well come to resent the machine with all his heart; he may come to wonder who he is. The absence of true community in mass society causes men to assume that they have no power to influence events. Such men lose sight of their own value and identity.

There are signs that modern urban enmassment also has a paralyzing effect upon the will and emotions of the city dweller. For several years, two university psychologists have been studying the psychology at work in urban crowds which seem completely immobilized when confronted by a situation in which a fellow human being needs help. John Darley and Bibb Latane, in their *The Unresponsive Bystander: Why Doesn't He Help?*, have pondered such cases as:

> Andrew Mormille is stabbed in the head and neck as he rides in a New York City subway train. Eleven other riders flee to another car as the

---

[3]William H. Whyte, Jr., *The Organization Man* (New York: Simon and Schuster, 1956), p. 288.

17-year-old boy bleeds to death; not one comes to his assistance, even though his attackers have left the car. He dies.

Eleanor Bradley trips and breaks her leg while shopping on New York City's Fifth Avenue. Dazed and in shock, she calls for help, but the hurrying stream of people simply parts and flows past. Finally, after 40 minutes, a taxi driver stops and helps her to a doctor.[4]

The most shocking example of irresponsibility in an urban throng which the psychologists cited was the story of Kitty Genovese, ". . . set upon by a maniac as she returns home from work at 3:00 A.M. Thirty-eight of her neighbors in Kew Gardens, N. Y., come to their windows as she cries out in terror; not one comes to her assistance, even though her assailant takes half an hour to murder her. No one so much as calls the police." The conclusion to be drawn from these studies might well be a warning that men act responsibly only when they are aware of their individual identity and responsibility, an awareness increasingly denied them by modern mass society.

The Antinatural Order

Meanwhile, we rob men of their birthright in other ways as well. Have you ever noticed that the normal instinct of a child is to enjoy weather — rain and snow — and the natural elements? It seems that the adult, "civilized" world must teach the child to dislike such things as a "normal" part of growing up. The close connection between man and nature is so apparent that modern urban man must shut his eyes very tightly to hide this from himself. The Bavarian critic Joseph Hofmiller has caught the essence of the connection between children and natural things with truly beautiful imagery:

A metropolitan child doesn't even know what it means to be a child. To be a child means to play in the fields, amidst grass and trees and birds and butterflies, under the endless canopy of a blue sky, in a great silence in which the crowing of a neighbor's cock is an event, as is the Angelus bell or the creaking of a wheel. To be a child means to live with the seasons, the first snow and the first colt's foot, the cherry blossom and the cherry harvest, the scent of flowering crops and dry grass, the tickling of the stubble in ones' bare feet, the early lighting of the lamp. [To be a child in the city] is a surrogate, shabby, cramped, musty, an adult's life *en miniature.*

[4]John M. Darley and Bibb Latane, "Why People Don't Help in a Crisis," *Readers Digest,* May 1969, p. 65.

Today's urban development, and its offshoot, the suburban development, work toward destruction of that natural order, substituting asphalt, concrete, and endless sameness in its place. In the process, we defeat the human spirit by undercutting its proper environment. Even our suburban developers unknowingly give testimony to this effect: The higher priced a piece of suburban property, the more privacy, isolation and natural beauty it is likely to retain.

Sadly enough, the march of economism across our landscape enforces quantity, not quality. City and country are run together in an amorphous blur, as we destroy our trees and devastate our landscape, the better to build row upon row of identical houses on "suburban tracts." In such fashion we do not escape from the city — we bring the city with us. First we destroy our natural surroundings, then we plan "vacations" from that urban sameness by going further and further afield to recapture what we have lost in our lives. And make no mistake, what we are losing is far more than a tree or a bird or a flower or a running stream . . . we are losing touch with Creation itself:

> The spoiling of man seems always to begin when urban living predominates over rural. After man has left the countryside to shut himself up in vast piles of stone, after he has lost what Sir Thomas Browne called *pudor rusticus,* after he has come to depend on a complicated system of human exchange for his survival he becomes forgetful of the overriding mystery of creation. Such is the normal condition of the deracine. An artificial environment causes him to lose sight of the great system not subject to man's control. Undoubtedly this circumstance is a chief component of bourgeois mentality, as even the etymology of "bourgeois" may remind us. It is the city-dweller, solaced by man-made comforts, who resents the very thought that there exist mighty forces beyond his understanding; it is he who wishes insulation and who berates and persecutes the philosophers, the prophets and mystics, the wild men out of the desert, who keep before him the theme of human frailty.[5]

The great urban complex is antinatural in another way as well. It is so completely artificial in itself that it must reach further and further afield to sustain itself in its physical needs. As urbanization and technology pollute their own atmosphere, the city must spend more and more to attain a sufficiency of clean water. As urban sprawl covers more and more ground,

[5]Richard M. Weaver, *Ideas Have Consequences* (Chicago: University of Chicago Press, 1948), p. 115.

the traffic problem into the so-called "core city" becomes more and more uncontrollable. More cars demand more roads; more roads open new areas of suburban development; and more suburban development leads to more cars on the way to the city; more cars demand more roads — and so on until we appear to be moving toward the totally paved society.

As the urban complex draws talent and labor into it, it also draws into its vortex all the natural resources which it cannot produce for itself. The city is a great consumer of natural *and* human resources, drawing upon the world outside for its continued existence and then spewing the waste products of its consumption into its slums, its garbage, its polluted air and water.

In such an artificial environment, the mass-man is divorced from nature and from the life of the earth. He finds himself eating adulterated, artificial foods, living by artificial light, breathing conditioned air, drinking water made pure by chemical additives. How far can we depart from our true nature?

Antipersonal "City Planning"

The progress of urbanization makes all of us steadily more and more a part of this unnatural order, with predictably disastrous results. Today the "urban crisis" is on everyone's lips. We are told that the frightful mess we have created was due to insufficient planning. For the sake of efficiency, we must no longer allow the selfish individual to interfere with the complex workings of the urban structure. We must think of the "total society" — the individual is an anachronism, we are told. But we have been told that before. Karl Marx had a vision of the technological, urbanized society of the future. Communism has always been a faith of the cities.

From Marx's viewpoint, he was quite correct to build his technological paradise around the urban idea. The city in the twentieth century has been built upon technological standards. We think in technological terms, not always in accord with human purpose. Archibald MacLeish describes the results:

Wildness and silence disappeared from the countryside, sweetness fell from the air, not because anyone wished them to vanish or fall but because throughways had to floor the meadows with cement to carry the automobiles which advancing technology produced first by the thousands and then by the hundred thousands. Tropical beaches turned into high-priced slums where thousand-room hotels elbowed each other for glimpses of once-famous surf not because those who loved the beaches wanted them there but because enormous jets could bring a million tourists every year — and therefore did.

The result seen in a glimpse here, a perception there, was a gradual change in our attitude toward ourselves as men, toward the part we play in the direction of our lives.[6]

The part we play in the direction of our lives is indeed changing in urbanized, technological society. We consign steadily more of our responsibility to the planner, with amazingly antipersonal, sterile results. As Jane Jacobs has made clear in *The Death and Life of Great American Cities*, if city life is to have any meaning, it must take the form of multiple human meetings. Cities must be for people, not people for cities. When urban renewal and city planning fail to allow for that diversity, for that vital human characteristic of being uniquely ourselves, it transforms society into a homogenized mass in which public impersonality takes the place of private personality.

The public impersonality of the planner seems forced upon us today because the city's problems seem far beyond the capacities of individual or private solution. Tests in the water reservoirs of one urban center showed the progression of pollution to such an extent that, during the low-water winter months, the city's water supply was one-half straight sewage! In 1952, 4,000 people died during a London smog disaster. Disposal of garbage has become an urban problem of such magnitude that we no longer know how to dispose of the waste which engulfs us. Can the individual urban dweller handle problems of such magnitude? A negative answer to that question seems self-evident. Enter the public planner.

Ultimate Political Effects

When political alternatives and the ideal of public planning are offered as the solution to our urban problems, another possibility should at least be considered. Would the dreadful enmassment which produces the blight of urbanization ever have occurred, or would it continue, without politically enforced central planning? For example, would New York's automotive traffic problem be possible without the enormous public subsidy of roads leading into New York City, roads which we were told would "solve" the traffic problem? Would a million people be on relief in New York City, with all the soul-destroying effects upon those individuals and their society, if public relief payments didn't make it profitable to move to New York? Would there be such an enormous shortage of moderate-cost housing in New York City if publicly planned rent control had not for years made it completely unprofitable to build such housing? Examples of this sort can be multiplied almost indefinitely; and what applies to New York City applies to our other urban centers as well. New York serves as such a horrible example only because the processes of centralization and public

[6]Archibald MacLeish, "Crossing the Line," *Manas, XXI,* 33 (August 14, 1968).

control have proceeded furthest there. Is public planning a solution to the urban problem or is it the cause of the problem itself?

Whatever the effects of public planning and centralized political authority upon urban society, urban society has another effect of its own upon our political processes. Throughout the history of Western civilization, there has always been a strong presumptive tie between virtuous republican government and the decentralization of a nonurban society. In this century, that decentralization has ceased to exist and a new mass society has been substituted in its place.

Ortega writes of a distinguished Roman of the Imperial era who visited Rome, where he pondered the massive structures representative of the Eternal City's position as supreme arbiter of all temporal affairs. Surely such a magnificent edifice, with all power, all civilization, all culture, centralized in its hands, could never fail! Yet Rome did fall, perhaps because the very centralization which built the Empire killed the Republic. And the end of the self-governing Roman citizen of the Republic meant the beginning of the urban mass-man, dependent upon political processes for his well-being and amusement.

Whatever parallels might be drawn between Rome and America, one other idea deserves careful consideration. The progressive disappearance of any remaining distinction between city and country, plus the increasing urbanization of American culture, has become the accepted fact of our times. This follows the Marxian sociological ideal almost precisely, in that it provides a growing proletarian population, rootless and adrift. Such a society opens the door to applications of political power which would be deemed totally unacceptable in a traditionally decentralized society, where the people enjoyed a sense of personal identity, an accepted place in a genuine community, and a scale of living and social organization more nearly human and individual in its scope. We have departed dangerously far from that ideal.

IV

MASS PSYCHOLOGY

In the monstrous confusion of modern life, only thinly disguised by the reliable functioning of the economic and State-apparatus, the individual clings desperately to the collectivity. The little society in which he was embedded cannot help him; only the great collectivities, so he thinks, can do that, and he is all too willing to let himself be deprived of personal responsibility: he only wants to obey. And the most valuable of all goods — the life between man and man—gets lost in the process; the autonomous relationships become meaningless, personal relationships wither; and the very spirit of man hires itself out as a functionary. The personal human being ceases to be the living member of a social body and becomes a cog in the "collective" machine. Just as his degenerate technology is causing man to lose the feel of good work and proportion, so the degrading social life he leads is causing him to lose the feel of the community — just when he is so full of the illusion of living in perfect devotion to his community. . . .

Martin Buber,
Paths In Utopia

"Monstrous confusion" does indeed seem to be a distinguishing characteristic of modern life. Never before have men exerted such apparent domination over the forces of nature. Scientific progress promises to make man master of his environment. Yet, despite all this awesome power, we sometimes display signs of wondering just what our lives are *for*. Perhaps there are aspects of human nature for which a highly technological society does not necessarily provide all the answers.

Some of those hard-to-discover answers concerning human conduct are ultimately moral in nature. And one of the most easily discernible features of our present society is the steady regression from *personal* to *social* morality. Individual conscience is regarded as "old-fashioned" by some, and as a luxury by others. In the wake of something loosely called "Progress," many moderns have come to imagine themselves the measure of all things. The progress presumably displayed by mass society, a society coming into existence as the result of technological and political capacities for mass organization, has apparently demonstrated (for some men, at least) that the new forms of social organization simply supersede individual conscience and responsibility. And yet it may be true that the mysterious humanness which we all possess does not so easily lend itself to uniformity and social manipulation. It may be that men demonstrate their common humanity precisely by exercising their uncommon personalities. If so, an all-encompassing social organization which denies the development and exercise of individual personality is the road to inhumanity. A social system which does not allow for diversity on all levels may thus become inhumane, and peculiarly ill-suited to the needs of the individuals who must live within the system.

There are a number of signs that we are reaching such an inhumane stage today. If so, our civilization is dying — and no amount of "prosperity" or technological achievement should be allowed to disguise the fact:

> The apostles of modernism usually begin their retort with catalogues of modern achievement, not realizing that here they bear witness to their immersion in particulars. We must remind them that we cannot begin to enumerate until we have defined what is to be sought or proved. It will not suffice to point out the inventions and processes of our century unless it can be shown that they are something other than a splendid efflorescence of decay. Whoever desires to praise some modern achievement should wait until he has related it to the professed aims of our civilization as rigorously as the Schoolmen related a corollary to their doctrine of the nature of God. All demonstrations lacking this are pointless.[1]

Perhaps it is the very pointlessness of such demonstrations which causes us to place such a great emphasis upon change for its own sake. We moderns are rarely satisfied with the present, preferring to live in a future which is doled out to us piecemeal from a technological and sociological cornucopia — with magazines available weeks in advance of their stated publication date, with automobiles available as "next year's models" months before the previous year has ended. This same rush to be "up to date" pervades our reading matter, our material concerns, our taste in ideas, our values and standards. Today we tend to reject all previously accepted norms. Thus we pursue normality without norms.

Is it any wonder that the dropout and the copout typify so much of our current thinking? If all norms are to be discarded, can we be surprised when the young distrust all authority, all standards?

[1] Richard M. Weaver, *Ideas Have Consequences*, (Chicago: Univeristy of Chicago Press, 1948), p. 12.

No one knows towards what centre human things are going to gravi-
tate in the near future, and hence the life of the world has become
scandalously provisional. . . . He will be a wise man who puts no trust
in all that is proclaimed, upheld, essayed, and lauded at the present
day. All that will disappear as quickly as it came. . . . Nothing of all
that has any roots. . . . Men do not know what institutions to serve
in truth. . . .[2]

Is it possible that today we live in such an abnormal and inhumane
framework, a framework which demands behavior so unsuited to the individual nature of human personality, that we have lost the power to distinguish between normal and abnormal reactions? How does one distinguish
a "normal" reaction or an "abnormal" situation when all norms have been
set aside?

Modern Education

The material concerns which dominate the lives of so many young people
accurately reflect the values of our society as a whole. The decline of
individual personality which epitomizes modern mass education is also
consistent with the pattern imposed by modern mass society. We can
scarcely blame the young for being such faithful disciples of the system. Our
educational system removes discipline and standards from the lives of the
young, and society assumes the role of the indulgent parent — satisfying all
appetites and massaging all egos — until a generation has been raised which
actually believes that its every impulse is proper, that every restraint, including self-restraint, is unwarranted.

A society which rejects fixed standards and self-discipline will predictably
reject the religious impulse, since that impulse is the ultimate source of all
norms and inner discipline. Thus the secular emphasis of state-funded
education. Strictly material concerns replace spiritual concerns: Mass replaces individual conscience. Modern education appears bent upon substituting "adjustment" for standards, society for personality:

The advocates of the permissive home and the progressive school
believe that the child who is brought up permissively and progressively will become a well-adjusted adult. Vocational counselors guide
their clients into those occupations in which they will be best adjusted.
Marriage counselors endeavor to adjust the husband to the wife and
the wife to the husband. College and university admissions officers
favor the high school graduate who is rated well adjusted by his

[2]José Ortega y Gasset, *The Revolt of The Masses* (New York: Norton, 1957), pp. 181–182.

teachers and principal. And the personnel directors of large industrial and business enterprises often consider social adjustment the major criterion in the selection of new employees.[3]

Any educational and social system which makes "adjustment" the primary social goal will breed people who are afraid to be themselves. Such people seek their self-esteem in the values and attitudes of others. Group identity becomes dominant.

Nihilism Among Today's Youth

In the absence of guidelines, many moderns have abandoned hope in the social order. Such hopelessness is especially prevalent among the young. Today we hear far more about destruction than creation. There seems to be a great emphasis upon protest, upon criticizing what other people and "society" are doing wrong. By comparison, we see almost no action from these same protesters which would indicate that they *personally* feel capable (or even willing) to assume any burden of responsibility themselves.

It may be true that, in Eric Hoffer's phrase, "Faith in a holy cause is to a considerable extent a substitute for the lost faith in ourselves." Perhaps all the mass meetings and the four-letter words tell us more about what we are doing to our young people than they tell us about our "sick society." Perhaps our willingness to discard traditional norms and standards of behavior has undercut personal responsibility and a sense of personal identity to the point where the hippie and the yippie are themselves living examples of how even nonconformity can become hopelessly conformist. A society which denies individual values should not be surprised when it generates valueless individuals.

"Who am I?" and "What shall I do with *my* life?" may well prove to be the most vital questions our young people have to ask; and we are doing precious little to answer. Perhaps no society can answer such questions, but in many cases we are failing to provide our young people with the standards and the discipline whereby they might arrive at their own answers.

When a generation of young people are raised and educated in a society which denies them the development of their own capabilities, and when these young people are then confronted with a world in which the older sense of community has been swept away to be replaced by the new mass-oriented society, operating on an increasingly inhumane scale, we should not be surprised when many of those young people retreat to a nuerotic world of their own making. In the process, true freedom and individuality are the first casualties. A man no longer responsible to his own *personal* being is a man no longer responsible to anyone or anything. Such men are

[3]Richard LaPiere, *The Freudian Ethic* (New York: Duell, Sloan and Pearce, 1959), p. 131.

empty. They quickly become ideal raw material for massive organizations designed to run society or equally massive organizations designed to wreck society. Thus both "The Establishment" and "The Antiestablishment" become different aspects of the same problem:

> Emptiness is a specific ego reaction which accompanies the failure of the ego to establish identity. It is felt by a person who has a poorly developed sense of I AM I. People who are empty have accompanying physical symptoms of apathy, fatigue, and a general "washed-out" feeling. Emptiness is a self-descriptive term. This rather common ego reaction in our society implies a feeling of nothingness, lack of personal worth or esteem, lack of confidence in oneself as a person. In the concept of David Riesman, it indicates a lack of "inner direction." The individual lacks a feeling of self-worth which is not dependent on others. To depend on others for self-worth, e.g., other-directed people, is a compromise which works for many people only as long as they stay in a social situation where such other people exist.[4]

There seems no shortage of such empty men in our present society. The great paradox is that the men facing each other across the barricades of our disrupted social order all too often share that same emptiness whether they defend or attack the existing "system." The one absolutely certain fact concerning the empty men who epitomize modern society: Such men always run in packs, apparently the larger, the better. The age of the mass-man has arrived.

Collective Decision Making

Today we are fascinated with the group. The committee is the dominant organizational form, even for the tiniest church or community project. Business and government proliferate an unbelievable number of committees. In one recent year, the President of the United States decided there were too many committees in the highest levels of the executive branch. He brought his enormous authority to bear, and abolished 163 such committees within the year. While this housecleaning was underway, 203 new committees were set up. At year's end, the man reputed to hold the most powerful office on earth found that the committees had defeated him. Final score: 40–0.

Why this lust for group-think? People can do many things in groups. The one thing they *cannot* do in groups is think. Could it be that our taste for committees is based upon the all-too-common trait of avoiding thought and responsibility? Could we be hiding in groups? Perhaps it is also true that

[4]William Glasser, M.D., *Mental Health or Mental Illness?* (New York: Harper & Row, 1960), pp. 24–25.

the noncreative, unthinking conformity which characterizes the group is an expression of the distaste which the noncreative man always displays toward the creative.

> The worst thing I see about life at the present time is that whereas the ability to think has to be cultivated by practice, like the ability to dance or to play the violin, everything is against that practice. Speed is against it, commercial amusements, noise, the pressure of mechanical diversions, reading habits, even studies are all against it. Hence a whole race is being bred without the power to think, or even the disposition to think, and one can not wonder that public opinion, *qua* opinion, does not exist.[5]

The very closeness of living which present-day society forces upon us mitigates against decisive and self-directed individual action. The result has been a mental and moral paralysis in which we have lost faith in ourselves to act. None of us can live long without faith in something. As modern men lose faith in themselves, they substitute faith in governments, in technology, in organization on a massive scale. Unfortunately, our faith in collective processes soon proves disillusioning. A million zeros massed together still amount to nothing. A conclusion achieved by political consensus has no necessary connection with the right or wrong of a given situation. Such a system leaves too little room for individual character.

Mass-man of course is quick to applaud such collective substitutions for individual character. The assumed worthlessness of the individual and an accompanying preference for collective solutions seems an almost universally accepted idea today:

> Under these circumstances it is small wonder that individual judgment grows increasingly uncertain of itself and that responsibility is collectivized as much as possible, i.e., is shuffled off by the individual and delegated to a corporate body. In this way the individual becomes more and more a function of society, which in its turn usurps the function of the real life carrier, whereas, in actual fact, society is nothing more than an abstract idea like the State. Both are hypostatized, that is, have become autonomous. The State in particular is turned into a quasi-animate personality from whom everything is expected.[6]

Considering the tragic demonstrations of what can happen when masses of men are organized and trained to respond to the orders of a leader, it is

[5] Albert Jay Nock, *A Journal of These Days* (New York: Morrow, 1934), p. 245.
[6] C. G. Jung, *The Undiscovered Self* (New York: New American Library, 1964), p. 26.

amazing that today we continue so cheerily on our road to the totally organized life, firmly convinced that mass organization holds the solution to all our problems.

The Anonymity of Corporate Life

One reason the committee and group-think have such a hold on the American imagination is the strong desire evidenced by the typical white-collar worker "to belong," to be an identifiable part of a group. The modern "organization man" is likely to be a master of adjustment and "human relations." Those skilled at adjustment become the most common social types — they fit themselves to the new needs peculiar to group-think and organizational empire building. In the process, "adjustment" becomes an obvious tool for achieving popularity and advancement, a surefire means of winning friends and influencing people.

Sadly enough, adjustment doesn't always fill the bill. After finding his place in big business, big labor, big government, big education, or some other bigness, today's employee finds himself an interchangeable part in a gigantic machine which *he needs,* but which can get along very well without him. Suddenly one day, the employee, and he could be a man far up the decision-making ladder, looks in the mirror to discover that he is faceless. Adjustment may be the road to success in today's bigness, but that same adjustment demands that the individual adapt his form, his life-style, to external conditions. We all do this to a certain extent to live in the world around us; but when that process of externalization becomes too great, nothing of the individual remains within — the internal man, the unique personality, ceases to exist.

Depersonalization

In fact, mass society might be best defined as any form of social organization which denies men the claim to a unique spiritual and moral personality. It is well-nigh impossible for a man to be truly a person unless he exercises some measure of independence and responsibility in the conduct of his own life. Today many men pass their lives in a giant urban complex, totally divorced from their natural environment and dependent upon a highly artificial social and technological system for the conduct of their daily lives. These same men are frequently rootless and propertyless, employed to perform some chore entirely divorced from the satisfaction which comes from a completed task and cut off from the dignity which characterized the older craftsman or professional man. Is it any wonder that such men, as they make their weary rounds inside the cage which modern society has created for them, often seem glum and sullen? It seems that many men have been called upon to abandon some of the most basic satisfactions of their nature in order to keep the social system in operation.

Most moderns may sense this deprivation only dimly, reacting with a sort of vague dissatisfaction and a nostalgic yearning for "the good old days." But there are other indices. The reaction of the modern artist is a case in point. Many literary figures have been keenly aware of the assault upon men's dwindling sources of personal dignity. Most literature since the First World War bears witness to that recognition. Huxley, Orwell, Kafka have all exploited this theme. Perhaps it is peculiarly fitting that many of these early critics were Europeans, since Europe has preceded us down the road to bigness and collective solutions.

In America the trend toward enmassment has been especially comfortable and security-oriented. Further, the process has been achieved at such a gradual pace that little public outcry has been raised:

All mass movements, as one might expect, slip with the greatest ease down an inclined plane represented by large numbers. Where the many are, there is security; what the many believe must of course be true; what the many want must be worth striving for, and necessary, and therefore good. In the clamor of the many there lies the power to snatch wish-fulfillments by force; sweetest of all, however, is that gentle and painless slipping back into the kingdom of childhood, into the paradise of parental care, into happy-go-luckiness and irresponsibility. All the thinking and looking after are done from the top; to all questions there is an answer; and for all needs the necessary provision is made. The infantile dream state of the mass man is so unrealistic that he never thinks to ask who is paying for this paradise. The balancing of accounts is left to a higher political or social authority, which welcomes the task, for its power is thereby increased; and the more power it has, the weaker and more helpless the individual becomes.[7]

As the individual has become more helpless, personality has been lost in statistical averages. The individual goals and meanings of life have been lost in "total social goals." The person is increasingly deprived of control as to how he should live his life and becomes a social unit whose various needs are met by one form or another of social organization. Increasing importance is attached to numbers. The individual finds his insignificance drummed into him on every hand, in mass communication, mass entertainment, mass education.

Having lost both personality and community, the mass-man is offered not

[7] *Ibid.,* pp. 70–71.

only a "big brother" in the form of government, but similar "friends" in various functions of the private sector which touch his life. Today we find banks which assure us in the most ingratiating TV manner that we can "find a friend" at Bank X. In fact, we are surrounded at every hand with "public relations experts" whose principal job it apparently is to sell us denizens of mass society on the idea that government, business, labor, education, or some other wing of the existing system, exists solely for our benefit. Still there are moments when each of us may feel a trifle dwarfed by all this, rather as though the whole system would function exactly the same without little old us. There is something strangely disheartening about having one's social significance measured by the bureau of statistics, a Nielsen rating, a turnstile, or a collection of marketing figures. It appears that we can become an infinitesimally important part not only in the assembly line of production which services man's society but can also be an equally small and inconsequential part (an interchangeable part, without personal identity) in the process of consumption as well. Thus the individual is ground down into the mass.

Anxiety

The process of depersonalization seems to generate anxiety, making anxiety essentially a group phenomenon in present-day society. Our literature is filled with the anxiety theme — our time is labeled "the age of anxiety." Visit one of our cities and spend a few minutes in traffic, or in a crowded restaurant or department store. You will discover tension and pent-up emotion at every turn, resulting in rude, irritable, often irrational behavior on the part of many people. The role which this anxiety plays in aggravating racial tensions is probably too little acknowledged.

Anxiety is generated within the individual by loss of control over his affairs and by a parallel loss of personal identity. As mass society encroaches upon a man's identity, he comes to feel himself in the grip of forces beyond his control. Such a man tends to await with anxiety the course of events and the actions of various collective forces which will determine his existence for him.

This anxiety has its roots deep in the social changes of the twentieth century. Beginning with the First World War, family structures loosened, the father lost his central role in the family, women were "emancipated." The death and destruction of the war was followed with the further social upheaval of the Roaring Twenties, and the social disintegration of the Depression Thirties:

> The whole nation, gripped by anxiety, elected a "radical" president and a Congress who, acting upon the need to alleviate the national anxiety, legislated measures which are the basis for much of our present political structure based on security. After the Depression

came World War II and with it the completion of much of the loss of sexual identification and family structure initiated by World War I.[8]

While family ties and personal identity have been progressively weakened by enmassment (undercutting family, community, and personal responsibility), the rush for "security" has continued. As we move along that road, it is worth remembering that the growing necessity for new sources of security bears a direct relationship to the decline in existing security. In short, our security anxiety appears to stem from a failure to maintain those aspects of social organization which previously made us feel secure. We are looking for security in enmassment when it is that very enmassment which has caused our insecurity. Like Alice and the Red Queen, we must run faster and faster to stay in the same place. Unfortunately, the outcome of such a race is predictable:

Not actual security, but want of security produces those powerful organizations we see growing up around us, not only labor parties and unions but also private insurance combines and governmental social security bureaus. However, he who craves security, he who calls for protection, can in no way escape from paying the price it costs. To the same extent to which protection is granted, the individual becomes dependent upon the organization that gives the protection. The whole weakness of the human being who lives within the technical organization, his whole peculiar uprootedness, his crying need for guidance and aid, his isolation — they find expression in this striving for security that shrinks from no act of subjection, that surrenders itself into dependence with a definite eagerness. Moreover, since the craving for security grows as fast as actual security declines, we notice a peculiar vicious circle at work: Technical progress increases the craving for security, while mushrooming organizations for a sham security produce a decline of actual security.[9]

Even when technological development and large-scale organization provide a higher standard of living, too often we fail in making that higher standard of living (or the large-scale organization which achievement of that standard supposedly necessitates) responsive to the needs of the individual human beings involved. Perhaps efficiency in greater material production, or the "bigger is better" assumption which usually accompanies such efficiency, is inefficient or even misleading as a guideline. Perhaps the whole system can become so enormous and so complex that the men living

[8]Glasser, pp. 77–78.
[9]Friedrich Georg Juenger, *The Failure of Technology* (Hinsdale, Ill.: Regnery, 1949), p. 171.

within it lose their way and suffer severe anxieties as the result. If so, the
price is too high, the system inhumane:

> It is to simplify, but there is much validity to the view that the
> individual has been dwarfed by nationalized, consolidated, and cen-
> tralized businesses; swallowed up in giant corporations, vast bureau-
> cracies, and huge armies; battered by total war, economic depressions,
> governmental and business propaganda; made apparently insignifi-
> cant by his life in impersonal cities; replaced by the machine, or
> required to adjust at its demands; baffled by the complexity of the
> operations in the world in which he lives; manipulated by salesmen,
> advertisers, politicians, announcers, and assorted confidence men.[10]

Love

Having thus been assaulted by his society, today's American has taken
refuge in what D. H. Lawrence called "abstract caring." We no longer think
of individuals, but of "Causes," of abstract political principles. We no
longer emphasize man–wife, parent–child, teacher–student, friend–friend
relationships. Such interpersonal relationships terrify us. Today the word
love has been bastardized until it refers not to individual personalities, but
to broad social issues and all-consuming "causes." How little we love —
how little we are loved!

Some time ago I attended a luncheon in midtown Manhattan. Arriving
early, I found myself alone in a second-floor dining room which overlooked
a teeming business district intersection at the noon hour. From my vantage
point I could see the faces of the crowd but could hear nothing of the traffic
noises filling the street. Thus, unaware they had an audience, the office
workers of New York City acted out a pantomime as they rushed on their
way. With an occasional and heartwarming exception, these people were
uniformly grim, tense, hurried, and ugly — perhaps ugly even to themselves
and certainly ugly to one another. Try the same experiment some day
yourself and then inquire: "What price 'Progress'?"

> It has become very rare for one person to open up spontaneously to
> another. He holds back, observes, calculates, and criticizes. The other
> no longer is a personal world like myself, a world which I can under-
> stand and affirm from the vantage of my own; he is a sum of qualities
> which are more or less useful to me; he is an aggregate of forces which
> I regard as excellent or poor prospects for my exploitation.[11]

---

[10]Clarence B. Carson, *The Fateful Turn* (Irvington, N.Y.: Foundation for Economic Education, 1963) pp. 68–69.
[11]Martin Buber, "The Prejudices of Youth," *Israel and the World* (New York: Schocken,
1948), p. 48.

We seem to feel more and more bewildered as we perceive that the mass of people for whom we "have no time," whose personal needs the system does not consider in its "efficient" operation, also includes ourselves. If we abandon love in the old sense, in the sense of concern for other specific personalities who touch our lives, the result is an acute spiritual isolation which bids fair to destroy us all.

The Loss of God

One of the primary reasons for that acute spiritual isolation has been the way in which our society and its secular educational system has carefully ignored religion. So long as each individual maintains the idea of a personal responsibility and a direct contact with God, man cannot be totally dissolved into society. A portion of each man remains uniquely his own. Remove that power of faith, and the individual no longer has that sanctuary from which to confront mass society.

Today we are told that God is dead. The corollary of that doctrine is that *we* are now in charge. In practice, of course, this turns out to be a *very* collective "we." There is a blemish on this new certificate of title to the universe which we have bestowed upon ourselves. Dr. Edmund Leach, provost of Kings College, Cambridge, reminds us, "Unless we teach those of the next generation that they can afford to be atheists only if they assume the moral responsibilities of God, the prospects for the human race are decidedly bleak."[12]

The patent absurdity of the present generation of social and political leaders assuming *any* serious moral responsibilities, let alone filling in for God, has caused many men to retain at least some portion of their instinctive religious impulse. Thus, church attendance has never been better.

Unfortunately, when religion is cultivated and organized, sometimes the I–Thou, individual-to-his-Maker, relationship in religion declines and is replaced by the same sort of social technique and organizational giantism that afflicts other aspects of our modern social order. Today organized religion in America is doing well indeed, but in the process it may have become just another big institution. Big religion may well have joined big government, big business, big labor, big education, and big communications as a molder of men's minds and a manipulator of men's fortunes:

Curiously enough, the Churches too want to avail themselves of mass action in order to cast out the devil with Beelzebub — the very Churches whose care is the salvation of the individual soul. They too do not appear to have heard anything of the elementary axiom of mass

[12]Malcolm Muggeridge, "Men Like Gods," *The Christian Century*, February 5, 1969, p. 176.

psychology, that the individual becomes morally and spiritually inferior in the mass, and for this reason they do not burden themselves overmuch with their real task of helping the individual to achieve a *metanoia,* or rebirth of the spirit — *deo concedente.* It is, unfortunately, only too clear that if the individual is not truly regenerated in spirit, society cannot be either, for society is the sum total of individuals in need of redemption.[13]

Social religion thus seems to be on the wrong tack. Society cannot redeem the individual — individuals must redeem society. The virtue of the saints in past society rested squarely on their capacity to go their own way, with no regard for "public opinion." It is precisely the loss of that individual quality in modern organized religion which promises to eliminate both virtue and personality from our social order.

In their unending effort to know God and thus define their own experience, men have traditionally pursued the development of their own personalities. Those who have failed to set about the task of developing their own personalities have usually been described as morally incomplete. It is precisely that moral incompleteness which plagues modern society. Perhaps the social and psychological problem involved in enmassment has been best expressed by the late Whittaker Chambers:

> I did not understand that the malady of the life around me from which I retreated into the woods, and the malady of the life of my family, from which I was about to retreat into the world, were different manifestations of the same malady — the disorder that overtakes societies and families when a world has lost its soul. For it was not its mind that the life around me had lost, though I thought so as a boy and was to continue to think so for almost twenty years, but its way, because it had lost its soul.[14]

[13]Jung, p. 68.
[14]Whittaker Chambers, *Witness* (Chicago: Regnery, 1952), p. 149.

V

MASS CULTURE

The desire not to be impinged upon, to be left to oneself, has been a mark of high civilization both on the part of individuals and communities. The sense of privacy itself, of the area of personal relationships as something sacred in its own right, derives from a conception of freedom which, for all its religious roots, is scarcely older, in its developed state, than the Renaissance or the Reformation. Yet its decline would mark the death of a civilization, of an entire moral outlook.

Isaiah Berlin,
Two Concepts of Liberty

The liberal ideology which today permeates our social and political order has historically functioned best as an agency of reform. It has the most to tell us when in opposition to the status quo, or when locked in struggle with the "Establishment." Put another way, liberalism seems peculiarly ill-suited to itself becoming the Establishment, since the ideology is most effective when it can be against something, when it can play an essentially negative role. When a social and political order takes its guidance and its values from a negative ideology more skilled in criticism than in offering workable alternatives, it should surprise no one that the society in question is likely soon to feel itself surrounded by serious and possibly insoluble problems. The desperation thus induced leads men to doubt their culture:

As men lose confidence in and enthusiasm for their culture, they are, so to speak, left hanging in midair and incapable of opposing anyone who affirms anything, who makes himself solid and secure in anything — whether it be true or be said in jest. Hence there are periods in which it is enough only to give a shout, no matter how arbitrary its phrasing, for everyone to surrender themselves to it. These are periods of *chantage* in history.[1]

[1]José Ortega y Gasset, *Man and Crisis* (New York: Norton, 1958), pp. 146–147.

The shout of our time, heard again and again, is for "action," for "reform," for "positive programs." Needless to remind the reader, all this "action" and "reform" is always assumed to be necessarily collective in nature. Usually government action is urged by the politicians of all parties; but the assumption runs a close second that organized business, labor, religion, or some other large institution might perhaps also be called in to do the job. The possibility never seems to cross anyone's mind that any individual might ever satisfy his own needs, if given the opportunity to do so without organized bigness intruding itself into his affairs.

Thus for several generations life in America has become more and more collectively organized. The period of increasing collectivization has also been a period of increasing disorder. The connection seems more than coincidental. Still, the *chantage* described by Ortega goes on. As society's problems become more and more severe, we shout louder and louder for collective solutions, and grow more and more suspicious of anyone who suggests that collective measures may be causing social dislocations rather than correcting them.

Our distrust of individually-oreinted solutions and values has deepened until it has become a hatred. Unfortunately, hatred is an emotion which leads to the end of all values and all critical thinking. This is true because hatred of a man or an idea allows us the luxury of blaming all our troubles on the object of our hatred. Thus our society, already far-gone in enmassment and collectivization in all sectors, public and private, is able to make itself believe that some unreconstructed individual or another is responsible for our difficulties. A society which has bound the individual hand and foot now cries out for new powers and new organizational forms to protect itself from him.

Of course, it is those who have not yet been fully absorbed into the benevolent system of totally organized life who need the real protection:

Readers who are all too familiar with popular works on anthropology may be interested to learn that some recent investigations have involved a completely novel approach. The ordinary anthropologist is one who spends six weeks or six months (or even sometimes six years) among, say, the Boreyu tribe at their settlement on the Upper Teedyas River, Darndreeyland. He then returns to civilization with his photographs, tape recorders, and notebooks, eager to write his book about sex life and superstition. For tribes such as the Boreyu, life is made intolerable by all this peering and prying. They often become converts to Presbyterianism in the belief that they will thereupon cease to be of interest to anthropologists; nor in fact has this device been known to fail. But enough primitive people remain for the purposes of science. Books continue to multiply, and when the last tribe has resorted to the singing of hymns in self-defense, there are still the poor of the backstreets. These are perpetually pursued by questionnaire, camera, phonograph; and the written results are familiar to us all.[2]

Today we pursue the poor relentlessly. The characterization of "those who have learned to love the poor, profitably" is not far from the literal truth. Often we are not genuinely concerned about improving the quality of life in the "poverty pockets" which are discovered; we prefer to bring the poor to the great urban complexes which are already so pitifully over-crowded, storing the unemployed like so much cordwood. All this is done in the name of the "welfare" of the poor. Predictably, such people are treated as members of a sociological group, not as individuals.

Often the "Progress" which the modern economic system brings to an area is nearly as ugly as the government's definition of welfare. How many of us have returned to a lovely place of our remembrance (perhaps "poor" by sociological standards) and found that loveliness reduced to billboards, gas stations, and cheap new housing developments, decaying almost before they are completed? According to per capita income, property tax base, or other such sociological standards, the people of such an area are presumably better off. Are they indeed? The economistically and collectively oreinted age which has made sociology a tool of prime importance to the social planner, both public and private, has led us to replace individual values with "welfare projects" and "market analysis." We no longer like to use such words as man or woman, preferring to discuss "income groups." None of us is exempt from this loss of individuality. The poor are only most disad-vantaged because of their especially vulnerable position when the collec-tivity is casting about for a likely object of "reform."

Education

Nowhere is this desire to remake society and all its members more in evidence than in our educational institutions. Bigness in education has long since exceeded all rational bounds. Education has become almost totally institutionalized and anti-individual. Should anyone doubt the extent to which enmassment has dominated education, a short visit to the massive public high school or giant university campus of his choice should quickly demonstrate how small and unimportant the individual student has become and how enormous is today's "system." In the face of such bureaucracy and punch-card anonymity, the wonder lies in the fact that anyone emerges with a mind of his own.

[2]C. Northcote Parkinson, *Parkinson's Law* (Boston: Houghton Mifflin, 1957), p. 91.

This entire subject has already been analyzed in some detail by a number of critics. I have even ventured such an analysis myself.[3] It is hardly necessary to reiterate such criticism here. But there is a connection between educational enmassment and our present social crisis which deserves special mention. Education in general and the university in particular has been made a servant of the existing system. Intellectual independence has been set aside so that educational institutions can be used to provide properly adjusted social animals, ready to take their place in the system. The governmental–industrial complex needs its technicians, skilled workers, bureaucrats. Lest the reader think this an exaggeration, I refer him to no less a prophet of modern American society than Harvard professor John Kenneth Galbraith, who urges that our primary educational purpose should be the provision of such properly trained human material for the governmental–industrial complex, since Galbraith wishes to make "human beings as privileged, for purposes of investment, as are machines."[4]

Professor Galbraith's somewhat narrow view of educational purpose has been expanded to include not only our training for production, but our training for consumption as well. Today our high school and college age youths are taught how to shop, how to entertain themselves, even how to deal with the opposite sex. In fact, our young are taught the proper means of living life in all its facets. We are turning out properly "programmed" social machines, ready and willing to conform to "social needs," needs defined by the current crop of social planners:

> . . . the twentieth-century State has finally accepted the responsibilities of statism. In totalitarian countries, this is obvious. In the liberal democracies of the West, the State enlists the cooperation of the collectivity, including institutions, agencies, the press, business, entertainment media, and of course, the schools, which are chronologically the first and probably the most decisive influence in the lives of individuals. Thus schools must now perform before the public eye and establish their own goals for society, namely the *production of technicians* at various levels of skill and competence and the *formulation of social virtues* upon which the State and the collectivity may agree.[5]

Thus the social process finally becomes political. Though the Russians were the first modern people to mold deliberately the culture of an entire

---

[3]George Charles Roche III, *Education in America* (Irvington-on-Hudson, N. Y.: Foundation for Economic Education, 1969).

[4]"Man and Capital," "Adventures of the Mind," No. 47, *Saturday Evening Post,* March 5, 1960, p. 99.

[5]Thomas Molnar, *The Future of Education* (New York: Fleet, 1961), p. 60.

society, they are no longer alone in that ambitious undertaking. Deweyite instrumentalism, which dominates American education, favoring "adjustment" and "social goals" while demanding conformity from the individual, is quite as ambitious in its social engineering as its Russian counterpart.

The spread of compulsory "education" and the extension of education to the higher levels, primarily in public institutions, has promoted uniformity of indoctrination favorable to the welfare/illfare state. Experimental tests of the effect of the prolongation of schooling seem to demonstrate conspicuously that the longer the schooling, the higher the score in terms of stereotyped answers to the standardized tests. The customary interpretation of these facts, however, has represented them as proving that the higher scores meant a higher level of thinking intelligently about public questions. The "joker" in that conclusion lies in the nature of the questions and the "correct" answers. Certainly the "correct" answers were suspect. In one such study cited, they reflected the prevailing "liberal" sentiment in academic circles during the period immediately preceding the experiment. The outcome reflected, not independent thinking, but conditioned reactions to a stereotype.[6]

Mass Communication

"Conditioned reactions to a stereotype": Thus does mass education prepare us for life in mass society. Meanwhile, mass communication provides a lifetime postgraduate course of its own in stereotypes, mass values, and conformity.

For example, the impact of advertising and propaganda has contributed greatly to the concentration of political and economic power. Mass communications has done far more than the armies and police forces of the modern world in saddling the masses with ruling organizations and ersatz values. The term "brainwashing" is generally applied to political indoctrination as practiced by the Communists. The element of physical force present in such brainwashing makes it especially repugnant to the Western world, but it should be remembered that we also possess enormous capabilities for reaching the minds of men, capabilities which we are quite willing to use.

In a nation in which 19 of every 20 families has a television set, it should be of more than passing interest that there are 6,858 full-time public relations employees in the executive branch of the federal government. It is the

[6]James C. Malin, "Adventure into the Unknown: Relativist, 'Man-Afraid-of-His-Mind,' " *Relativism and The Study of Man,* Helmut Schoeck and James W. Wiggins, eds. (Princeton, N. J.: Van Nostrand, 1961), p. 179.

purpose of these PR people to sell the big-brotherly qualities of government to the taxpayer. Lest the reader still think this a small operation — the budget for this work is $425 million a year! Meanwhile, the private advertisers are quite as busy as the government propagandists. The nonsense jingles of the advertisers, nearly as offensive as the tasteless programming which they sponsor, form a conspicuous place in the consciousness of the average American. Who of us does not know that "Winston tastes good, like a cigarette should?"

The newspaper extends its influence over an area nearly as large as television:

> In countries where the press is said to be free, newspapers are subsidized primarily by advertisers, and to a lesser extent by political parties, financial or professional groups. In countries where the press is not free, newspapers are subsidized by the central government. The man who pays the piper always calls the tune. In capitalist democracies the popular press supports its advertisers by inculcating the benefits of centralized industry and finance, coupled with as much centralized government as will enable these institutions to function at a profit. In totalitarian states all newspapers preach the virtue of governmental omnipotence, one-party politics and state control of everything. In both cases progressive technology has strengthened the hands of the local bosses by providing them with the means of persuading the many that concentration of political and economic power is for the general benefit.[7]

Thus massive organization breeds mass communication, and mass communication breeds massive organization. Throughout this process, the claims of advertising and propaganda escalate to higher and higher levels. There seems no end to claims concerning what "the system" is doing for us. The amount of humbug involved in these claims has become so enormous that larger and larger doses are required to achieve the proper effect. Thus the increasingly strident and hysterical tone, whether we are being sold soap by the private sector or seat belts by the public sector. Today the sheer volume of this selling job has become so great that it is difficult to escape. Turn off the TV, close the newspaper, ignore the great flood of periodical literature — you are likely to discover that a transistor radio is in your neighbor's hand. Conversation, Sunday's sermon, or your child's comments when he returns from a day at school are likely to bring you more of the same.

[7]Aldous Huxley, *Science, Liberty and Peace* (New York: Harper and Brothers, 1946), pp. 9–10.

The Dream World

The rebuttal to this criticism usually is a standard plea that mass communication serves to keep people informed and abreast of their world. All this information is thus a means of providing a properly informed electorate. If only that were so!

One reason the public is not properly informed by mass communication is the biased ideological position of many communications people. That ideological presupposition regards the current mass-oriented direction of our society as the only correct and moral position which an honorable man can support. Thus there is no embarrassment whatsoever in presenting only those "facts" which appear to lend credence to such a view. One wag has summarized the situation nicely by recalling several lines of Hilaire Belloc, lines well suited to the contemporary American scene:

> You cannot hope to bribe or twist,
> Thank God, the British journalist,
> But seeing what the man will do
> Unbribed, there is no reason to.

Another problem which mass communications introduces into our society might be termed "problem-enmassment." Just as enmassment has removed so many aspects of our lives from an individual scale, so have mass communications and modern technology escalated problems and their solutions from a human scale to a scale where individual action is no longer psychologically or practically possible.

In the nineteenth century, a man's problems were centered on the well-being of himself, his family, his neighbors, his community. If his neighbor's barn burned to the ground, he pitched in and helped rebuild it. Today we live in what James Burnham has called "the global village." Technology now permits mass communications to tell us what the entire world is suffering, generally telling us with an unbelievable amount of bathos. Thus we are introduced to new problems hopelessly beyond meaningful solution by the individual. What is therefore required? Collective solutions, of course!

A number of serious observers — Mr. David Riesman, in his study *The Lonely Crowd,* eminent among them — have grown alarmed at the increasing indifference of a great part of our population to even the most urgent issues of our time. I am equally alarmed, but I am not in the least surprised. For one thing, nearly everyone is deluged daily by a mass of "facts" and opinion, heaped upon him by the newspaper press, the radio, television, and motion pictures; he is urged to decide and act at once upon everything under the sun, and of course he cannot do anything of the kind. Thus most people, despairing of taking any intelligent part in the concerns of mankind, grow tired of hearing "wolf, wolf" cried out in frenzy every day, and sink into their own petty concerns for relief.[8]

A world in which everything is a constant and insoluble problem becomes a world in which all responsibility is finally totally rejected. Today when our neighbor's barn burns down, we assume that "the proper authorities" will deal with the problem. More and more of us make that assumption even when the barn in question is our own. The result is a society ugly and irresponsible beyond belief, a society whose members are unwilling to act to help one another or even to help themselves.

The End of Quality

Mass communication has also played its role in vulgarization of our culture. Once the sense of community and personal identity is undercut by enmassment, the drifting mass-man needs an anchor, a new sense of identity. This has been provided in modern America by the press, television, radio, and mass entertainment of all types. When mass-man meets mass communication, it is no longer clear, however, who is master. Judging from some of the comments made on the subject by such prophets of the new order as Marshall McLuhan, mass-man may prove to be a means by which the communications media pursue their own development. If medium and mind become so interchangeable, perhaps the two will one day become one.

And the union of medium and mind seems to be taking place on a very low plane indeed! It seems that "mass taste" is assumed by most advertisers and entertainment programmers to be on such a low level that one must stoop very low indeed to reach his audience.

There never was a time of so many and so powerful competitive distractions contesting with culture for the employment of one's hours, and directly tending towards the reinforcement and further degradation of the natural taste for the bathos. One has but to think of the enormous army of commercial enterprisers engaged in pandering to this taste and employing every conceivable device of ingenuity to confirm and flatter and reassure it.[9]

As quality suffers in our mass programming, an irony presents itself. Technological progress can produce a miracle such as television, bringing the sight and sound of a cultural or sporting event into our homes at the

[8]Russell Kirk, *Prospects for Conservatives* (Chicago: Regnery, 1956), p. 67.
[9]Albert Jay Nock, *On Doing the Right Thing, and Other Essays* (New York: Harper & Brothers, 1928), pp. 86–87.

instant of occurrence, yet this miracle is used largely to broadcast the most dreadful garbage imaginable.

Do the gross tastelessness and low standards so common to technological entertainment have their origins in the misuses and misdirection of technology — or in the nature of technology itself? Technology, remember, has its greatest triumphs in mass production and mass distribution. It just may be true that technology and mass communications can never rise above the low common denominator of their origins. Perhaps mass-men and mass communications deserve one another.

Whoever may be to blame, our modern culture continues on its rather depressing route. As Albert Jay Nock once remarked: "The sale of a book, however, at least in this country, is no guarantee of its good quality, but rather the opposite." Of course there are still good books being written and read, but the mass-man of our society has created does not read them. "Nowadays Demos, having learned to read, reveals an infantile taste by what he reads, the greater part of it rubbish and not a little of it garbage."[10]

Anyone dispassionately examining our broadcasting and our publishing in the last third of the twentieth century would agree, I think, that it leaves much to be desired. Many of the publishers and broadcasters would be the first to agree, but would defend their actions with the plea that the market dictated a demand for the sort of rubbish which is currently produced.

> The things they put out are what they are because we, the customers, are the kind of people we are and will buy nothing more reputable, at least in large enough quantity to bring in to the owners a sure and considerable profit. They print and broadcast what will build up mass circulation and so secure advertising, from which alone comes any large return on their investments. Surely, they insist, no reasonable American can fault them for being so typically American.[11]

Thus the mass communications media display economism, enmassment, technological dominance and the rest of the characteristic features of modern society. Each characteristic is occasionally described as the cause for the system's shortcomings; yet together they produce what we call the "American Way of Life."

The one additional lack of quality consistently demonstrated by American mass communications is the vicious attack upon privacy which the system reflects. The more heart-rending a mine disaster or an accident, the more certain that the television and newspaper reporters will examine every detail of the scene, every facial expression of the bereaved. Our public figures are allowed no privacy. No human act, from birth to death, is safe

---

[10]Bernard Iddings Bell, *Crowd Culture* (Chicago: Regnery [Gateway Edition], 1956), p. 15.
[11]*Ibid.,* p. 14.

from the prying eye of the media. Here again, mass communications is no more than a reflection of mass-man himself. Men tend to invade the privacy of others only when they fail to value their own privacy.

Culture Perverted

As men in their primitive environment reacted to the problems that inevitably arose, they evolved solutions to those problems. Over time, those solutions which best met human needs and fulfilled human longings have been institutionalized by society. That institutional structure is what Ortega defines as culture:

> But this culture, on being received by later generations, becomes more and more complicated and loses more and more of its genuineness. It turns into affectation and a concern with the topical, into cultural narcissism and the dead letter. Man then loses himself again, becomes demoralized, not now in the primitive forest, but in the excessive vegetation of his own culture.[12]

Something of that sort may be happening to America in our time. We may have begun to worship the forms of our society and forgotten the human meaning which those forms once had. For example, a technology originally designed to free people from the material limitations of their existence may have become a god-term in its own right, demanding the sacrifice of human values for its continued operation. We should be sure that the "Progress" which we have enshrined at the center of contemporary life is truly the route to human fulfillment for the individuals who compose society. In Irving Babbitt's phrase, before we completely give over our imaginations to "Progress," we should be sure we are "not progressing towards the edge of a precipice."

> Nor is being "progressive" inevitably virtuous or always shrewd. Sometimes progress is toward death. The mammoths of old time progressed. From century to century they became ever bigger and better armored. It was this progress that led to their extinction. They progressed until they could no longer handle themselves quickly, readily; and then a lot of funny little creatures, our semihuman ancestors, put the big brutes out of existence forever. More recently, we all have known of cities which prided themselves on "progress," meaning thereby growth in population, with no understanding that the price of their numerical development was the deterioration of charming and urbane communities into ugly, unorganized, uncivilized conglomer-

---

[12]Ortega y Gasset, *Man and Crisis*, pp. 127–128.

ates of human insects living without dignity. Theirs was a progress in degeneration.[13]

Assuming that modern America is launched upon such "a progress in degeneration," the next question is whether or not our society truly wishes to survive. No amount of critical analysis will cause us to change our direction until the values of the individuals composing society have changed. Until then, rest assured that we shall continue to cry for more and more of those forms which present society deems desirable.

The American Way of Life

The American cultural pattern becomes steadily more rigid and monolithic as time passes. We accept our present cultural forms with an amazing complacency. We are equalized and standardized to an extent which would have astonished any of our nineteenth-century social observers. For that nineteenth-century observer, indeed, for the typical nineteenth-century America, the world was a bright place:

The world, they felt, was a safe place, watched over by a kindly God, who exacted nothing but cheerfulness and goodwill from his children; and the American flag was a sort of rainbow in the sky, promising that all storms were over. Or if storms came, such as the Civil War, they would not be harder to weather than was necessary to test the national spirit and raise it to a new efficiency. The subtler dangers which we now see threatening America had not yet come in sight — material restlessness was not yet ominous, the pressure of business enterprises was not yet out of scale with the old life or out of key with the old moral harmonies. A new type of American had not appeared — the untrained, pushing, cosmopolitan orphan, cocksure in manner but not too sure in his morality, to whom the old Yankee, with his sour integrity, is almost a foreigner. Was not "increase," in the *Bible,* a synonym for benefit? Was not "abundance" the same, or almost the same, as happiness?[14]

Today the quest for material satisfaction and the desire for power has transformed America — and not for the better. That small cloud which George Santayana saw on the horizon a few decades ago has become the dominant fact of our culture. With that material emphasis has come a parallel emphasis upon conformity. With the advent of advanced tech-

[13]Bernard Iddings Bell, *Crisis in Education* (New York: Whittlesey House, 1949), p. 9.
[14]George Santayana, *Character and Opinion In The United States* (Garden City, N. Y.: Doubleday [Anchor Books], 1956), pp. 8–9.

nology, we all tend to do the same kind of work, read the same books and
newspapers, use the same soap. We have even become a bit suspicious of
anyone who does not choose to participate in this "Progress."

Sometimes this material emphasis and conformity is blamed on the sheer
quantity of people in present society. Surely the problem of numbers is
important, but the change in our society is less in *how many* of us there are
than in *who* and *what* we have become. For example, New York City had
as large a population 30 years ago as it does today. Yet compare the clean,
efficient, *very human* city of the late 1930s with the filthy, hopelessly
clogged and viciously inhumane mess it has become today. Somewhere
along the line, we have become so concerned with money, power, and
enmassment that we have lost sight of what we are living *for*. That fact, and
not the coincidental fact of more people, is the cause of our discontent.

Read a daily paper, watch television, take a stroll past a paperback book
display on a newsstand. Consider for a moment the sort of people at whom
such rubbish is directed. Then ask yourself what the American people have
become.

> . . . we contend, with an ingenuous provinciality, that all the world
> wants to be American. And by "American" we mean industrialized,
> motorized, Hollywoodized, capitalized, federalized, corporatized,
> synchronized, and modernized. Displaying an impatient perplexity
> which is wholly sincere, we decry as reactionary or conspiratorial or
> Russian-influenced anyone in foreign parts who dissents from The
> American Way. We manifest a yawning ignorance of the venerable
> principle that cultural form and substance cannot be transported
> intact from one people to another. We claim that everyone except
> feudal barons or Reds longs for tractors, Bob Hope, self-service laun-
> dries, direct primaries, cloverleaf intersections, high-school extracur-
> ricular activities, two evening newspapers, Coca-Cola, and a stylish
> burial at Memory Grove Cemetery.[15]

But while we sell ourselves on the American Way of Life, it is well to
recall that such a way of life has brought with it not only a cheapening
crassness, but also an amazing selfishness. Today many Americans seem to
live for comfort, luxury and amusement. We believe that we can buy our
way in anywhere, quite forgetting that not everything is for sale. We overin-
dulge our children and then are surprised when they turn out to be the
brattish pills that such undisciplined upbringing is so likely to produce.
What's the matter with our kids? What's the matter with our culture?
Exactly the same thing that's the matter with us!

[15]Kirk, pp. 178–179.

Bigness for Its Own Sake

One of those cultural forms which we have come to worship at such peril is sheer mass. "If it's bigger, it must be better." As a culture, we have come to *prefer* mass for its own sake. We lust after bigness — in Roepke's phrase, "the cult of the colossal."

The cult of the colossal pervades all our social institutions. Our churches are social to such an extent that many religiously inclined people no longer feel their church a place to which they can turn for spiritual guidance. Our organized charity has become organizational to an amazingly antipersonal extent. A campaign to raise and distribute millions of dollars for charitable purposes may be "private" (that is, nongovernmental), but can hardly be called personal in any true sense of the world. Our obligation to serve as our brother's keeper is not so easily discharged. Whether the massive organization of the State, or of a private institution, takes over, our charitable function is not really discharged. Either way, we are made less as persons through the absorption of a measure of our personal responsibility. At this point, those who have been poor enough at some time in their lives to have experienced firsthand contact with an officious social worker or bureaucrat will quickly add that the recipient of "organizational charity" also often finds himself made less as a person by the transaction. Both giver and receiver are thus depersonalized.

The cult of the colossal undercuts our culture in other ways as well. The intoxication with quantity leads us into setting our standards and values on such a basis. We often tend to determine personal or artistic merit exclusively on dollar value. The colossal and the commercial thus run hand in hand. In the process, Gresham's Law applies to cultural affairs. It seems that the bad drives the good from circulation in all areas of human endeavor.

Another closely related trap which quantification has set for us is the excessive reliance upon statistics which dominates modern society. Today we are concerned with volumes, averages, indices, often without sufficiently careful thought as to what goes to make up the categories. We are so concerned with numbers that we often forget the real people, people with innumerable personal differences and spiritual values which cannot be quantified, who go to make up those statistical aggregates which we praise so highly.

We are told that measurement of what 50,000 television viewers, carefully selected from around the nation for their representative characteristics, are watching on a given day will tell us all we need know to discover what television programs 200,000,000 Americans are watching. This may tell us a great deal about the mass-oriented nature of television. I hope it tells us little or nothing about the personalities and the individual capacities of 200,000,000 people. However buried the personalities of those

200,000,000 may be in our age of mass organization, the urge to be real people, real human beings, is still present, despite the American Way of Life:

> To be poor in order to be simple, to produce less in order that the product may be more choice and beautiful, and may leave us less burdened with unnecessary duties and useless possession — that is an ideal not aritculate in the American mind; yet here and there I seem to have heard a sigh after it, a groan at the perpetual incubus of business and shrill society.[16]

The Loss of True Leisure

Just as our culture suffers from quantitative values in its institutional structure, so it suffers a parallel decline in the standards of art and entertainment. Our sports events are largely mass spectacles suitable for a Roman arena, though we have gone the Romans one better by bringing such events "live and in living color" into nearly *all* American homes. Even our cheering at the football game is organized. The "cheerleader" is a phenomenon peculiar to American society.

Our social life is equally organized. We have books on how to win friends and influence people, how to "handle" groups, how to raise our children according to the best approved methods. We even have books telling us how to read books! And, in the perfect capstone of organized and nonspontaneous existence, we then form groups to read and discuss these books. Name the activity, at any point between birth and death, and a book exists to tell you how to conduct yourself, while a group gives you moral support and social acceptance in that particular activity.

Irving Babbitt, one of the most perceptive social critics of this or any other age, some 40 years ago detected this abuse of leisure time which we have perpetrated upon ourselves in the twentieth century. Even while technology has freed us from the basic material concerns, we have not used our new-found free time as true leisure, but instead have subordinated our every waking moment to new material concerns, preferably pursued in the company of a herd of other people. If one questions our society's appetite for more material gadgets and more regimented, stereotyped existence, one automobile trip on a Sunday afternoon at any point within 100 miles of any large American city should soon remove any lingering doubts.

To lose any idea of how one's time might be put to *personal,* nonorganized use, to become afraid of any moment of time in which one is not surrounded by gadgets and groups, is true decadence, because a sense of true leisure has always been the mark of a civilized man.

[16]Santayana, p. 117.

Life can be drab in a world caught on a technological treadmill, a world in which the object of human existence has been lost:

Each day for most people is like the last, each week is like the week before, each month a repetition of the previous month, each year a tale retold to an audience which has aged twelve months since the last performance. Men rise, shave and breakfast, travel to work, eat and work again, travel and eat, relax and exercise, make love or quarrel, gamble or read and so to sleep. Women rise, breakfast and cook, wash dishes and make beds, do their shopping and tend their children, cook and eat, gossip, relax and sleep. More fortunate at first, children are soon involved in the same stale sequence with the classroom instead of the factory, with homework instead of play. While the pattern may vary with the income group, the day's routine has captured us all in some degree. We must eat in order to work and work in order to eat. And having done what we must, we lack time or energy to do what we want.[17]

A number of social commentators have recognized that such a life is finally no life at all. Some recommend relief via "consumership," which turns out to be working harder and harder for the means to employ more gadgets, while surrounded by larger and larger groups of people. Surely no true leisure, no genuine personality, is present in such an extension of our mass society.

Another suggested approach to relieving the boredom of modern society is through "cultural advancement" for the masses. We have recently been informed of a newly created post in the United States Government: a presidential advisor on art affairs, presumably to bring the organized powers of government to bear on the collection and "appreciation" of art. This idea is not as new as it might appear. Some such notion of "enriching the life of the masses" has always been present in the vast, expensive, organized library and museum projects, both public and private, which dot the modern scene. For some individuals, such opportunities will indeed enrich their lives; for them, the contact with art will lead to personal development because of the energy and the portion of self which the individuals involved will give to that aspect of their lives. Put another way, the proper use of the individual's leisure can give the libraries and museums meaning — but the burden still rests with the individual, not the mass.

Without individual incentive to cultivate artistic endeavor, all the mu-

[17]C. Northcote Parkinson, *Left Luggage* (Boston: Houghton Mifflin, 1967), pp. 169–170.

seums on earth will not raise popular culture one iota; nor will true leisure
be utilized; nor will any new artistic achievement occur:

> Our megalopolitan agglomerations, which make great ado about art,
> are actually sterile on the creative side; they patronize art, they mer-
> chandise it, but do not produce it. The despised hinterland, which is
> rather carefree about the matter, somehow manages to beget the great
> majority of American artists. True, they often migrate to New York,
> at considerable risk to their growth; they as often move away again,
> to Europe or some treasured local retreat. Our large cities affect a
> cosmopolitan air but have little of the artistic cosmopolitanism that
> once made Paris a Mecca. They do not breed literary groups; the
> groups appear in the hinterland.[18]

Modern planners who would "enrich" our lives should face one fact.
Enmassment and mass values do *not* produce art. Only people, individuals,
have that capacity. Meanwhile, for the rest of us, the artistic level of
enmassed modern life leaves much to be desired:

> The shopgirl does not recite Shakespeare before breakfast. Henry
> Ford's hired hands do not hum themes from Beethoven as they go to
> work. Instead, the shopgirl reads the comic strip with her bowl of
> patent cereal and puts on a jazz record while she rouges her lips. She
> reads the confession magazines and goes to the movies. The factory
> hand simply does not hum; the *Daily Mirror* will do for him, with
> pictures and titles that can be torpidly eyed. The industrialists in art
> — that is, the Hollywood producers, the Macfadden publications, the
> Tin Pan Alley crowd, the Haldeman-Julius Blue Books — will natu-
> rally make their appeal to the lowest common denominator. They
> know the technique of mass-production, which, if applied to the arts,
> must invariably sacrifice quality to quantity.[19]

Quantity as the Enemy

Just as the worship of quantity and the cult of the colossal have warped
our institutions and have robbed us of true leisure, so has quantification
attacked us in our purely physical existence. We are drowning in things —
we are burying ourselves beneath a mountain of trash.

We all desire a decent home, food, and clothing. We all wish to have those
comforts and amenities which allow us to live our lives in peace and satisfac-

---

[18]Donald Davidson, "A Mirror for Artists," *I'll Take My Stand* (New York: Harper [Torch-
book], 1962), p. 57.
[19]*Ibid.*, p. 35.

tion, with sufficient surplus to meet the needs of our loved ones. I carry no brief for poverty. But when the politicians and the sociologists describe the American Way of Life as they envision it, I believe they are less concerned with the alleviation of true poverty than with an endless flood of material goods, pouring out upon society to satisfy an endless escalation of human appetite.

How ugly such a world becomes! Visit Yosemite, Yellowstone, or some other lovely natural treasure. Watch the trash pile up, smell the cook stoves and the chemical toilets, listen to the transistor radios.

We have just ended the most productive decade, in material terms, of our entire American history. That productivity has developed a new American habit: throwing things away. The parkways surrounding New York City are littered with abandoned cars. Too junky to bother with, the cars are stripped of identification by their owners and left for the local government to handle. The economics is extremely simple: When it costs $30 to have a car towed to a junkyard where it can be sold for $10, the owner comes out $20 ahead by leaving the car on the street. The same pattern dominates our technological society. The parts to repair an automobile, a television set, or most of the devices which surround us are usually in so-called "sealed units." It is cheaper to replace whole segments of our machines than it is to repair them. This may be "economic," but it makes for junkpiles and waste beyond all belief. Today it is usually cheaper and easier to throw our broken toys away than to mend them. And how many toys we have, young and old alike! Every conceivable activity carries with it a list of "necessary" gadgets, conveniences, accessories, and what-have-you, many of them "disposable." Use it once and discard it — why be bothered?

Meanwhile, due to modern technological "progress," the new aluminum beer cans, discarded everywhere across the face of our land, will now resist the elements for fully 30 years, serving as a semipermanent monument to our new affluence. Our waste keeps pace with our material production: Each year we discard a billion and one-half tons of animal waste, over a billion tons of mineral waste, over one-half billion tons of agricultural waste, a quarter billion tons of household and commercial waste, over 100 million tons of industrial waste — a total of 3.5 billion tons of waste a year and growing yearly! Meanwhile, what we are doing to our air, our water, and our living space, is literally beyond belief. We are making a pigsty of our world.

As we wallow in the problems generated by mass-man and his mass society, the central problem remains: How do we tell the vital difference between a culture oriented to *people* and a mass culture? The central distinguishing feature of mass culture may be the love of quantity for its own sake. If so, mass culture in American society has come into its own.

Epilogue

The bigger the crowd the more negligible the individual becomes. But if the individual, overwhelmed by the sense of his own puniness and impotence, should feel that his life has lost its meaning—which, after all, is not identical with public welfare and higher standards of living — then he is already on the road to State slavery and, without knowing or wanting it, has become its proselyte. The man who looks only outside and quails before the big battalions has no resource with which to combat the evidence of his senses and his reason. But that is just what is happening today: We are all fascinated and overawed by statistical truths and large numbers and are daily apprised of the nullity and futility of the individual personality, since it is not represented and personified by any mass organization.

C. G. Jung,
The Undiscovered Self

Technology is neither good nor bad in itself. Urban growth, like bureaucracy, may be a cooperative social effort which benefits those involved; or it may be a monstrosity which strangles the individuals who compose society. Technology, bureaucracy, and urbanization are all no better or worse than the uses to which they are put. We all have benefited from many technological advances; we all find occasions when centralized organization and administration accomplish goals we cannot achieve alone; and man's psychological and cultural needs can often be better served by life in the city. Nothing in the preceding pages is intended to deny these facts.

Still, it is also true that the tools of bureaucracy, technology, and urbanization can be misused. They can become brutally oppressive of the individual citizen. It is my contention that exactly this has been happening in twentieth-century America. We have forgotten that men are individuals as well as social beings. We have pursued a course of enmassment, of contrived "bigness" for its own sake, that threatens to depersonalize our society and our culture, robbing us of our most precious possession: traditional American self-reliance and self-determination. No amount of alleged "Progress" can fill the void thus created.

The damage thus done to the individual, and to his society, touches every part of our lives. Mass society and mass values are having immeasurably adverse effects upon the quality and the personality of our existence. Today the typical American finds himself confronted with "bigness" on an unprecedented scale. Our lives are institutionalized and regulated on every hand. Each of us is becoming a smaller and smaller chip floating on a more and more enormous ocean. The individual finds himself under great pressure from every quarter to "adjust" to the new life — to find a place in "the system."

Since all the institutions of our society — ranging from organized religion to organized amusement and touching all points between the two — make the same demand, the individual has no place to turn. He is confronted with a truly bewildering situation. On every hand he meets a denial that the individual is genuinely significant; on every hand he is confronted with vast institutional enmassments that seem beyond both his control and his comprehension. He truly lives in "The Age of Bewilderment."

2

The Politics of Bewilderment

Prologue

> . . . many traditional positions in our world [have] suffered not so much because of inherent defect as because of the stupidity, ineptness, and intellectual sloth of those who . . . are presumed to have their defense in charge.
>
> Richard Weaver,
> *The Southern Tradition at Bay*

Most observers would perhaps agree that the traditional American emphasis upon individual values has generated an enormous achievement during the past 200 years, providing a great deal of material prosperity for the "common man," while leaving him largely free to determine his own way of life. At least our record in terms of both prosperity *and* freedom compares favorably with any other social system ever devised. Still, many of those same observers are highly critical of our present society. The charge is frequently heard that we have departed from those values which made us great — that the common man is no longer free and is steadily less likely to be prosperous. More and more Americans apparently feel trapped in a bewildering age which suffers from some basic malady. Some of the problems which give rise to these doubts have been discussed in the first portion of this book.

The resultant Age of Bewilderment is closely connected to the Politics of Bewilderment. Our problems seem so far beyond our individual depth that today we ever more frequently turn to bigness and to collective solutions. It seems that any age which thus favors collective solutions is tailor-made to guarantee politics a dominant role in ordering society, since political solutions are irrevocably collective in nature.

As the result:

> Throughout the world, in the name of progress, men who call themselves communists, socialists, fascists, nationalists, progressives, and even liberals, are unanimous in holding that government with its instruments of coercion must, by commanding the people how they shall live, direct the course of civilization and fix the shape of things to come. They believe in what Mr. Stuart Chase accurately describes

as "the overhead planning and control of economic activity." This is
the dogma which all the prevailing dogmas presuppose. This is the
mold in which are cast the thought and action of the epoch. No other
approach to the regulation of human affairs is seriously considered,
or is even conceived as possible. The recently enfranchised masses and
the leaders of thought who supply their ideas are almost completely
under the spell of this dogma. Only a handful here and there, groups
without influence, isolated and disregarded thinkers, continue to challenge it. For the premises of authoritarian collectivism have become
the working beliefs, the self-evident assumptions, the unquestioned
axioms, not only of all the revolutionary regimes, but of nearly every
effort which lays claim to being enlightened, humane, and progressive.[1]

The rationale for this collective political bigness, this enmassment of
political power over the lives of men, proceeds on the assumption that the
complexity of modern society necessitates central planning. The individual
is presumed to be faced with such organized bigness, such enormous concentrations of power, that only the bigness of government, acting in the
name of the individual, can properly protect his interests. We are being told,
in effect, that the old truths and the traditional American fabric of society
simply no longer apply in the modern world.

Before we abandon ourselves unreservedly to this new order in human
affairs, it might be instructive to ask how all this has come about. What is
the source of the bigness which threatens us on every hand? Why are we
becoming more comfortable with mass values than with the traditional
individual values of an older America? My thesis is easily stated: Bigness
in American life, the enmassment which surrounds us, has its origins in
political interventions which have occurred in our society on a steadily
increasing scale for the past 100 years. In short, today we are being told that
political intervention is the only answer for problems which have actually
been caused by previous political interventions!

It is true that some few voices have been raised in our country against
further expansion of political authority. Unfortunately, many of these are
the voices of men who are unwilling to practice what they preach. The
businessman who is an ardent "free enterpriser" at Rotary luncheons and
who simultaneously advocates political measures which improve the position of his business is an all-too-familiar figure in America today. We also
give away the case for freedom when we fail to speak from the right premise.
If we limit ourselves to the exclusively economic, exclusively materialistic
emphasis, we are dealing in the same terms used by the architects of the new

[1] Walter Lippmann, *The Good Society* (New York: Grosset and Dunlap, 1943), pp. 3–4.

mass society. More bathtubs and more color TV sets are an insufficient basis for the defense of human freedom.

Whatever the failings of freedom's defenders, the collective ideal has been having its way in American society. To engineer a reversal and to chart a course toward the individually-oriented society, the first question we must ask ourselves is difficult: Is the present American society which we see around us in the latter third of the twentieth century an inevitable development? Are bureaucracy, antipersonal organizational structure, materialism, conformity, and enmassment all part of an irreversible historical trend? Most historians who form our opinions in this area apparently believe this to be so. Dealing too exclusively with effects rather than causes, they tend to confuse sheer bulk with healthy growth, positing enmassment as the wave of the future.

Such history books give us a photographic image of our times; they catch a surface image. But they fail to penetrate beneath that surface of events, thus giving us only continuing reinterpretation of the same old image. In the process, they miss the point.

It is my contention that America might have been a far different place today were it not for the distortions introduced into our society by large-scale government intervention. Further, it seems clear to me that we cannot hope to reverse the trend of our times unless we first understand what has been done to us by The Politics of Bewilderment.

VI

WHO WERE THE AMERICANS?

Rural Americans, that is most Americans before the Civil War, produced most of the necessities of life on the farm and in the home. They grew most of their food, hunted and fished for a portion of their meat, spun their yarn, wove and fashioned homsepun clothes, churned their butter, made the soap and the lye that went into it. A family often "got by" with only an occasional trip to the store to purchase spices, salt, powder, and shot, and delicacies or trinkets. The farmer was by necessity a jack-of-all-trades, adept at everything from carpentry to wood splitting. The farm wife was expected to be accomplished in everything from fancy needlework to gardening.

I describe neither utopia nor pastoral bliss. There was much hard and lonely work, much suffering; the rains fell on the just and the unjust alike. My point is that here were people who had a way of life built upon independence, who had a significant liberty to dispose of their time and resources, and were profoundly aware of their responsibilities for their own well-being. Self-respect and community respect depended upon maintaining independence.

Clarence B. Carson,
The Fateful Turn

Who were the Americans? Once we thought we knew who we were. We were proud of our country and proud of ourselves. We were an independent bunch, quick to act, a bit restless and eager to "get a move on." Perhaps all that living space, all that room to grow, gave us a sense of freedom and a sense of freedom's importance that made us independent. Whatever the reason, Americans very early began to display a preference for tending to their own affairs.

Colonial America

The American colonial experience is too familiar to require extensive retelling here. The period of our thirteen colonies has another name in British colonial history: "The Period of Salary Neglect." That is, Britain was so busy with so many other things that she left the colonies largely to their own devices for much of their history. The result was a prosperity and an independence to which the new Americans soon became accustomed. We were a free people developing a new pattern of life in a new and largely unoccupied continent.

From the first, we were not bound by the restraints of bureaucracy and the economic regulations which plagued Europe. We were free of the tight European class structure, free to form a truly open-ended society. It is true that the seaboard colonial towns witnessed attempts to reinstitute the old European ways, but the vast unoccupied land mass to the west offered an excellent and constantly available source of individual independence.

American society left ample opportunity for the individual to achieve economic independence. Thrift, hard work, and self-reliance were virtues which bore direct rewards. Americans might not yet have achieved their every desire, but they did feel that they had discovered a system which left doors open for the individual and which left each man free to pursue his own desires.

Later, when the British Crown decided that the colonies should no longer be "neglected," but instead regulated according to the planned-economy mentality then labeled as mercantilism, England attempted to redirect the colonial patterns of life into new channels. The older social mobility, individual opportunity and independence which had characterized colonial life was now regarded as subversive to mercantilist policy. As a boy, George III had been told by his mother, "George, be King." Unfortunately for the first British Empire, he took his mother seriously and, in his attempted reimposition of royal authority, lost the American colonies.

Thus the American War for Independence was not a radical uprising designed to remake society according to some new master plan. It is far more accurately described as a struggle to preserve an open society which had already been largely achieved. Perhaps the easiest way to see the American Revolution for what it actually was would be to compare our development with the other great revolutionary uprising of the late eighteenth century. One of the distinguished political scientists of our time has made that distinction crystal clear:

If we compare the French Revolution, characterized by democratic radicalism with its quest for centralization, by bloodshed and infringements upon liberty and property, with the American Revolution characterized by democratic restraint with its desire for federalism, and a protection of the individual's life, liberty and property, then the value of federalism for freedom suggests itself strongly. This impression is enhanced by a comparison between the turbulent political development in France which often challenged the rights of the individual, and the quiet evolution in America which in general has been conducive to a protection of those rights.[1]

The same emphasis upon individual rights also characterized the deliberations of the Constitutional Convention. The Founding Fathers have often been criticized for antidemocratic attitudes. And it is true that the distinguished social, political, economic and intellectual leaders who came together to form the political framework of our nation were strongly suspicious of unlimited democracy; they were strongly suspicious of *any* system of government which centralized so much power that it became the exclusively determining factor in the lives of the individuals composing society. No one, not even a majority, should have control over the lives of other men. Or so Americans once thought.

Felix Morley has originated a valuable distinction to clarify the word "democracy." He divides the concept into *political* democracy and *social* democracy. Viewed in this light, it is clear that the innumerable roadblocks thrown up in the path of the majority by the Founding Fathers in the writing of the Federal Constitution and their creation of American federalism were not intended to set up a *political* democracy. Yet America has traditionally been the land of great social mobility and individual opportunity, that is to say, a *social* democracy. Thus the American tradition of federalism has deliberately limited the exercise of political power, not to suppress individual liberty, but to enhance it. Put another way, the very real success story of America has hinged upon the limitation of political power rather than its exercise.

This nation has been consistently hostile to monopoly power, whether social, religious, or political. The Constitution outlawed titles of nobility (social monopoly) and an established church (religious monopoly), and made a particular point of outlawing excessive centralization of political power, as for example in the Ninth and Tenth Amendments to the Constitution:

Ninth: The enumeration in the Constitution of certain rights shall not be construed to deny or disparage others retained by the people.
Tenth: The powers not delegated to the United States by the Constitution, nor prohibited by it to the states, are reserved to the states respectively or to the people.

The social mobility and room for individual difference which characterized colonial America and was institutionalized in the Constitution became the dominant theme for American life in the nineteenth century. Strong

[1]Gottfried Dietze, *America's Political Dilemma* (Baltimore: Johns Hopkins Press, 1968), p. 87.

statement of such sentiment appears again and again in the works of such key intellectual leaders as Thomas Jefferson and John Adams. In fact, whatever else Americans may have found to quarrel over, individual independence and opportunity were so universally accepted as fundamental to the American system that those values were simply not called into question.

The Age of Jackson

The American emphasis upon individual independence and opportunity coincided with the development of modern capitalism. Naturally enough, the entrenched local capitalists already established in the eighteenth century were not always eager to share their privileged position with rising new capitalists. Also quite naturally, those rising capitalists who were insisting upon their own place in the sun were unwilling to allow the old government-granted monopolies (for example, The Charles River Bridge or The Bank of the United States) to stand in their way. This led to the political and legal struggles of the 1830s and 1840s — sometimes characterized by historians as an embryonic New Deal — struggles presumably between "the people" and the "vested interests."

Nothing could be further from the truth. It is much more nearly correct to see the political conflicts of the Age of Jackson as a struggle between "new" capitalism and "old" capitalism. The Bank of the United States, for example, was attacked not in an assault upon capitalism, but as a complaint by members of a rising middle class who protested a monopoly situation limiting their opportunities within the burgeoning American system.

The assault on economic privilege carried over from the banking struggle and came to include tariffs and subsidies. The Jacksonians were squarely in the American tradition of insisting upon free competition and a minimum of interference, whether public or private, with the independence and opportunity of the individual. Jackson himself was a westerner whose primary appeal to a rising middle class was equality before the law and resistance to unwarranted centralization, whether in economics or politics. Nothing could make it clearer that the Jacksonian movement was well within the dominant American tradition than the fact that upon John Marshall's death Andrew Jackson appointed such a man as Roger Taney to fill the Supreme Court vacancy. As Chief Justice, Taney served for nearly 30 years, from 1835 to 1864, producing a series of decisions steadily strengthening the contract clause of the Constitution and consistently enforcing property rights as a prime guarantee of individual liberty.

Meanwhile, American life before the Civil War continued to be heavily influenced by the Western frontier. The West was a source of individualism and opportunity. The image of the American frontiersman as a free man, as a man responsible for self, fitted well with the frontier's function as a safety valve for those Americans who wanted or needed a new start.

As the Civil War approached, the essence of Abraham Lincoln's position on slavery came to rest upon the great importance which he and most Americans attached to independence and opportunity in the American West. Lincoln's own life epitomized both the virtues of the frontier and the open quality of American society. We were proud of a nation in which a rail-splitter could become President of the United States. Lincoln was insisting that the door be left open to westward expansion. That was a large part of the argument against allowing the spread of slavery into the territories. Many Americans were afraid that slavery in the territories would spell the end of the frontier as a source of independence and opportunity for the small American freeholder. Thus one of the compelling reasons for the war may well have been an insistence that the United States remain a land of opportunity and freedom.

Fragmented Political and Social Power

Even the tragedy of the Civil War did not shake the enormous optimism of Americans. We felt our nation to be a Promised Land, a land in which the little man truly had the opportunity to chart his own course. Most Americans felt a sense of genuine security. Men feel secure not when others have promised to care for them, but when they are conscious of their freedom, a freedom which brings with it a sense of personal dignity and responsibility. It is little wonder that we look back with nostalgia on a happy era free from the menace of foreign invasion, an era in which, except for the brief aberration of the Civil War and its immediate aftermath, we were spared the burden of standing armies and bureaucratic manipulation which plagued the nations of Europe throughout the nineteenth century.

By mid-century, Americans had a history stressing social mobility and individual independence. We thought we had proven that such a system could work. We thought we had a vast and still largely undeveloped frontier to insure that the system would continue to work, that the little man would continue to have a chance to chart his own course.

We Americans were justifiably proud of our society. The nation's relative decentralization of power, political and economic, astonished nineteenth-century Europeans. The resultant freedom had given a social balance of aristocratic and democratic elements, and a chance to develop a deep and abiding love for local community and family:

> The heart of American democracy was local autonomy. A century after France had developed a reasonably efficient, centralized public administration, Americans could not even conceive of a managerial government. Almost all of a community's affairs were still arranged informally.[2]

[2]Robert H. Wiebe, *The Search for Order* (New York: Hill and Wang, 1968), p. xiii.

Status, wealth, and power were widely diffused in the America of 100 years ago. Leadership was likely to be based upon high standards of conduct, upon close professional and social ties within each community. The great centralizations still lay in the future. Americans were still responsible to self and society. They still felt themselves confronted with problems and institutions on a scale adaptable to real people and individual needs.

Loss of the Old Ways

All that was destined to end. A largely agrarian and decentralized society was about to be industrialized, bringing with it such centralization and standardization that the individual would no longer be allowed a place to shield himself from bigness, no longer allowed to lead his own life. The problem was not exclusively American. The European community was rushing ahead of us down the same road. In the words of a distinguished social historian of the comparable period in German history:

> Indeed, no one who compares the Germany of the first part of the nineteenth century with that of the second part, can escape the disheartening impression that this country . . . became a victim of the general intellectual and moral disintegration . . . [T]he second half of the nineteenth century . . . was a period of progressive vulgarity, gloom, and disintegration.[3]

It is true that industrial development and modern technology were destined to bring vast material wealth to Americans. The advances in medical science, the improvements in living standards stagger the imagination. All such progress is to the good. However, this does not necessarily tell us anything about the comparative quality of the old and the new social orders. Industrialization itself is neither good nor bad. Like all social developments, it can never rise higher than the means and ends which dominate its practical application. The shortcomings of the late nineteenth century were to stem from the new values which accompanied industrialization on its march through society. Whatever else may be said about the simpler, largely agrarian social order of an earlier America, it should at least be conceded that the traditional America had functioned with values worthy of conservation. The nation had been a refuge of sentiment, honor, and dignity, a place in which "little men" had both the chance and the necessity of discovering their own solutions to the riddle of life. In the older framework, Americans knew who they were. In the period which lay ahead, they were no longer so sure of their identity.

[3]Wilhelm Roepke, *The Social Crisis of Our Time* (Chicago: University of Chicago Press, 1950), pp. 59–60.

VII

THE BIG CHANGE

The way was prepared for a new ethos in America. The intellectual foundations of liberty — belief in reason, freedom of the mind and will, natural law, and individual responsibility — were undermined by deterministic theories bolstered by Darwinism, by an increasing emphasis upon the role of the nonrational in human behavior, and by doctrines of force and necessity. Industrialization and mechanization, accompanied by the rise of the city, the influx of numerous immigrants from Southern and Eastern Europe, the concentration of wealth, and the growth of corporations and trusts posed new problems for the livelihood and independence of the individual.

Clarence B. Carson,
The Fateful Turn

Many historians view Mr. Lincoln's fight to save the Union as a fundamentally conservative effort to maintain American society in the face of sweeping change. This may be an accurate description of at least one principal Northern motivation during the Civil War. If so, it contains one of the great ironies of American history. If the Civil War was indeed a conservative attempt to prevent the disruption of the Union, it was also the vehicle for an enormous transformation in the fundamental character of American society — an attempt to avoid change, producing the most sweeping changes.

The War Between the States and the Reconstruction Period made abundantly clear that participation in the American experiment was no longer to be a voluntary process. The war itself and the constitutional amendments which came as the direct result of the war enormously extended the authority of central government. Notice was served that the states were no longer to be given authority in defining the rights and obligations of their citizens. Citizenship for the individual American became national. And yet the national government which now posed as the defender of individual rights was quick to violate those rights once it was enmeshed in the first total war of the modern era. The Civil War was fought to the point of exhaustion within the narrow confines of a single country. It should not be surprising that hatred and tensions mounted to a point which produced extensive violations of fundamental civil liberties by both the Northern and Southern governments.

The Civil War saw repeated cases of civilian arrest and imprisonment on completely arbitrary grounds. In the Confiscation Acts, the North granted itself the privilege of seizing private property, on the grounds that the property was being used to further Southern resistance. In this way, the concept of total war was extended from states to individuals. Total war was also extended to include rigorous censorship of the press, as even the minds of men were to be mobilized for war. Perhaps the single largest imposition which ran counter to previous American experience was the effect on the individual produced by the draft. During the Civil War, military conscription was used on a large scale for the first time in American history. Both the North and the South found themselves willing to adopt compulsory military service and centralized control over the individual.

In a variety of ways, the American Civil War saw the substantial growth of the power of centralized government to control the opinions, property, and persons of its citizens. The Union had been preserved, but only at enormous cost in terms of the erosion of the individual values which Americans had previously cherished. The door was opened to a wave of political centralization which promised to change the character of American life.

Seen in historical perspective, the effects of the American Civil War were only a local manifestation of a new mentality then on the rise throughout the Western world:

> If there is any one thing which typifies the latter part of the nineteenth century in a manner which carries its disastrous consequences over into our day, it is that "cult of political unity and national expansion." . . . It is nothing but the familiar urge for super-organization and centralization and the habit of attaching absolute value to it, while regarding any attempt to question it as heresy, treason, or malicious perversity. In the eyes of this cult it is despicable and a sign of reactionary and romantic stupidity to be moderate in one's wants, to stress the necessity for an integrated and varied social structure and to demand as much independence and autonomy as possible for the subsections which constitute the larger units (federalism) both in political and economic respects. This megalolatry is the common ideological breeding ground of modern nationalism, imperialism, socialism, monopoly capitalism, and statism.[1]

[1]Wilhelm Roepke, *The Social Crisis of Our Time* (Chicago: University of Chicago Press, 1950), p. 60.

Economism and the Rugged Individualists

Albert Jay Nock defined economism as an interpretation of ". . . the whole of human life in terms of the production, acquisition and distribution of wealth." In the period following the Civil War, such an exclusively materialistic interpretation of life became increasingly common in America. The concerns of economic production came to be considered apart from the legal, institutional, and ethical framework which made such productivity possible. Wealth became less a means to an end than an end in itself. Soon the political centralizations of the post–Civil War era were being used to further the economic centralizations of the late nineteenth century. In the process, room for individual difference and decision continued to shrink steadily in both the economic and political spheres:

> The old idea of rewards was vanishing, and instead of receiving a station dictated by a theory of the whole society, men were winning their stations through a competition in which human considerations were rulled out. Carlyle had bitterly indicted it in England as the age of the "cash-nexus." Everything betokened the breaking up of the old synthesis in a general movement toward abstraction in human relationships. The individual was becoming a unit in the formless democratic mass; economics was usurping the right to determine both political and moral policies; and standards supposed to be unalterable were being affected by the new standards of relativism. Topping it all was the growing spirit of skepticism, which was destroying the religious sanctions of conduct and leaving only the criterion of utility.[2]

The rationalist assumptions of Darwinism and relativism denied men the dignity of a spiritual heritage and the fixed standards by which their lives might be ordered. In return, the late nineteenth century promised that political and economic enmassment would replace such individually oriented groupings as the family, the neighborhood, and the parish, presumably bringing new material prosperity to all.

Meanwhile, the collective tendencies of the age were not yet always labeled as collectivism. The late nineteenth century saw the heyday of such defenders of "rugged individualism" as Herbert Spencer and William Graham Sumner. Despite their reputation as defenders of the individual, both men founded their concept of Social Darwinism on an essentially deterministic view of social evolution. The Social Darwinists thus forgot that when the individual is assumed to be subject to forces of social evolution totally beyond his control, such concepts as individual liberty and individual re-

---

[2]Richard M. Weaver, *The Southern Tradition at Bay* (New Rochelle, N.Y.: Arlington House, 1968), pp. 223–224.

sponsibility no longer have meaning. The long-range effect of much of the "rugged individualism" of the late nineteenth century was to generate a feeling of individual helplessness and lack of direction which paved the way for the collectivist theories of social control which followed in their wake. If society is indeed an organism rather than a collection of individuals gathered together in voluntary, cooperative associations, if man is only an animal and not also a spiritual entity, then little ground remains upon which the individual can make his stand against bigness. In the late nineteenth century, the ground upon which the individual could make such a stand grew steadily smaller as it was eroded simultaneously by two streams of thought, one flowing from those who would centralize all human functions and the other flowing from those who would atomize all human functions. A society based upon individual groupings and voluntary associations was thus adjudged impossible, by simultaneous attacks from both the friends and the enemies of individualism.

It seems clear that many of the so-called "conservative" forces of post–Civil War America did far more to destroy the existing order than any other single group of thinkers:

We may wonder whether, in the entire history of thought, there was ever a conservatism so utterly progressive as this. Some of the peculiarities of social Darwinism as a conservative rationale become apparent if one compares Sumner with Edmund Burke. As thinkers the two, of course, have something in common: both show the same resistance to attempts to break the mold of society and accelerate change; neither has any use for ardent reformers or revolutionaries, for the conception of natural rights, or for equalitarianism. But here the resemblance ends. Where Burke is religious, and relies upon an intuitive approach to politics and upon instinctive wisdom, Sumner is secularist and proudly rationalist. Where Burke relies upon the collective, long-range intelligence, the wisdom of the community, Sumner expects that individual self-assertion will be the only satisfactory expression of the wisdom of nature, and asks of the community only that it give full play to this self-assertion. Where Burke reveres custom and exalts continuity with the past, Sumner is favorably impressed by the break made with the past when contract supplanted status; he shows in this phase of his work a disdain for the past that is distinctly the mark of a culture whose greatest gift is a genius for technology. To him it is only "sentimentalists" who want to save and restore the survivals of the old order. Burke's conservatism seems relatively timeless and placeless, while Sumner's seems to belong pre-eminently to the post-Darwinian era and to America.[3]

[3]Richard Hofstadter, *Social Darwinism in American Thought* (Boston: Beacon Press, 1962), p. 8.

Here again an irony presents itself. The virtues that Sumner and Spencer extolled — hard work, self-sufficiency, personal responsibility — were essentially middle-class ideals far better suited to pre–Civil War America than to the dawning age. But the determinism and the relativism which the Social Darwinists also espoused were the very ideas destined to sweep away the kind of society in which the virtues preached by Spencer and Sumner could hope to survive. It is sometimes true that we kill what we most love.

Dissent

Not all nineteenth-century intellectuals lent their approval to the new direction of affairs. The same struggle between the new order and the old order was going on throughout the Western world. In Britain, the debate has been described by the British scholar R. J. White as best epitomized in the varying views of Jeremy Bentham and Samuel Taylor Coleridge. White describes this difference as "the difference between the man [Bentham] who takes social institutions as so many pieces of furniture that can be moved around, rearranged, refashioned, or even chopped up for firewood, and the man [Coleridge] who sees them as elements in the total concrete experience of a people — not as the furniture of life, but as life itself." The difference then is between the conservative who senses an order in society which makes individual life possible, and the radical who is impatient with such distinctions. It is true that the radical who sees no virtue in such traditional patterns of life may for a time appear to favor economic freedom, as did Bentham, Sumner, or Spencer; but this is all too often only a passing phase. The radical favors change and what he calls "growth." And growth is more easily measured in material than spiritual terms. Thus the emphasis upon what Albert Jay Nock defined as "economism."

The critics of economism were in the field long before Nock arrived on the scene. The value-free social order which measures the worth of society in exclusively material terms was sharply attacked by Matthew Arnold in the field of culture and education, by Coleridge in philosophy, by Disraeli in politics, by Newman in religion. Thomas Carlyle coined the phrase "cash-nexus" as a critical description of the materialist emphasis of life a generation after Edmund Burke had extolled the "unbought grace of life."

Thus a few English thinkers had examined the possibilities of the new economism, and had found it wanting, much earlier than had the Americans. After the Civil War, when Americans began to realize what the cash-nexus really meant, the American intellectuals who opposed an exclusively materialistic emphasis in American society and who warned of the dangers to the individual stemming from such an emphasis, had available an ample reservoir of thought on which to draw.

As the century moved on, the earlier American optimism of a Walt Whitman was destined to become the pessimism of a Mark Twain. Some post–Civil War Americans began to suspect that the direction their society was taking was not necessarily the direction which would enhance the quality of individual life. As Albert Jay Nock comments:

Even Whitman lapsed from his "barbaric yawp" of faith in economism to the desponding observation that the type of civilization which economism had produced was "so far, an almost complete failure in its social aspects, and in really grand religious, moral, literary and aesthetic results. . . . It is as if we were somehow being endowed with a vast and thoroughly appointed body, and then left with little or no soul."[4]

America was producing great wealth, and this measure of advancement was widely extolled. But the matter of soul is somehow a highly individual concern, and in this area some Americans questioned what the future would hold. No one better epitomized that questioning spirit than the sons of Charles Francis Adams, the grandsons and great-grandsons of two American presidents. Brooks Adams spent his life writing books which consistently displayed hostility toward the principle of centralization. Adams had no use for the centralizers or the socialists, and suspected that mass production and mass values would bring about the very political and economic centralization which he so distrusted. Still, the changes seemed to be coming at such a furious pace in the American society of his time that Brooks Adams expected the eventual triumph of bigness. He saw no way to avoid the resultant disasters for the individual which he expected as the inevitable result of centralization. As his brother, Henry, described it:

Loving paradox, Brooks, with the advantages of ten years' study, had swept away much rubbish in the effort to build up a new line of thought for himself, but he found that no paradox compared with that of daily events. The facts were constantly outrunning his thoughts. The instability was greater than he calculated; the speed of acceleration passed bounds.[5]

This sense of acceleration and enmassment was also the dominant theme in the life of Henry Adams. As yet another Adams (James Truslow) writes in the introduction to the classic autobiography of modern times:

Henry could only watch the body politic swinging at incredible speed away from the family into the waste spaces beyond. "We, the people"

[4]Albert Jay Nock, *The Memoirs of a Superfluous Man* (Chicago: Regnery, 1964), p. 113.
[5]Henry Adams, *The Education of Henry Adams* (New York: The Modern Library, 1931), p. 339.

had become marvelously "we, the plunderers." To be sure, most of the people were rather the plundered, but hope was in the air; any day the role might be reversed in the individual case, and meanwhile it would be best to let the game go on in case Fate should throw trumps to us some day. The really great and noble American dream, the dream of a better and fuller life for every man, had become a good deal like the stampede of hogs to a trough. Such a stampede, like the subway rush, is no place for the development of the finer elements of life and thought.[6]

Henry Adams finally became an expatriate from the modern world. The brilliant intuitions that allowed him to prophesy our future so precisely led him to believe that the individual could not resist the enormous enmassment which was taking place. Few of the events of the twentieth century would have surprised Adams. Writing in 1897, Adams warned, "The reaction of fashionable society against our old-fashioned liberalism is extreme, and wants only power to make it violent. I am waiting with curiosity to see whether the power will come — with the violence — in my time. As I view it, the collapse of our nineteenth-century J. Stuart Mill, Manchester, Chicago formulas will be displayed — if at all — by the collapse of Parliamentarianism, and the reversion to centralized government." Thus he correctly predicted the subsequent course of American society in the twentieth century, at a time when most Americans still gave lip service to the standard assumptions about "progress" and "free enterprise."

Adams stressed that the movement from the unity of a simpler era to the ever-accelerating multiplicty of the modern world was becoming so unmanageable that the individuals within society would be forced to turn to centralizing, depersonalizing institutional forms as a haven from that multiplicity. In *The Education of Henry Adams,* he described his view of America's largest city as it appeared in the early twentieth century:

The outline of the city became frantic in its effort to explain something that defied meaning. Power seemed to have outgrown its servitude and to have asserted its freedom. The cylinder had exploded, and thrown great masses of stone and steam against the sky. The city had the air and movement of hysteria, and the citizens were crying, in every accent of anger and alarm, that the new forces must at any cost be brought under control. Prosperity never before imagined, power never yet wielded by man, speed never reached by anything but a meteor, had made the world irritable, nervous, querulous, unreasonable, and afraid. All New York was demanding new men, and all the new

[6] *Ibid.,* (Intro. by J. T. Adams), p. ix.

forces, condensed into corporations, were demanding a new type of man — a man with ten times the endurance, energy, will, and mind of the old type — for whom they were ready to pay millions at sight. . . . As one jolted over the pavements or read the last week's newspaper, the new man seemed close at hand, for the old one had plainly reached the end of his strength, and his failure had become catastrophic. Everyone saw it, and every municipal election shrieked chaos. A traveller in the highways of history looked out of the club window on the turmoil of Fifth Avenue, and felt himself in Rome, under Diocletian, witnessing the anarchy, conscious of the compulsion, eager for the solution, but unable to conceive whence the next impulse was to come or how it was to act. The two-thousand-years failure of Christianity roared upward from Broadway, and no Constantine the Great was in sight.[7]

America has been searching for its Constantine the Great ever since, with a conspicuous lack of success.

It is probably not fair to place too much blame on the Spencers and the Sumners who advocated their particular variety of "rugged individualism." They never really had the opportunity to implement their system. The new-style promoters who prospered in the new environment were quick to use the power of government to achieve their own ends. And why not, if the determinism preached by Sumner and Spencer was a true description of society's workings? If the new system was foreordained, why not go to the top, as one of Henry Adams' "New Men"? Thus determinism and the "survival of the fittest" bred economism, and economism changed the face of American society.

American Business — New Style

Changes were occurring in all aspects of American economic life. In the period following the Civil War, the energy of the American people had been absorbed in a burst of material development. Entrepreneurs and settlers had poured into the vast Western land. The country had been filled coast to coast with an enormous railway network, while production and consumption of every conceivable material had increased by leaps and bounds. The development of a national market, with its growing transportation system, financial system, and corporate structure, brought great changes to the late nineteenth century. The growth of a national market also brought with it the growth of businesses national in scope.

Denver, Portland, Minneapolis, St. Paul, Kansas City, and a dozen more cow towns grew into substantial communities. While the rural population

[7] *Ibid.*, pp. 499–500.

of America doubled between 1860 and 1910, the urban population increased sevenfold. Chicago doubled its population between 1880 and 1890, while Minneapolis–St. Paul tripled its population in the same period. As America became a national market, it also became an essentially urban market:

> The economic triumphs of urban industrialism naturally were accompanied by the victory of city culture over the folkways of village, town, and farm. By 1890 erstwhile "lords of the soil" had become "hayseeds," "bumpkins," and "rubes." Crossroads merchants and yeoman farmers who, a few generations before, had run the United States, now had as little cultural influence as they had economic power. In control were manufacturers, bankers, railroad executives, and corporation lawyers, under whose influence the American people had developed urban modes of dressing, living, speaking, and thinking. General mail order catalogues after 1872 spread city customs while personal contact undoubtedly brought about much of the change. Traveling salesmen, national business executives, and workers visiting their families back home were missionaries of urban culture; and their influence was all the greater because the wealth of city businessmen and the bigness of city affairs gave prestige to all things pertaining to the metropolis. In addition to these subtle, untraceable influences, however, journalism and public education were continuously at work spreading the gospel of the city.[8]

Another decisive factor in the formation of late nineteenth-century America was the rising new technology. Following the Civil War, a network of telegraph, telephone, and railroads revolutionized intercontinental communication and transportation. Americans discovered new ways of releasing industrial energy, new ways of extracting minerals, new techniques for preserving food. Without the development of the refrigerator car in the concluding quarter of the nineteenth century, the increasingly large urban populations perhaps could not have been fed. Without the development of structural steel, the heart of urban America could not have been constructed. In these and countless other ways, technology played a greater part in shaping American society than in any previous civilization.

Accompanying the revolutionary changes in technology were equally revolutionary ideas concerning the management of the new industrial machine. Frederick W. Taylor pioneered in what became known as "scientific management." Labor was divided into more and more minute particles. The actions of men were to be mechanized. As the machine gained dominance

---

[8]Thomas C. Cochran and William Miller, *The Age of Enterprise* (New York: Harper and Brothers, 1961), p. 268.

in the late nineteenth century, the decision was increasingly taken to mold man to the needs of the machine. Thus a "job" was less an expression of a man's skills than it was a means of earning money by hiring out as an essentially interchangeable part. The psychological consequences of this decision did much to undercut the individuality of the worker.

As industrial America bred a new sort of worker, it also bred a new leadership. Great fortunes accumulated in steel, oil, meat, railroads, and all the other areas of industry dominating the American scene. The growth of urban America and the new national market brought with it the growth of giant new industries to serve the new vision of American society. Morgan, Rockefeller, Harriman, and Carnegie became household words. By 1893, it was estimated that nine percent of the families in America owned 71 percent of the nation's wealth.

Leaving aside for the moment the question as to whether or not the interests of the American people were best served by this industrial enmassment, it is interesting to note the sociological impact of the new super-rich industrial leadership which emerged. In one of his more prophetic moments, Alexis de Tocqueville predicted the rise of an "aristocracy of manufacturers" as the inevitable result of a democratic society. Tocqueville noted that the emphasis upon material welfare for all, an emphasis which always puts in an appearance in a democratic society, creates a situation in which the demand for goods is likely to increase without end. He also noted that the accompanying equality of opportunity which seemed a feature of the American democracy was likely to encourage talent to enter the area where the greatest material rewards could be expected to accrue. In an industrial age, with a rising demand for material goods, those material benefits were most likely to accrue in various industrial occupations connected with mass production. Thus the best talents would go into business, rising higher and higher above the democratic mass as the industrial empires they erected grew larger and larger. Meanwhile, the mechanical and repetitious job of the industrial worker would become steadily narrower and progressively more dehumanizing and anti-individual. The employer in such a situation becomes more and more the "administrator of a vast empire." In such a situation, Tocqueville suggested, ". . . one seems as much born to obey as that other is to command. What is that but aristocracy?"

Tocqueville's 1830 prophecy, appearing in *Democracy in America,* seemed to be borne out by the events of the late nineteenth century. Certainly the rising new industrial aristocracy were quite assured of their own capacity to guide the affairs of the nation over which they presided. George Baer, spokesman for the owners in the coal strike of 1902, appeared to be perfectly serious when he declared, "The rights and interests of the laboring man will be protected and cared for, not by the labor agitators, but by the Christian men to whom God in His infinite wisdom has given the control of the property interests of this country, and upon the successful management of which so much depends."

Modern industrialism has completely reordered American society. The control of wealth was rapidly passing from its older, rural, middle-class bases to a new industrial and financial class. Since the numbers involved in the new leadership community were so much smaller, America was in the position of passing from a broadly based, highly individualistic situation in which the typical citizen largely charted his own course, to a narrowly based situation in which fewer and fewer men had greater and greater influence in the lives of all Americans.

The American Dream — New Style

Since the nineteenth century came to emphasize primarily material values, the nature of what Americans were losing was not immediately apparent to them:

> What they saw about them were more tracks and more factories and more people, bigger farms and bigger corporations and bigger buildings; and in a time of confusion they responded with a quantitative ethic that became the hallmark of their crisis in values. It seemed that the age could only be comprehended in bulk. Men defined issues by how much, how many, how far. . . . Increasingly people were judged in the public arena by dollars, raw not refined. A man rose or fell in common parlance according to the slide of his bank balance, and the cult of the millionaires arrived, focusing rapt attention upon how many there were and how much money each had.[9]

As the North rushed headlong into the new age of enmassment, the "New South" leadership moved heaven and earth to encourage the development of the same rationale in the defeated provinces. Northern manufacturing capital, government support and subsidy, were eagerly courted by the Southern counterparts of the new industrial aristocracy. Progress became the goal of American society, and "Progress" was defined exclusively in quantitative, material terms.

The style of the period assumed the existence of opportunity. Small capital and talent could achieve recognition and could build a fortune of its own — or so we fondly believed. With the rapid increase in wealth which actually did occur for most Americans, something else was also occurring. As the standard continued to rise, the average American found himself on an endless treadmill of rising expenses as well. It was true in a sense that the possibilities for material advancement were almost limitless, that an

[9]Robert H. Wiebe, *The Search for Order* (New York: Hill and Wang, 1968), pp. 40–41.

upward push of income could be achieved. But this upward push generated great pressures in the direction of an exclusively monetary and material concern. The point of life became to "make money" — never mind how, and never mind the quality of the individual's life while he was making and spending that money. In the midst of this frenzy for more and more wealth, Mark Twain and Charles Dudley Warner wrote *The Gilded Age,* a comic overstatement of everything wrong with the late nineteenth century. The title of their novel serves as an appropriate title for the age.

Many of the business practices of the age were as coarse and as dishonest as so often has been suggested, but the really significant feature of the era was not the conduct of the Jay Goulds, the Jim Fisks and the Uncle Dan Drews. The tastes and standards elevated to notoriety by the actions of a few men were also the tastes and standards of all too many Americans. The emphasis upon quantity and size for its own sake, the massive and overornate architecture and oratory, became typical of the life-style in America's Gilded Age. Economism had come of age in America.

VIII

BUSINESS AND POLITICS

Certainly in America the roles of the liberal and the conservative have been so often intermingled, and in some ways reversed, that clear traditions have never taken form. This will go far to reveal not only why our nonconservatives have such a hard time explaining themselves today but also why social Darwinism has such a peculiar ring as a conservative social philosophy. In the American political tradition the side of the "right" — that is, the side devoted to property and less given to popular enthusiasms and democratic professions — has been throughout the greater part of our history identified with men who, while political conservatives, were in economic and social terms headlong innovators and daring promoters. From Alexander Hamilton through Nicholas Biddle to Carnegie, Rockefeller, Morgan, and their fellow tycoons, the men who held aristocratic or even plutocratic views in matters political were also men who took the lead in introducing new economic forms, new types of organization, new techniques.

Richard Hofstadter,
Social Darwinism in American Thought

Thanks largely to Matthew Josephson, the term "robber baron" has become part of the American language. Patterning their ideas after the Marxian determinism of Charles and Mary Beard, Josephson and a generation of American scholars largely convinced this country that the American businessman was the living embodiment of what Karl Marx had called "the expropriators." More recently, a school of entrepreneurial history has grown up which insists that the American businessman of the nineteenth century was essentially a builder, not a destroyer. William Miller, Thomas Cochran, and Allan Nevins, among a number of American historians, have now popularized this more positive view. Schools of historical interpretation being what they are, both positions probably contain elements of the truth.

While it is true that the big were getting bigger during the second half of the nineteenth century, it is also true that the wage rate of the average

American worker was rising rapidly and that the number of small firms was continuing to grow at a very rapid rate. The assumption that only the rich were profiting from the new order of things is simply not borne out by the facts. It would appear that many of the "robber-baron" charges were more emotional than factual in nature.

There could be no better illustration of this than the historical debate which has centered upon the record of the Standard Oil Corporation. Rockefeller has always been given top billing as a particularly brutal robber baron, ever since Henry Demarest Lloyd's publication of *Wealth Against Commonwealth*. Lloyd, Ida Tarbell, and such modern defenders of the muckraker position as Professor Chester McArthur Destler have consistently refused to see any good whatever in John D. Rockefeller or his Standard Oil, despite the mass of evidence presented which exonerates Rockefeller from most of the charges leveled against him and emphasizes his role as a builder of modern industrial society. Allan Nevins' two-volume biography of Rockefeller has been especially effective in laying to rest much of the Standard Oil demonology. Nevins has received major confirmation of his thesis in the work of Ralph and Muriel Hidy, *Pioneering in Big Business, 1882–1911*. The studies of the Hidys and Nevins make it abundantly clear that the "robber baron" view of Standard Oil ignores an imposing array of factual evidence in an effort to grind its bitterly antagonistic ax. On net balance it seems clear that those historians who view such nineteenth century businessmen as Rockefeller as essentially *builders* have by far the better of the case. The older "robber-baron" view still persists, primarily due to the strong emotional attachment it evokes.

A number of other nonrobber-baron biographies have also been published, setting in perspective the constructive careers of other key nineteenth century business figures such as McCormick, Armour, and Carnegie. An imposing body of literature has grown up suggesting that the second half of the nineteenth century was less populated with robber barons than with industrial statesmen. It is sometimes forgotten that the great industrial development of the late nineteenth century could not have been accomplished without the vital skills of the entrepreneur who knew how to organize and pioneer in areas where no one had gone before. Perhaps the era should be rechristened "the age of the entrepreneur." Certainly the task which such men performed in our society brought with it substantial material benefits for the great majority of Americans.

Every age has its style. The nineteenth century had its own version of the Renaissance adventurers, men facing the risks of the era with their special élan:

This was the work and the accomplishment of America's first generation of industrial capitalists who owned and managed their concerns, took risks, made enormous profits, and reinvested most of them in new and improved plants, the acquisition of raw materials, and the financing of market agencies. They were enterprisers, adventurers, and innovators, for the great forward strides of technology were possible only as the results of their risk-taking. There is no doubt they engaged in cutthroat and unfair means of competition; there can be no question that in many areas monopoly practices were developed. On the other hand, they lowered costs, reduced prices, and kept wages high.[1]

Surely some distinction must be made between the colorful rogues — Jim Fisk, Jay Gould, Uncle Dan Drew — and the builders. Presumably the complaint against the "robber barons" centers not upon the material progress which took place, but only upon the accompanying abuses. And, if we are to believe the "robber-baron" theorists, these abuses unfailingly occurred in league with government. Matthew Josephson's work, for example, is filled with suggestions of the uses to which government power was put for private business advantage. Thus the charge most often advanced against the nineteenth-century business community concerns the abuse of coercive power when used by one sector of society at the expense of the others. The critics of such uses of government during the second half of the nineteenth century always make the accompanying assumption that government should have been (and should be) used as an agency to further the interests of some other sectors of society besides business. More to the point is the question, "Why grant *any* sector such privileges?"

The businessmen of the nineteenth century *are* to be blamed for courting government to gain special privilege, though perhaps the fault rests less with businessmen than with society as a whole. The late nineteenth century was an era conspicuously dominated by the assumption that government could be used to achieve various special interest projects, whether it was the building of a railroad or the development of an "infant industry." Probably one should be surprised that those special interests took advantage of such an open door to public power and the profitable monopoly situation stemming from the exercise of that power:

> . . . there was the American idea . . . that there was somehow virtue in making money and "developing" the country as fast as possible, which had as its corollary the belief that the main point was to get a thing done regardless of how it was done or its larger social implications. This had become a marked American characteristic, inherited from the frontier "get rich quick and develop fast" state of mind. It

[1]Louis M. Hacker, *American Capitalism* (Princeton, N. J.: Van Nostrand, 1957), p. 57.

was as marked in Roosevelt, who fought the big business leaders, as it was in those leaders themselves. We shall note later his grab of the Panama Canal Zone, but may quote here his alleged remark, when circumventing an Act of Congress in regard to the building of the canal, "Damn the law. I want the canal built." That was precisely the spirit of the men who were ruling the world of business in America at the same period.[2]

Sometimes it is assumed that all the material benefits of modern industrial society would have come our way automatically. Nothing could be further from the truth. We willed into existence the kind of society which would make that material progress possible. The builders of industry played a hand, but we all played a hand in the careful destruction of old customs and associations by our willingness to throw the full resources of government behind the various economic enterprises which we deemed important. The trouble with the robber barons was not their impact upon society, an impact which was essentially productive, but rather that they (and the society which made them possible) were both products of an emphasis too narrowly economic, too self-interested, resulting in an inevitable proletarianization which left the individual at the mercy of forces far beyond his control. The resultant rush to collectivism since that time is no more than the inevitable reaction to that proletarianization. In short, we all helped in changing the face of American society, and then were so frightened by that new face that we were quick to call for protection against our new creation. In that creation, the businessman is no more and no less involved than the rest of us.

The Uses of Government

Corruption soon followed the new American acceptance of highly centralized political power as a problem-solving device. The process quite clearly began with the American Civil War. Nationally, the Civil War produced a monopoly political situation for the Republican party. In the repressed and resentful South, local politics came to be a monopoly of the Democrats. Even some oases of Democratic support remained in the North (for example, Boss Tweed's New York City), due primarily to the inevitable reaction against the monopoly situation of the Republican party in national politics. The age of machine politics thus stemmed from an undue centralization of political control.

One-party domination of American political life robbed the Republic of that flexibility and variety that had traditionally been its strength, thus

[2]James Truslow Adams, *The Epic of America* (Garden City, N. Y.: Garden City Publishing, 1947), p. 320.

producing the very monopoly political power that our tradition had previously tried to avoid. It is true that a time of tremendous building did occur in industry, communication, and transportation across our American continent following the Civil War. But it is also true that the era brought with it the spoilsmen in politics and the exploiters in economic life who were quite willing to work hand in glove in taking the American people for a ride. A half century of abuses stemmed from this monopoly situation. Boss Tweed and Jim Fisk were all too symbolic of their era.

The growing enmassment of American population also furthered the situation:

> The city, with its immense need for new facilities in transportation, sanitation, policing, light, gas, and public structures, offered a magnificent internal market for American business. And business looked for the sure thing, for privileges, above all for profitable franchises and for opportunities to evade as much as possible of the burden of taxation. The urban boss, a dealer in public privileges who could also command public support, became a more important and more powerful figure. With him came that train of evils which so much preoccupied the liberal muckraking mind: the bartering of franchises, the building of tight urban political machines, the marshaling of hundreds of thousands of ignorant voters, the exacerbation of poverty and slums, the absence or excessive cost of municipal services, the cooperation between politics and "commercialized vice" — in short, the entire system of underground government and open squalor that provided such a rich field for the crusading journalists.[3]

The Civil War itself had greatly extended the activities of government and multiplied political officeholders. New taxes demanded a host of new tax collectors. Military contracts demanded government agents, inspectors, and clerks. Homesteading and railway grants brought more surveyors and clerks. City government grew apace with national government. In the years following the Civil War politics itself became one of the giant businesses of the American nation.

With that political growth came political corruption. Jay Gould attempted his famous corner of the gold market, relying primarily upon inside information from President Grant's personal secretary. Some of the traders on the market who were quick to condemn Gould for his attempted corner in gold were themselves recipients of fortunes built primarily upon blood-soaked army contracts garnered during the Civil War. It seemed that all

[3]Richard Hofstadter, *The Age of Reform* (New York: Vintage Books, 1955), pp. 174–175.

American politicians were invited to what became known as the "Great Barbeque":

> While industrial business was being consolidated into great units and winning for itself unassailable national supremacy, the business of politics, for a decade and a half after the Civil War, levied a heavy toll upon it. The general public, through federal, state, and local taxation, continued, of course, to contribute the largest amounts toward the support of professional politicians. But industrialists and railroad men especially were forced to pay extraordinary sums for political benefits, and frequently were blackmailed by threats of regulation or withdrawal of government aid. Faced with dissolution under the sectional and religious pressures of the fifties, the two-party system had now been firmly reestablished, with the new Republican party almost as strong in the federal government as the Democrats were later to become in the "Solid South." Victory in the war and paternalistic legislation during the conflict had won for the Republicans a stanch nucleus of party regulars, and expanding government functions had given Republican leaders much new patronage to barter for the support of opposition bosses as well as thousands of new officeholders to tax for lavish contributions to party chests. The politicians in power, therefore, could treat businessmen simply as customers, selling political support at the highest price the traffic would bear, depending mainly upon a nation's gratitude and party discipline for the perpetuation of their tenure.[4]

Never before in American life had the temptation for corruption been so great. Following the Civil War, politicians found themselves dealing in land grants, tariffs, mail contracts, subsidies, mining claims, pensions. The power of taxation gave them power to protect or detroy individual businesses. It is often alleged that bussinessmen came to control politics. In reality, it is far from clear who controlled whom. Deeply immersed in land grants and government loans connected with the construction of the Central and Southern Pacific Railway, Collis P. Huntington wrote one of his associates an irate letter in November 1877:

> You have no idea how I am annoyed by this Washington business, and I must and will give it up after this session. If we are not hurt this session, it will be because we pay much money to prevent it, and you

[4]Thomas C. Cochran and William Miller, *The Age of Enterprise* (New York, Harper and Brothers, 1961), p. 154.

know how hard it is to get to pay for such purposes; and I do not see
my way clear to get through here and pay the January interest with
other bills payable to January 1st, with less than $2,000,000 and
probably not for that. . . . This Washington business will kill me yet
if I have to continue the fight from year to year, and then every year
the fight grows more and more expensive; and rather than let it
continue as it is from year to year. . . . I would rather they take the
road and be done with it.[5]

In the fierce heat of competition to procure government assistance for
various projects, the legislative process took on the appearance of an auc-
tion.It is this aspect of the late nineteenth century upon which the robber-
baron philosophy rests most strongly. In Gustavus Myers' *History of the
Great American Fortunes,* great stress is placed upon the low level of
political morality which was evidenced in the rush to accommodate the
highest bidder from the business community. Describing the situation in
New York State, Myers charges, "Laws were sold at Albany to the highest
bidder."[6]

In an article prompted by the Credit Mobilier scandal, E. L. Godkin,
editor of the New York *Nation,* warned that the only possible lasting
answer to bribery and corruption would be an end to the power of congressmen to bestow great privilege upon private individuals and corporations.
Godkin wrote: "The remedy is simple. The Government must get out of the
'protective' business and the 'subsidy' business and the 'improvement' business and the 'development' business. It must let trade, and commerce, and
manufactures, and steamboats, and railroads, and telegraphs alone. It cannot touch them without breeding corruption."[7] There were few to listen to
Godkin's advice.

Who Corrupted Whom?

Advocates of centralized authority and economic control in the twentieth
century look back to the so-called era of reconstruction and big business to
point out its evils with great glee and to suggest that those evils are a *prima
facie* case for the necessity of more political control of business. The very
reverse is actually the case. It was a monopoly of political power, and an
exercise of that power by one element of society, that did the damage. All
of the significant scandals of the late nineteenth century were closely connected with the exercise of political power. This is true with the Credit

[5]*Ibid.,* p. 158.
[6]Gustavus Myers, *History of the Great American Fortunes* (New York: Random House, 1937),
p. 310.
[7]Arthur A. Ekirch, Jr., *The Decline of American Liberalism* (New York: Longmans, Green,
1955), p. 151.

Mobilier, a scandal which deeply involved many members of Congress. The entire fraud stemmed from the capacity of the government to issue valuable land grants to the private individuals composing the Union Pacific Railroad. As the beneficiary of 10,000,000 acres of public land, the Union Pacific and the holding company set up by the insiders, the Credit Mobilier, were obviously in such a privileged position that enormous profits were likely to channel themselves into a few pockets, and, not surprisingly, some of those pockets proved to be in the halls of Congress.

Not all corruption evidenced so *direct* a form of larceny. The new view of government as an agent of material good, coupled with the political monopoly following the Civil War, had led to the passage of a collection of laws which would appear to demonstrate a positive dependence of business upon politics during the heyday of "free enterprise." The situation was not peculiar to America. The very system which was to produce such disastrous results in America was being pursued throughout the Western world. For example, a comparison of the interventions in Bismarck's Germany during the same period makes American efforts at state capitalism pale by comparison.

In the areas of land policy, regulatory activity, subsidies, tariffs, and government finance, the new era of special privilege is most readily apparent. The accelerating process of public land disposal began even before the Civil War was over. The Homestead Act of 1862 provided free 160-acre farms to any settler who would agree to cultivate the land for five years. Unfortunately, the law also declared that the settler could purchase his land for $1.25 an acre with full and immediate rights of resale. The result was that the Homestead Act did little to provide small settlers with their own piece of land. Instead, speculators were enabled to buy up large tracts of land, already worth far more than the $1.25 price, by using dummy settlers to go through the legal requirements of the Act. The homesteading land, the land put on the market in connection with the land grant colleges of the Morrill Act, and the land grants used to encourage construction of railroads all met with the same general fate. The public lands moved into private ownership, but the private ownership turned out to be narrowly based upon special privileges which often made the large even larger and did little or nothing for the small man.

Again and again in the years following the Civil War, great emphasis was placed upon the "poor settler" and how the various land grants would advance his position. Yet few, if any, of the public land policies in operation during those years demanded actual settlement upon the land. Thus the railroad builders, the lumber corporations or some other insider to the seats of political power usually profited instead. The Desert Land Law, the Stone and Timber Act, and similar laws promised that the forces and resources of government would be brought to the aid of the individual landholder.

Again and again the promise was not fulfilled. Under the various federal acts designed to distribute public lands, 300,000,000 acres were thus distributed. The small settlers who actually used the land as farmland received one in ten of those acres. The Republican campaign slogan "Vote Yourself a Farm" thus proved to be only another demonstration that government power and money, when it promises to come to the aid of the "common man," often seems to have peculiarly uncommon beneficiaries, composing a group quite different from those for whom the program was allegedly designed.

Government land policy was not the only instance of this noteworthy trait. Most of the regulatory activity of the late nineteenth century, presumably designed to protect consumers from rapacious businessmen, was in most cases actually urged by the very businessmen supposedly regulated. A number of historians, most recently Professor R. H. Wiebe in his soundly researched *Businessmen and Reform* (1962), have made it abundantly clear that in case after case, ranging from railroad regulation to the manufacture of cigars, regulatory activity was most often urged by competitors already in the field who wished to prevent new competition from disrupting the *status quo*. Meanwhile government subsidy provided extremely lucrative returns to the few insiders capable of benefiting from the public largess. Mail subsidies serve as an excellent illustration. Railroads were paid rental allowances for mail cars which were annually double the total price of a new car. The steamship subsidies involved in carrying the mails to California were nearly double the actual costs involved. It seemed to matter a great deal whom one knew in Washington.

Tariffs offered another fertile field for exploitation. The tariff, of course, is a classic case of governmental power giving a privileged position in the market to a producer or distributor, and thus penalizing all the consumers of that particular product. The Civil War saw the beginning of a series of rapid upward revisions of the tariff. The average tariff rate in the United States nearly tripled between 1861 and 1864 and continued at great height for the rest of the century. Copper, coal, iron, steel, and woolens were soon taxed to the point where further importation became almost impossible. Americans were beginning to discover some of the workings of political power.

The Double Standard

Thus there evolved the dichotomy which saw businessmen preaching *laissez-faire* doctrine for everyone else, while asking for government assistance in their own particular case. The peculiar situation did not escape the attention of many observers, among them Lord James Bryce, a celebrated English observer of American politics who commented:

One half of the capitalists are occupied in preaching *laissez faire* as regards railroad control, the other half in resisting it in railroad rate matters, in order to have their goods carried more cheaply, and in tariff matters, in order to protect industries threatened with foreign competition. Yet they manage to hold well together.[8]

In Sidney Fine's *Laissez Faire and the General-Welfare State . . . 1865–1901* (1956) it becomes clear just how widespread this double standard was during the late nineteenth century. Andrew Carnegie could suggest that the legal *status quo* was perfect, *until* he decided to advocate a federal subsidy for the construction of a canal which would enable his Pittsburgh steel mills to receive raw materials more economically. The National Association of Manufacturers could condemn federally financed cattle vaccine as a violation of "free enterprise" at the same time it called for federal subsidies to underwrite foreign export markets for United States manufacturers.

Signs of the Times

In his socialist and bitterly anticapitalist *History of the Great American Fortunes,* Gustavus Myers spoke with more than a grain of truth when he suggested: "Government was nothing more or less than a device for the nascent capitalist class to work out its inevitable purposes, yet the majority of the people on whom the powers of class government severely fell, were constantly deluded into believing that the Government represented them." In another of his oft-quoted passages, Myers suggested that ". . . the whole of governing institutions served the interests of plutocracy."[9]

Myers is not far from the mark in his description of the late nineteenth century. But if Myers and the other critics of capitalism are correct (and I believe they are substantially correct on this point) in their assumption that many fortunes were built by government intervention and favors, isn't that an argument *against* government intervention? Unfortunately, in the late nineteenth century, as well as in our own century, society has managed to come to the opposite conclusion. We assume that political force can be used to solve private problems, and then are scandalized when exactly that is done with various government programs.

In looking back on the late nineteenth century, we might remember that businessmen, then as now, were in business primarily to make a profit, and should therefore not be blamed for taking that profit in transactions with the government at a time when transactions with the government were the dominant and accepted mode of society. The blame lies with our intellectual

[8]James Bryce, *The American Commonwealth* (New York: Macmillan, 1937), *II*, p. 304.
[9]Myers, pp. 238, 251.

leadership: So long as our society accepts the level of morality involved in using public power as a means to satisfy private interests, we will have more of the same morally ugly results. Businessmen did not force such a society upon us 100 years ago. They were no more nor less guilty than society at large.

IX

THE CORPORATION

... it is untrue that modern corporate capitalism is a predestined development due to some mysterious necessity of the machine process, or to some inexorable tendency to the agglomeration of wealth and power. The promoters of the giant corporation were not giants to whom ordinary men had to yield. They were ordinarily enterprising men who made the most of legal privileges with which legislatures and courts had inadvertently endowed them. The essential elements out of which the giant corporations were assembled were titles to land and natural resources and patents, limited liability for debts and damages, perpetual succession, their chartered right to set up an internal government of the corporate organization.

> Walter Lippmann,
> *The Good Society*

One governmentally granted privilege usually not considered in discussions of corporate empire building deserves special consideration. What was the role of the limited liability corporation in building the corporate giants of the late nineteenth century?

The corporation is not a uniquely American development. Indeed, it has an interesting history of its own. Coke, Blackstone, and most of the commentators on English common law for the past several hundred years have expressed a variety of opinions about the corporation and its legal rights. Because of these special legal rights, Blackstone described the corporation as "a little republic." These "little republics" had their origins in loose forms of partnership between and among merchants, spreading the risk of various joint ventures. As the process of such partnerships became more formalized, the English named them "joint stock companies." And, beginning with the reigns of Elizabeth and James I, the British Crown began to grant monopoly privileges to joint stock companies engaged in various risky enterprises. It is in this fashion that the famous East India Company came into being. Sometimes the risks involved in these worldwide ventures were greater, far greater, than any individual had either the inclination or the resources to bear alone. In response to this situation, there came into being another quality which we associate with the modern corporation: limitation of liability, a specially granted legal privilege which relieves a corporate stockholder from any corporate debts above the amount of the stockholder's investment. No such privilege has been accorded the individual businessman, either in Stuart England or modern America. Unlike the corporation, no legal immunity is extended to any portion of the individual's debts, barring complete bankruptcy.

Actually, limited liability had its origins in Renaissance Italy, and was only taken up later by the joint stock companies of England. However, during the past several hundred years, limited liability and the corporation have been tightly welded into a single concept throughout the Western world. From that concept grew the enormous extension of corporate enterprise which we now take so much for granted.

Some recollection of this brief history of the corporate idea is helpful in gaining perspective of just what legal privileges have become connected with the corporate concept.

> It is very useful to recall that in monopolism's early days and right up to the nineteenth century, certain legal rights were established by granting individual privileges which today, due to a most regrettable trend of events, have lost their character of being exceptional and have become a matter of course, so much so that most people have completely forgotten that these rights were originally based on privileges granted by the state and, in spite of their everyday legal aspect, are still that. We are thinking in particular of the legal status of patents and corporations which have proved to be of such importance for the development of modern monopolism. Today we accept both as a matter of course.[1]

The Corporation in America

The authors of the Constitution had been concerned to avoid factional control over the new American society. Madison, in particular, had warned that representative government could be destroyed if it ever found itself used for strictly partisan ends. One of the groups held most suspect in early-day America was the corporation.

At first, corporations were little more than specifically chartered private groups, empowered by special legislative act to achieve a particular community purpose, such as constructing a bridge or providing a strictly limited banking service. In a new and undeveloped country, the number of those

[1]Wilhelm Roepke, *The Social Crisis of Our Time* (Chicago: University of Chicago Press, 1950) pp. 230–231.

specific purposes grew rapidly, and the resultant corporations also grew rapidly. Initially, the states had few precedents with which to work, but a body of law gradually developed, based partially upon common law doctrine, and partially upon the modifications necessitated by a new era and by previously unencountered conditions. Meanwhile, the corporate form continued to grow in both size and numbers.

All such corporate legal questions were at first exclusively on the state level. Studies of this early corporate development make it clear that a much closer connection existed between corporations and the state government than we would today readily grant. Oscar and Mary Handlin have described the case in Massachusetts:

> The attributes of peculiar economic efficiency, of limited liability, and of perpetual freedom from state interference were . . . not present at the birth of the American business corporation. Divested of these characteristics, the form assumes a new significance. At its origin in Massachusetts the corporation was conceived as an agency of the government, endowed with public attributes, exclusive privileges, and political power, and designed to serve a social function for the State. Turnpikes, not trade, banks, not land speculation, were its province because the community, not the enterprising capitalists, marked out its sphere of activity.[2]

Soon the proliferation of corporations turned this quasi-governmental function into a business form, quickly destroying the apparent contact between the corporation and the state. But it should not be forgotten that a close connection originally existed. The unifying theme in the history of the corporation is the fact of its close ties to specially granted legal privilege. For centuries, the corporation was viewed as a governmentally granted monopoly, holding special privileges of immunity from the legal restraints which bind individuals. The pre–Civil War origins of corporations continued to show the same quasi-public motivations. The corporation is a creature of state intervention and specially granted privilege, clearly political in its origins.

A New Image for the Corporation

> Our economic world has in the main assumed its present shape because certain legal forms and institutions have been created — the stock company, the corporation, patent law, bankruptcy law, the law

---

[2]Oscar Handlin with Mary Flug Handlin, "Origins of the American Business Corporation," *Journal of Economic History, V* (1945), p. 22.

relating to trusts, and many others — and because legislation, the administration of justice, and custom have evolved these forms and institutions in a way which today we can often describe as nothing but harmful to the community and to the economic system itself.[3]

The modern business corporation is not and has never been a "little republic" with powers independent of government. The corporation is now and has always been derived entirely from power granted by the state, power directly dependent upon continued enforcement of the laws providing it with its special privileges and immunity. Since the Civil War, the area of special privileges and immunities granted to corporations has been greatly expanded. American corporations have been quick to turn to both the state and national governments for sweeping grants of power, and have been equally quick to avoid governmental interferences with exercise of that power by playing off the state and national governments, one against the other. The result has been the encouragement of bigness for its own sake, and the creation of an institutional structure so large as to alienate much of the American public. In this way, the legal advantages granted to corporate bigness may have proved to be the worst possible enemy of the corporation, since corporate bigness has aroused the fears and animosities of increasingly large numbers of Americans.

Despite the fact that one of the principal motivations in the writing of the 1787 Constitution had been to disarm groups and to keep factions from running roughshod over the American political, economic, and social scene, within 100 years we had completely changed that original concept and were actually catering to the various special interests which James Madison and his colleagues had so feared. Exactly 100 years after the writing of the Constitution, the Interstate Commerce Act became law, thus instituting the first of a series of governmental regulatory activities designed to protect the interests of special groups. The Interstate Commerce Commission regulated activities within the transportation industry so that new competitors were prevented from entering the marketplace by means of requirements for government licensure. Meanwhile, price competition was also eliminated, since the government regulatory agency set rates. All the populist rhetoric emphasizing that the Interstate Commerce Commission was designed primarily to "protect the consumer" should not obscure the fact that monopoly conditions were injected into the marketplace as the result of this government intervention. A special group was receiving special privileges backed by government. Of course, the Interstate Commerce Act was only the first in a series of similarly motivated special interest bodies. In years

[3]Roepke, pp. 117–118.

to follow, the Federal Trade Commission, the Federal Communications Commission, the National Labor Relations Board, the Securities Exchange Commission, and a number of similar agencies came into existence. The effect for the competitors and corporations already entrenched in these industries was the virtual guarantee of a semi-monopolistic position. The partnership between business and government was coming of age in America.

The interpretation of American history which views the late nineteenth-century businessman as a free enterpriser, while describing government activity as an attempt to restrain *laissez-faire*, is simply not borne out by the facts.

> Big business has more often taken refuge behind the national government than behind the state. I have only to call attention to the way in which corporations take refuge behind the Fourteenth Amendment to avoid state legislation, to the numberless cases brought before the Supreme Court of the United States by corporations whose charters have been vitiated or nullified by state action, to the refuge sought by the railroads in national protection against the state granger legislation, and to the external whine of big business for paternalistic and exploitative legislation such as the tariff, the ship and railroad subsidies. Historically, then, the vested interests of industrialism have not had any great use for state rights. They are the founders of the doctrine of centralization. . . .[4]

Businessmen of the late nineteenth century knew full well how to take best advantage of the new centralization. Richard Olney, the corporation lawyer who a few months later was to become Attorney General of the United States, wrote a letter in 1892 to one of his colleagues in which he epitomized the new corporate style concerning government regulation. He defended the Interstate Commerce Commission and went on to say:

> The Commission, as its functions have now been limited by the courts, is, or can be made, of great use to the railroads. It satisfied the popular clamor for a government supervision of railroads, at the same time that that supervision is almost nominal. Further, the older such a commission gets to be, the more inclined it will be found to take the business and railroad view of things. It thus becomes a sort of barrier between the railroad corporations and the people and a sort of protec-

[4]Frank Lawrence Owsley, "The Irrepressible Conflict," *I'll Take My Stand* (New York: Harper [Torchbook], 1962), p. 86.

tion against hasty and crude legislation hostile to railroad interests.
... The part of wisdom is not to destroy the Commission, but to utilize
it.[5]

Perhaps the best single illustration of the close partnership which developed between the corporation and government can be seen in the Fourteenth Amendment and the use to which it was put in the late nineteenth century. The Fourteenth Amendment was of course originally designed to protect the personal rights of the newly manumitted Negro, insuring him due process of law. Soon, however, it was put to a new and most peculiar use. The "persons" presumably protected by the Fourteenth Amendment were also interpreted to include corporations, since corporations are "legal persons." Thus any state attempt to control the actions of corporations was interpreted by federal courts as an interference with the rights of those "legal persons," and a violation of due process of law.

In this fashion the corporations, originally mere legal creatures incorporated for specific purposes by the state governments, were now completely removed from any and all state control. The new centralization in Washington served as a close working partner for the giant new American corporations. Small wonder that corporations continued to multiply in size and number. These new "persons" could not be deprived of life, liberty, or property without due process of law. Before the 1880s, such a view of the corporation would have been considered absurd. After the 1880s, the assumption was so "self-evident" that the matter was regarded as closed. Chief Justice Waite of the United States Supreme Court, deciding a case in 1886, dealt with the matter in some exasperation:

> The Court does not wish to hear argument on the question whether the provision in the Fourteenth Amendment to the Constitution, which forbids a state to deny to any person within its jurisdiction the equal protection of the laws, applies to these corporations. We are all of the opinion that it does.[6]

The perfection of centralization for the benefit of corporations was largely completed by 1890. The Interstate Commerce Act was passed in 1887, pioneering in the new concept of government regulatory activity in league with the corporations. By the late '80s, the new and perverse definition of the Fourteenth Amendment had also been accepted as the law of the land. The corporation, originally a creature of government, had now been ex-

[5]Arthur A. Ekirch, Jr., *The Decline of American Liberalism* (New York: Longmans, Green, 1955), p. 169.
[6]Carl Brent Swisher, *American Constitutional Development* (Cambridge, Mass.: Riverside Press, 1943), p. 405.

tended the further blessings of immunity and special privilege by the same agency. As the result, by 1900 two-thirds of all manufacturing in the United States was carried on by corporations. During the same period, consolidation of the trusts also continued at breakneck speed. Of the 318 trusts listed by Moody in 1904, 234 of them had been organized between 1898 and 1904. Thus the great consolidations which were to cause the political reactions of the Progressive era took place in the largest part only after the perfection of the partnership between government and the corporation.

Nothing in the above should be interpreted as an attack upon the corporation. There can be no question of the fact that many of the large corporations involved in business in the late nineteenth century were, as described earlier, essentially builders of our present material prosperity. The nature of the complaint that I am making centers on the peculiar double standard which developed, assuming one set of rules for the corporation and another for the individual. In such an unfair double standard, it is not surprising that the individual has come out a bad second best, and that in the process he has become highly resentful of the American corporate structure. An understanding of the political results stemming from that antagonism is one of the basic elements necessary to understanding American history in the twentieth century.

Entrepreneur or Organization Man?

From the foregoing, it should be clear that a close connection exists between the high degree of institutional centralization present within the modern business community and the legal system which made that centralization possible. However, it does not necessarily follow that the enmassment of American business is an absolute prerequisite for large-scale production. Neither does it follow that the accumulation of capital necessary for the development of modern technology can be achieved *only* by a highly centralized business system built by special legal privilege. It *is* true that labor-saving machinery and the money necessary to provide such machinery constitute what would be a very large investment for the individual; but it should be remembered that most of the necessary accumulations of capital, and most of the plant sizes necessary to achieve so-called "economies of scale," are far smaller than the present size of most corporate giants. There is a point beyond which larger factories are not necessarily more efficient. When United States Steel enlarges its productive capacity, it need not enlarge its Pittsburgh plant. Instead it may build a new plant in some entirely different location. Walter Lippmann placed his finger upon a very sensitive point of our modern economic structure when he pointed out that, "What holds together these various plants is not the technic of mass production but the legal device of incorporation."[7]

[7] Walter Lippmann, *The Good Society* (New York: Grosset and Dunlap, 1943), p. 14.

To defend the present corporate structure with the plea that, without the structure, we could not enjoy our present productive capacity, is to accept illusion in place of reality. The same capital formation and economy of scale could take place in far smaller units than we presently accept as necessary.

Thus the fundamental feature of the modern giant corporation is not that it offers us productive capacities which we would not otherwise have available, but that it offers great legal advantages for that giant corporation in comparison with unincorporated individuals:

> We shall not . . . fall into the error of regarding the existing law of property, of contracts, of corporations, as marking a realm in which the state does not or should not intervene. We shall recognize it for what it is, as a structure of rights and duties, immunities and privileges, built by custom, judicial interpretation, and statute, and maintained by the coercive authority of the state. We shall not think of all this as subsisting somehow outside the law, and then become involved in an empty debate as to whether the law may interfere with it. The whole of it, all property, and everything which we include in the general name of private enterprise, is the product of a legal development and can exist only by virtue of the law. This is evident enough in periods of social disorder when for want of law observance and law enforcement the whole private economy may collapse in a day.[8]

At this point, the reader may well inquire how, in the absence of the modern corporation in its present form, might we achieve our material production and distribution. I don't know, but surely believers in the efforts of free men would be compelled to answer that some means must exist to provide what we need without granting rights to some at the expense of others, through the power of government. An earlier America had faith in the entrepreneur, in the individual with a new idea.

Historically, this intervention granting special privileges to the corporate structure at the expense of the individual may well have been the key leading to many of the subsequent interventions and institutional enmassments of the twentieth century. Special privilege for business is precisely as wrong as special privilege for labor unions, special privilege for established churches, or special privilege for any other interest group in society. This simple fact, recognized by Madison and the writers of the Constitution, is a fact we have forgotten only at our own great peril.

Meanwhile, the individual entrepreneur with a new idea was also increasingly handicapped *within* the new business structure. One of the most basic changes brought about by the rise of the giant corporation and the close

[8] *Ibid.*, p. 273.

contact with government bureaucracy was a growing bureaucratic quality within business itself. The enormous, centralized enterprises which came to constitute American business brought with them hierarchical structures of their own, structures within which the older entrepreneurs found less and less room for maneuver. Many of the early-day pioneers remaining in post–Civil War American business were unable to make the change to the new bureaucratic system. Thomas Alva Edison was an idea man and an entrepreneur in his age, but was never able successfully to control or direct General Electric. In fact, had Edison been born a generation later, he would either have had no impact at all, or would have had his impact as a salaried employee of General Electric. The old day was passing, and the new day seemed to leave less and less room for the individual within business. Many of the largest companies in America, companies the size of Marshall Field, F. W. Woolworth, and A & P, had been partnerships or family businesses; but the new corporate organization had changed those traditional relationships. A wall was being erected between ownership and control, and the organization man was replacing the entrepreneur.

As the nineteenth century wore on, it became increasingly clear that bigness had indeed come to American business. Whether this bigness had come as a result of entrepreneurial genius or political favoritism (and there was considerable evidence pointing to each conclusion), the reaction of the American people was largely antagonistic to the new giants which had arisen. Too many Americans felt excluded from the new sources of wealth and power, and sweeping political changes were about to occur.

X

THE FAILURE OF

NINETEENTH-CENTURY

PROTEST

For a century and a half we had been occupied in conquering and exploiting
a continent, and by 1890 the task was complete. It had been an adventure of
youth. Now it was over. There were plenty of empty spaces left to be filled,
chinks in the structure, but the country was ours, peopled, bound together,
politically organized from coast to coast. Henceforth the work would be one
of consolidation rather than expansion. The problems would be those of
ruling a vast population with divergent interests, not of organizing new States;
the economic and social problems of the new world era of machinery and the
conflicts between capital and labor; the problems of world markets and world
contacts; the supreme problem of whether a Jeffersonian democracy could
survive in a Hamiltonian economy.

James Truslow Adams,
The Epic of America.

As the nineteenth century drew to an end, the world seemed to be closing
in on the Americans. The old order was passing, and Americans seemed to
be waiting for the new order to overtake them. The pioneers and the
entrepreneurs had been replaced by cities and organization men, and the
quality of American life irrevocably changed. The early 1890s saw the
publication of Frederick Jackson Turner's *The Significance of the Frontier
in American History,* a classic serving scholarly notice that the older America was now a subject in the past tense, and had become a world not in which
people lived, but of which historians wrote.

The path toward bigness and centralization seemed inevitable. Charles
Francis Adams, Jr., an older brother of Brooks and Henry, had earlier
expressed all the same doubts and fears about the rapidly approaching new
world which so tormented his brothers. Yet, as president of the Union
Pacific Railroad in the waning years of the nineteenth century, he began to

insist that ". . . the principle of consolidation . . . is a necessity — a natural law of growth. You may not like it: you will have to reconcile yourself to it. . . . The modern world does its work through vast aggregations of men and capital. . . . This is a sort of latter-day manifest destiny."[1]

And, by the 1890s, it certainly seemed manifest that the big were destined to get larger and larger, consolidating themselves in area after area of American life. It was alleged that big business not only controlled business, but also controlled politics. Meanwhile, the new technology was revolutionizing American life. The gasoline engine was patented in the United States in 1878. Electric power and the means by which that power might be applied to everyday life increased and improved enormously in the 1880s. In every walk of life, the new age was coming, and those who seemed in charge of the new age were apparently far beyond the control of the individual American. Indeed, for much of the late nineteenth century, no one wanted to exercise any such control. The businessman had become a middle-class hero, the symbol of the dawning age.

The time came when the little men began to lose their confidence, however. The cartoonist discovered a new field for exploitation in the barrel-shaped capitalist with the top hat and the big cigar. Before the nineteenth century had ended, people were no longer so sure that the new era offered them the pattern of life which they really preferred. At least in the older America, the predominantly local pattern of men and events allowed a measure of understanding and participation:

> As long as Americans were content to operate within that familiar setting, the outside world posed no serious problems. They translated its events into the language of local power, then dismissed them. When they moved into a broader arena, however, they soon found that they could neither see, know, nor even know about the people upon whom they had to depend. The legal framework changed; new groups, some abiding by quite different values, complicated the pattern; and relationships often followed an alien logic. The system was so impersonal, so vast, seemingly without beginning or end.[2]

It was in the face of this bigness which Americans felt beyond their control that national groupings according to economic interests first made their appearance. The Knights of Labor were organized in the 1870s, with the American Federation of Labor following in 1886. The farmers also began to organize, with the Grange making its appearance shortly after the Civil War. New political parties designed to further group interests also

[1]Gabriel Kolko, The Triumph of Conservatism (Chicago: Quadrangle Books, 1967), p. 14.
[2]Robert H. Wiebe, *The Search for Order,* (New York: Hill and Wang, 1968), pp. 164–165.

made their appearance. The Greenback Labor party was organized in 1878, and the Populist party in 1891. Farmers, laborers, and many middle-class Americans were no longer sure that the major political parties and the existing political structure furthered their interests. It seemed that tariffs, land grants, and the various other items of special interest legislation, which had become so numerous, penalized anyone not organized to fight back as a group. Bigness was pressing on Americans and they were beginning to seek the power by which they might resist that pressure.

The Workingman

Factors peculiar to the United States had long retarded the growth of the trade union movement. In the first place, the availability of new lands, a place where the laborer could always turn from the industrial situation and make a new start of his own, resulted in a shortage of skilled labor for American industry. Since the demand for his skilled labor was so intense, the typical American workman could more easily increase his income by improving his skills than by organizing with other workers. In the earlier American climate when circumstances still favored the independent entrepreneur, an ambitious worker always had the option open to him of setting up shop for himself. So long as these conditions prevailed, unions were likely to have trouble in organization. Thus, in the land of opportunity, every man felt he had a chance open to him:

> The average competent and respectable workman was, and felt himself to be, a businessman. He successfully applied himself to exploiting his own individual opportunities, to getting on or, in any case, to selling his labor as advantageously as possible. He understood and largely shared his employer's way of thinking. When he found it useful to ally himself with his peers within the same concern, he did so in the same spirit.[3]

The great centralization of industrial America following the Civil War brought an increase in nonagricultural workers. There had been only slightly over 4,000,000 such workers in America when the War broke out, but by 1900 there were over 18,000,000. The large class of industrial workers which thus developed found itself closely tied to the fortunes of American industry. Employment fluctuated dramatically in the major depressions of the 1870s and the 1890s. Even in the best of times, the new style American workman found himself far less independent than before. True, a few men might aspire to rise from laborer to foreman, from foreman to supervi-

[3]Joseph A. Schumpeter, *Capitalism, Socialism, and Democracy* (New York: Harper and Brothers, 1950), p. 331.

sor, from supervisor to manager; but how few such opportunities were available for how many workmen! For the individual workman, the area of free choice in the ordering of his life was clearly narrowed. Modern industrial organization had brought with it a measure of mobility; the worker now could move about freely as he saw fit, from job to job, from industrial slum to industrial slum. But each new job and each new slum looked remarkably like the one which the worker had just left. He found himself forced to come to terms with a centralized industrial structure beyond both his control and his understanding. As the American worker became more mobile, he also became more mobilized. The reaction to that increasing mobilization was inevitable:

Those weavers who in a burst of blind and thoughtless hatred destroyed the power looms that have deprived them of their livelihood were not yet aware of the real menace. They tried to stop technical progress by brute force, a fruitless attempt to save themselves from proletarization. The realization that man has to pay a price for every increase in power the machine gives him, that he must give an equivalent in return, is a realization that had not yet dawned in the early days of technology. In those days boundless economic confidence predominated, an unshakable optimism about the future.[4]

As the twentieth century approached, that earlier optimism about the future was deeply shaken. The industrial workers began to cast about for their own form of collective bigness by which they might oppose the collective bigness which had come to dominate their lives:

The labor organizations spring up wherever laborers reach an awareness and an understanding of the fact that they have become dependent and that they must organize to offer joint resistance. All such organizations are marked by the hatred with which they look upon the unorganized worker, the worker who has not yet grasped the compulsion of mechanical labor and the necessity of surrendering his independence to organization. As the workers unite, however, they unwillingly fulfill a condition of technical progress, the condition that everything must be organized. Workers, thinking they are acting on their own volition, work with enthusiasm, but their organization into unions is only an expression of the mechanical compulsion to which they are subjected. These organizations which try to make certain types of work a preserve for their group, disintegrate as soon as the

---

[4]Freidrich Georg Juenger, *The Failure of Technology* (Hinsdale, Ill. Regnery, 1959), pp. 116–117.

perfection of technology mechanizes all work; when the organization of work becomes universal, when everybody becomes a
worker.[5]

For a time, the crafts unions seemed to offer a special form of organization to the skilled worker. However, the process of erosion which Juenger
described as the time "when the organization of work becomes universal,
when everybody becomes a worker," was not far off in the increasingly
centralized world of industrial America. The rise of industrial unionism
brought a bureaucracy controlling industrial workers which was quite as
well organized as the bureaucracy controlling business. One bureaucracy
was to prove as anti-individual as the other.

The Farmer

The census report of 1890 which declared the end of an official frontier
in the United States touched no other group so directly as it did the farmer.
For generations, the farmer had turned to free land in the West as the
traditional remedy for all of his problems. As the economy became increasingly centralized and industrialized, and as society became primarily urban,
the farmer found himself more and more associated with the past than with
the present. With the old safety valve of Western lands now largely closed
to them, the farmers found themselves trapped within a society which left
them few or no options. They were faced with the question which every
minority must face sooner or later: What happens when there is no longer
any place to run?

When the farmers could no longer run, they began to see themselves as
victims of a society beyond their control. They had some reason for feeling
as they did. Government land policy had generally done them far more
harm than good. Tariff policies which favored the new industrial America
left the farmer buying in a high-priced, protected market while selling his
agricultural production in a low-priced world market. In the long run, what
did the farmer more harm than any other single factor was the fact that the
farmers themselves came to desire a share in the new centralized, industrialized system and its urban values. The seductive promises of specialization
and modern technology led the farmer into a one-way street of steadily
higher capital investment and indebtedness. As the result, the farmer soon
learned that his "share in the new system" was always less than the demands which the new system placed upon him. The farmer was becoming
a businessman; but he was entering the new age with very bad timing. He
was becoming, or attempting to become, a small entrepreneur at just the

[5] *Ibid.,* pp. 60–61.

moment when modern society was becoming dominated by centralized corporate interests. Small wonder the individual farmer found it difficult to swim against such a strong tide.

As the American farmer became "progressive," he found that he must think more and more in terms of a money economy, and thus less and less in terms of farming as a way of life. This change brought a total revolution in traditional agrarian values. The older ideal of the self-sufficient farmer began to appear more a curiosity than a reality. The new urban America changed the farmer's image from yeoman to yokel.

The pressures of the new money economy brought real hardship to the American farmer wherever he lived, but it brought special burdens to the Southern agrarian. In an economy in which the small white farmer had been largely self-sufficient and had felt no sense of inequality with his larger planter neighbors, the earlier germ of American independence and individuality had been able to thrive. But in the new money economy, white tenantry developed, turning the plain man into the "poor white." With that change in status went the small farmer's independence. The case of the Southern farmer is only a particularly dramatic and unfortunate example of the direction of American agrarian society as the twentieth century approached. While the Northern farmer did not become a tenant in the literal sense of the word, he found himself closely tied to a banking and corporate structure completely beyond his control.

As a result of this lost independence and lost respect, the farmer lost his way as an individual and came, like the workingman, to hope that some form of organization and political activity might redress the balance which tilted so disastrously against him. The political movements of the 1870s, 1880s, and 1890s, were not an attempt to overthrow the traditional fabric of America, but an attempt to restore it to its original form. The men who would have been small capitalists in an earlier era, the skilled workers and the farmers, were waging a struggle against the centralization wrought by the new and dominant corporate structure. However mistaken the Populist movement might have been in its means, its ends were those of an earlier and more individualistic America:

> . . .the Populists were the first great social realists of the new era; the first to speak openly of the dangers of plutocracy; the first to convey something of the bewilderment a whole generation felt in the disillusionment that followed the Civil War; the first to influence a folk literature, crude as it often was, based upon the consciousness of common struggle; the first to proclaim, in a difficult period, the enduring worth of the submerged Jeffersonian democracy that was to re-

main the essential testament of a large section of the American people up to the First World War.[6]

The great tragedy was that those Jeffersonian ends were to be linked to Hamiltonian means. The resultant extensions of a strongly centralized government would prove to be the greatest anti-individualistic force of all. The Populists forgot that the very plutocracy that they so much feared had grown strong precisely *because of* its connection with government. Thus the underlying cause of farmer and worker discontent in the late nineteenth century, that is, strong centralized government, was now thought to be the means of salvation from those same discontents.

The Mugwump

A new word entered the American language during the Cleveland–Blaine campaign of 1884: "A Mugwump is a person educated beyond his intellect." Mugwump thus became a term of opprobrium directed at those educated members of the middle and upper classes who threw their influence against the dominant political currents of the day. The Mugwump found himself steadily less at home in either major American political party.

Middle-class and upper-class local leaders — clergyman, doctors, lawyers, small-town bankers, and other relics of an earlier America — felt that they no longer exercised the control or carried the economic influence which they had once possessed. Therefore the Mugwump found himself a ready ally with the workingman and the farmer in the quest for the return to the social values of an earlier day:

> The typical Mugwump was a conservative in his economic and political views. He disdained, to be sure, the most unscrupulous of the new men of wealth, as he did the opportunistic, boodling, tariff-mongering politicians who served them. But the most serious abuses of the unfolding economic order of the Gilded Age he either resolutely ignored or accepted complacently as an inevitable result of the struggle for existence or the improvidence and laziness of the masses. As a rule, he was dogmatically committed to the prevailing theoretical economics of *laissez faire.* His economic program did not go much beyond tariff reform and sound money — both principles more easily acceptable to a group whose wealth was based more upon mercantile activities and the professions than upon manufacturing and new enterprises — and his political program rested upon the foundations of honest and efficient government and civil-service reform. He was a "liberal" in the classic sense. Tariff reform, he thought, would be the sovereign

[6]Alfred Kazin, *On Native Grounds* (Garden City, N.Y.: Doubleday, 1956), p. 21.

remedy for the huge business combinations that were arising. His pre-eminent journalist and philosopher was E. L. Godkin, the honorable old free-trading editor of the *Nation* and the New York *Evening Post.* His favorite statesman was Grover Cleveland, who described the tariff as the "mother of trusts." He imagined that most of the economic ills that were remediable at all could be remedied by free trade, just as he believed that the essence of government lay in honest dealing by honest and competent men.[7]

For all of his classical liberal pretensions, the Mugwump shared the political and organizational bias of his times, believing with all his heart that the solution to America's problems was finding the "right man" for political office. He was the raw material from which the Progressive movement would grow in the early twentieth century.

The Mugwump completed the group of dissenters, a group of widely varying Americans who had almost nothing in common except their emnity to the existing system of centralized, corporate, urbanized industrialism which had changed the face of American society. Obviously enough, the small business and professional man had little in common with the farmer, who had in turn nothing in common with the average American workingman. It is also true that all the dissenting groups were on net balance better off economically than they had been before. The American workingman surely enjoyed a greater prosperity than earlier, at least in material terms. The farmer enjoyed conveniences and opportunities beyond the wildest dreams of his grandfather, and even the small businessman and professional man shared in the material prosperity of the late nineteenth century. What had changed most drastically for these people was the quality of American life, a quality which is ill measured in strictly material terms.

Now, reluctantly rather than enthusiastically, the average American tended more and more to rely on government regulation, to seek in governmental action a counterpoise to the power of private business. In his resentment against the incursions of business organization upon his moral sensibilities and his individualistic values, he began to support governmental organization and to accept more readily than he had been willing to do before the idea that the reach of government must be extended. Since the state governments, so long the central agencies of political action, had been clearly outdistanced by business interests (which were in any case constitutionally beyond the reach of state control), he looked to the federal government as his last resource for the control of business, thus ironically lending support to another

[7]Richard Hofstadter, *The Age of Reform* (New York: Vintage Books, 1955), pp. 141–142.

step in the destruction of that system of local and decentralized values in which he also believed. The long-range trend toward federal regulation, which found its beginnings in the Interstate Commerce Act of 1887 and the Sherman Act of 1890, which was quickened by a large number of measures in the Progressive era, and which has found its consummation in our time, was thus at first the response of a predominantly individualistic public to the uncontrolled and starkly original collectivism of big business.[8]

The Utopian

The worker, the farmer, and the Mugwump were beginning to recognize manifestations of a problem with roots deep in the economic and intellectual history of the modern world. Nineteenth-century Europe had already spawned a variety of protests against industrial capitalism, some on entirely different grounds than the American protest. Most of the European protests centered on variations of what came to be labeled "socialism." The potpourri of theories operating under that label had as their common thread an assault upon the principle of private property and an emphasis upon various forms of communal control at the expense of family and individual freedom. Most Americans of 1890 would have stoutly denied any affinity for the ideas of European socialism in any of its varieties, but the subject is worth consideration, since certain suppositions about the necessity for big government as a problem-solving device *were* present on both sides of the Atlantic. Witness the Populist platform of the 1890s, which contained demands for most of the measures previously urged by European socialists.

Most of the early-day European varieties of socialism suffered from ill definition:

> The reformers of the XIXth century used vaguely such formulae as "from each according to his capacities; to each according to his needs." They promised a society in which there should still be as much private ownership as would satisfy the equally vague instincts of their hearers, and attempted in some way to combine the principle of property with the implications of its opposite. They preached antagonism without conflict and wandered at large amid a host of similar self-contradictions.[9]

The communism of Karl Marx joined with the other varied strains of European socialism in protest against the existing industrial system. Marx and the rest of the nineteenth-century varieties of European socialism shared one common ideal, spiritual enthusiasm. Such spiritual enthusiasm

---

[8] *Ibid.*, p. 233.
[9] Hilaire Belloc, *The Crisis of Our Civilization* (London: Cassell,.), p. 181.

invariably releases a tremendous amount of creative energy, however bizarre the ideas stemming from that energy may prove to be. One form of creative energy which this protest released in the United States centered on utopian fiction. The second half of the nineteenth century brought to America a host of visionaries outlining the perfect society.

All utopians had two main points of reference which they held in common. First, they believed themselves to be staunch defenders of the individual; second, they believed that a uniformly controlled economic life was the only possible basis for an ideal society in which the individual could realize true freedom and independence. Like the Populists of their own time and the Progressives of a later generation, as well as the liberals of the twentieth century, the utopians failed to see that Step Two in their program invariably cancelled out any possibility of achieving Step One.

Morris' *News from Nowhere,* Howell's *Through the Eye of the Needle,* Hudson's *A Crystal Age,* and a host of similar works succeeded one another in rapid order. Each new utopian novel seemed to advance the ideal of a highly centralized institutional structure more passionately than its predecessor.

> In a period of almost unrestrained individualism, free enterprise, and "the less government the better" politics, utopists were anticipating the "welfare state," the nationalization of industries, "socialized" medicine and health programs, unemployment insurance, old-age pensions, and numerous other such proposals which were fantastically "radical," "dangerous," or "preposterous" in the latter nineteenth century, but which in 1950 have become a part of every man's political vocabulary.[10]

While it would be an exaggeration to suggest that the utopians had a determining influence in producing the turn of affairs which the twentieth century has witnessed, it is true that the role of the utopian novelist has generally been underestimated. The widely diverse strains of protest during the nineteenth century which found room to include the worker, the farmer, and the Mugwump, also found room for the utopian novelist, a breed who did much to provide an intellectual rationale, however farfetched it may have been, for the society which was then in gestation.

The sense of impending change hung heavy over the American society of 1890. As we became a nation of cities and factories, as old faiths dissolved in new enthusiasms, as the city replaced the country as the life-form for most Americans, the Populists and the Mugwumps were raising their voices

[10]Glenn Negley and J. Max Patrick, *The Quest for Utopia* (Garden City, N.Y.: Doubleday [Anchor Books], 1962), p. 14.

in complaint and shock and anguish. It was during the same time that the most distinguished utopian novels were being written. In a sense, for all their obvious shortcomings, the utopian had caught the spirit of discontent plaguing so many Americans. In William Dean Howell's *A Traveler from Alturia,* one character described the transformation of American life which had occurred between 1850 and 1890:

> If [in 1850] a man got out of work, he turned his hand to something else; if a man failed in business, he started again from some other direction; as a last resort, in both cases, he went West, pre-empted a quarter section of public land, and grew up with the country. Now the country is grown up; the public land is gone; business is full on all sides, and the hand that turned itself to something else has lost its cunning. The struggle for life has changed from a free fight to an encounter of disciplined forces, and the free fighters that are left get ground to pieces between organized labor and organized capital.[11]

Perhaps the single most influential utopian novel was Edward Bellamy's *Looking Backward,* published in 1888. Bellamy's ideal state was constructed like the corporation. He seemed to feel, not that centralization was wrong, but that it was in the wrong hands, and had not yet been carried far enough. For example, his ideal society included the concept of "an industrial army," anticipating the conscript labor forces of the Communists and Nazis. However ugly such ideas might appear in the late twentieth century, armed as we with nearly 100 years of hindsight, in his own time Bellamy met with instant acclaim. "Nationalist Clubs" sprang up across the country, filled with middle-class enthusiasts who thought they saw in Bellamy the organizational form by which "individualism" might be returned to American society.

The utopians are important primarily as an indicator of how desperate the American people had become to escape the situation in which they found themselves. Unfortunately, people failed to realize that the enmassment of society and the growth of privileged special interest groups were both due to increasing government involvement in their affairs. They turned to that same government as a device to solve their problems. Ideological forces were to move Americans very far and very fast down the road to more centralism than any of them had yet anticipated, and the utopians formed a small but significant wing in this movement.

The Failure of Nineteenth-Century Protest

Such "reforms" as were accomplished by the Populists and Mugwumps proved to have less than beneficial results. The Interstate Commerce Com-

---

[11]Kazin, p. 17.

mission became an instrument whereby a monopoly situation was maintained in transportation, clearly working in favor of the centralized power structure that had already grown up. The Sherman Anti-Trust Act was similarly a source of disappointment. In the immortal words of Mr. Dooley, "What looks like a stone-wall to a layman is a triumphal arch to a corporation lawyer." During the same period, the tariff situation also failed to improve, and those who had a stranglehold upon American banking were careful to maintain their hold upon capital. It seemed to a generation of small businessmen in the late nineteenth century that the only way one could afford to borrow money was to have it already. The processes of centralization, achieved largely through political means, continued on their merry way.

Theodore Roosevelt had reportedly favored a foreign war to give the nation "something to think about which isn't material gain." However commendable his antimaterialistic ideal may have been, it would seem that the Spanish American War only served to put the capstone on the existing system. By 1900 the United States had acquired Puerto Rico, Guam, Wake Island, Hawaii, and the Philippines. We were in the process of taking over American Samoa, plus protectorates in Panama and Cuba. We had become a Far Eastern power, a Caribbean power, and a Pacific power. Imperial America was now prepared to deal with the crowned heads of Europe. The internal centralization of enormous power now had its external manifestations as well.

The Spanish–American War and ensuing adventure in imperialism, coming on top of the hard times of the nineties, dashed even modest liberal expectations for the future. To conservative William Graham Sumner, the acquisition of the Philippines spelled *The Conquest of the United States by Spain*. And to the radical Tom Watson, the war doomed all reform hopes. "The blare of the bugle drowned the voice of the Reformer." Although the dismay of the anti-imperialist liberals was deepest, traditional liberals of whatever hue had little reason for optimism. Under the leadership of Theodore Roosevelt and Woodrow Wilson, the trend toward big government and big business was destined to continue. In the midst of the popular enthusiasm for progressivism during the first decade of the twentieth century this was perhaps not so clear. But from the perspective of a later age it is possible to see that the progressives were essentially nationalists moving to a state socialism along European lines and owing relatively little to the American tradition of liberal individualism.[12]

[12]Arthur A. Ekirch, Jr., *The Decline of American Liberalism* (New York: Longmans, Green, 1955), p. 170.

It seemed that reform had been a failure on all fronts. In most cases, even if more "reforms" had been pushed through and made law, the results would have been much the same, since the reforms partook of the same false ideals which were the original source of the problem for Americans of the late nineteenth century. The Mugwump, worker, farmer, and utopian had been united only in their opposition to the new system. Some had worked inside the existing parties, some had attempted to start new political parties, some had proposed ideal societies of their own imaginings. In terms of practical action, they had climbed on their respective horses and ridden off in all directions. Thus little or nothing of a lasting nature had come from the reform movements of the late nineteenth century. But in terms of a theoretical emphasis, a dangerous precedent had been set. "Reform" in America had come to mean political action, designed to substitute public enmassment for private enmassment. Within a few years, the fragmented, minority position of the Mugwumps and Populists was to become the unified, majority position of Progressivism. The way had been paved for a full-dress experiment testing whether or not wholesale political intervention in American society was the answer to our problems. Seventy years later we have not yet emerged from the experiment — one wonders whether or not such an experiment *can* end this side of social disintegration.

XI

THE PROGRESSIVES

The reformers of the period put me off, in the first instance, by their careless superficial use of abstract terms. They talked about the oppressiveness of capital, the evils of the capitalist system, the iniquities of finance-capitalism, and so on, apparently with no idea of what those terms mean. To me, therefore, most of what they said was sheer nonsense. I knew that no society ever did or could exist without employing capital, and my notion was that wherever capital is at work, there of necessity is capitalism and a capitalist system. As I saw it, there was nothing in the nature of capital that was unjust or oppressive, but quite the contrary. I could see that injustice and oppression were likely to follow when great capitalists were in a position of State-created economic advantage, like Mr. Carnegie with his tariffs or with the "railway-magnates" with their land-grants; but the same results seemed as likely to follow where small capitalists or noncapitalists were in a similarly privileged position. Spencer's *Social Statics,* published in 1851, had shown me that under such a government as he contemplated, — a government divested of all power to traffic in economic advantage, — injustice and oppression would tend to disappear. As long as the State stood as an approachable huckster of privilege, however, there seemed no chance but that they must persist, and that the consequent social disorder must persist also.

Albert Jay Nock,
The Memoirs of a Superfluous Man

One of the first and most significant changes of the Progressive era took place in the academic community. Prior to the twentieth century, the vast majority of American academicians had been completely out of sympathy with radical European thought. For the first time, during the Progressive era, a large minority of professors set themselves up as a braintrust to the protest movement. How great their impact was to prove is readily apparent from a roll call of these academicians. Such names as John R. Commons, Richard T. Ely, Thorstein Veblen, Charles Beard, J. Allen Smith, Lester Ward, and John Dewey were destined to be in the forefront of the new currents of thought coming to dominate twentieth-century America.

The new breed of professors made a great point of the economic bases of politics, stressing the deep involvement of government in business and business in government. For them the ultimate social sin of the modern world was the impersonality bred by the modern corporation. In E. A. Ross' *Sin and Society*, he stressed the fact that the corporation was a person for legal, but not moral, purposes. No one seemed to feel personal responsibility for corporate actions. The professors expected political intervention to fill this ethical gap. It was hoped that the new social sin of corporate enterprise could be dealt with when government acted as society's conscience. What the professors overlooked is that the "new political sin" would share the same impersonality and therefore continue to be divorced from any genuine ethical content.

The new situation which the professors met in the dawning twentieth century seemed to demand new academic departures. Charles Beard and Frederick Jackson Turner pioneered in the economic interpretation of history. John Dewey converted philosophy into sociology, making it a discipline directed primarily toward social planning. Veblen, Commons, and Ely converted the concepts of economics to new uses in propagandizing the virtues of a planned society. The result was an all-out attack on the traditional values of American society, coming for the first time from a new quarter:

Fully to appreciate the sweep of the assault it must be viewed as coupled with a much more subtle and broader attack. Philosophers such as William James and John Dewey worked to undermine the belief in a fixed reality. As they succeeded, the belief in natural law which had been at the heart of the American tradition crumbled. Frederick Jackson Turner, the historian, emphasized the changing and pragmatic character of American historical development. J. Allen Smith and Charles A. Beard took positions which helped to discredit the American Constitution. Biographers "debunked" men who had been heroes to earlier Americans. Justices Oliver Wendell Holmes and Louis D. Brandeis emphasized the evolutionary character of law and the importance of changing conditions.[1]

The changes thus produced in the American mind were to provide the predominant rationale for the twentieth century. It should not be overlooked that the greatest portion of that new rationale as it developed within the academic community drew heavily upon the European economic and social analyses of the nineteenth century. This European infusion of ideas,

[1]Clarence B. Carson, *The Fateful Turn* (Irvington, N.Y.: Foundation for Economic Education, 1963), p. 103.

coupled with the American discontent already described, carried America rapidly along a new road. The new ideas within the academic community were soon to find a wide audience among Americans, as they were spread through the classroom, popularized in the novel, and made to appear the exciting new rationale which offered solutions to all America's problems.

This new rationale drew heavily upon the assumption that the individual was powerless unless organized into larger groups which wielded political influence. The individual apart from these groups was assumed to lack the "belongingness" necessary, not only for effective political action, but even for proper "personal adjustment."

A close connection existed between the enmassment and superorganization of American life and the intellectual assault led against the older American values:

> In the great revolt against traditionalism that began around the turn
> of the century, William James, John Dewey, Charles Beard, Thorstein
> Veblen, the muckrakers and a host of reformers brought the ana-
> chronisms of the Protestant Ethic under relentless fire, and in so doing
> helped lay the groundwork for the Social Ethic. It would be a long
> time before organization men would grasp the relevance of these new
> ideas, and to this day many of the most thoroughgoing pragmatists
> in business would recoil at being grouped with the intellectuals. (And
> vice versa.) But the two movements were intimately related. To what
> degree the intellectuals were a cause of change, or a manifestation, no
> one can say for certain, but more presciently than those in organiza-
> tion they grasped the antithesis between the old concept of the ra-
> tional, unbeholden individual and the world one had to live in. They
> were not rebels against society; what they fought was the denial of
> society's power, and they provided an intellectual framework that
> would complement, rather than inhibit, the further growth of big
> organization.[2]

The Historians

Among the historians who achieved the greatest impact with the new ideas were Frederick Jackson Turner, Vernon Louis Parrington, and Charles A. Beard. Turner's *The Significance of the Frontier in American History* had an enormous influence upon the generation of Americans who first realized that the old frontier was gone forever, replaced by gigantic corporate structure and an urban society. Charles Beard furthered Turner's ideas by pioneering in a new approach to history, centering on economic

[2]William H. Whyte, Jr., *The Organization Man* (New York: Simon and Schuster, 1956), p. 20.

determinism. He read the ideas of 1900 backward through American history, creating the impression of a brutal and exploitive past in which the economic welfare of a few had been placed ahead of the total social welfare of all. Beard's economic interpretation became the almost literal expression of the Progressive mind:

> Into it went all the leavings of their nineteenth-century innocence, their brisk dissatisfaction with their own time, their yearning for a simple emancipation, and their fundamental goodness of spirit. Expose evil, the heavens commanded, and it shall vanish; prove the good and it shall be enacted; we who have stood at Armageddon with T.R., fought the bitter fight with Robert LaFollette, and left only Utah and Vermont in the election of 1912 to Big Business, may yet deliver America to virtue.[3]

Vernon Parrington's *Main Currents in American Thought* built upon the same theme of economic interpretation, applying it to American social and literary thought. The impact of his thinking upon twentieth-century American literature was most profound. For good or for bad, the literary intellectual of the 1930s took his fundamental tack primarily from Vernon Parrington. Alfred Kazin described the book and its influence upon American thought:

> . . . it represents the most ambitious single effort of the Progressive mind to understand itself, and can be understood only in reference to the idealism, prejudices, and characteristic sentimentality of that mind — all of which Parrington sought almost unwittingly, in the drive of his great idea, to impose upon intellectual history in America. For though Parrington often seemed to go beyond the diverse rebellions of the period, he was astonishingly loyal to them all, and often simultaneously. It was the grass-roots radical, the Populist, the Jeffersonian liberal, even the quasi-Marxist in him, that combined to make him so outstanding a Progressive intellectual.[4]

The Educationists

Though the historians had a great influence on American life, their influence pales in comparison with John Dewey and his cohorts. While many of the Progressives were expecting political reform to "save America from the plutocracy," John Dewey was working in quite a different direction. He advocated a system of education which would produce a new

[3]Alfred Kazin, *On Native Grounds* (Garden City, N.Y.: Doubleday, 1956), pp. 123–124.
[4]*Ibid.*, p. 125.

generation of Americans, Americans with a preference for group and social activity, who viewed themselves not as individuals but as members of a "total democratic society."

The new American was to be guided by the attempt to live in harmony with social processes. No individual values were to interfere with that social harmony. This relativist evaluation of the individual had its roots at least in part in the relativism of the pragmatic philosophy which John Dewey had borrowed from William James and then extended to total social goals. James had limited the application of his pragmatic principles to the concern of the individual. Nevertheless, the relativism and lack of fixed values which Dewey was to elevate in an entire social system was already present in James' work, removing all guidelines by which the individual might define himself and his goals. It is not surprising that members of the James family, including not only the psychologist and philosopher William James, but the novelist Henry James, should have found trouble defining the individual, since all the members of the family suffered from the same peculiar inability to sort out a final set of values whereby they might order their own lives. As one wag has suggested, "The psychology of William James is all fiction; the fiction of Henry James is all psychology."

The increasing loss of individual guidelines which was evident in the pragmatism of William James became even more explicit and evident when John Dewey applied the same ideas on a broadly social basis. The result was yet another version of the social enmassment which was already beginning to plague American life:

> . . . the individual was meaningless as a unit for investigation; only men's social behavior deserved analysis.. . . Public education reflected the changing psychology rather promptly. From anywhere inside the classical system, education meant mental discipline. Schools should train the good faculties, give them muscle in their fight against the bad. Now education implied the guidance of behavior in harmony with social processes. If destruction of the faculties eventually cleared the way for modern psychology, its most immediate beneficiary was social engineering.[5]

The Social Gospel

What John Dewey began to apply to the schools soon found its counterpart in the churches. Religion, which had once offered the most profound plea for individual liberty, was completely changed as the result of the Social Gospel movement. Environmentalism and economic determinism increasingly dominated the churches. Out of concern for the new social and

[5]Robert H. Wiebe, *The Search for Order* (New York: Hill and Wang, 1968), pp. 148–149.

economic innovations and under the influence of the academic theoreticians who were promoting a new view of American society, the ideas of Progressivism enveloped much of organized religion. The clergyman began to turn from theological to social questions. In the new emphasis upon "total social goals," even salvation was now to be collectivized.

The connection between the Social Gospel and the new current of ideas stemming from the utopians and the academic community is far more immediate than generally realized. For example, the utopian novelist Edward Bellamy had been raised in a Social Gospeling home and many of the ideas in his novels clearly derived from that source. The connections were particularly close between the Social Gospel and the new economic analysis. In the heyday of John R. Commons and Richard Ely, over sixty clergymen were listed as members of the new and highly Progressive American Economic Association. The new view of society would allow no areas of exemption.

Veblen

One of the most influential of the new economists was Thorstein Veblen. As a youth, Veblen had been in touch with an earlier America, at a time when a close personal relationship existed between the individual and his work. He never lost his affection for such a world. Describing that relationship as the ethical basis for society, he came to distrust and dislike the industrial world which had replaced that earlier concpet. Perversely, this same man also saw great potentialities in modern industrial society. While he resented the businsssman as an exploiter and a profiteer, Veblen was quite willing to allow the engineer to oversee and regulate society.

Veblen's perversity was not limited to wishing for a society which was simultaneously individual *and* engineered. He was quite capable of showing his personal and intellectual hatred and confusions in a variety of ways. He spent his entire life hating the existing system which repressed the sort of life he felt the individual was entitled to lead. Capitalism and all its institutional manifestations became his lifelong enemy. Reading his descriptions of business culture, as for example in *The Theory of the Leisure Class,* makes it clear how bitter and frustrated this son of a Norwegian emigrant ultimately became.

The conflict which Veblen was never able to resolve was between the individual workman and the efficiency of the engineered society. Veblen felt himself a defender of an earlier America, but, in his insistence upon the engineered society, he was as much a prophet of the new order which he so hated as any of the "profiteering businessmen" whom he constantly criticized.

America . . . never had suffered the misfortune of being reduced to uniformity of character. It would be ridiculous to pretend that Hawthorne, or Lincoln, or Josiah Royce, or Robert E. Lee, ever entertained such an affection for efficiency, utility, and pragmatic simplicity. Veblen stands for only one type of American; and that type is the devotee of aggrandizement whom Veblen's books denounce. There are men who kill the thing they love; there are others who become the thing they hate.[6]

Perhaps Veblen was led astray by his deeply rooted love of the machine. Even while he decried the results of modern technology upon the individual and his way of life, he saw society as dominated by the machine, and thus came to have an essentially mechanical view of social organization. If it is possible to separate what Thorstein Veblen was *for,* from the things Thorstein Veblen was *against,* it is perhaps not unfair to categorize his view of society as a gigantic, highly specialized, tightly coordinated human clockwork. On this point, Veblen sometimes is too much even for modern proponents of the new system:

Veblen's infatuation with the machine is a jarring note in a worldly philosopher otherwise so devoid of lyricism. It is true that machines make us think coldly, but they may end up by making us think too coldly. Let us not forget that the end of a "scientific" conduct of production may be the human robot and that while the machine process may exercise our technical judgment, it may stifle and frustrate our imaginations and emotions: Charlie Chaplin in *Modern Times* was not a happy or a well-adjusted man. A corps of engineers might well run our society more efficiently; that it would be more humanely run is a debatable proposition.[7]

Lester Frank Ward

What Charles Beard had done in history, and Thorstein Veblen in economics, Lester Frank Ward did in sociology. He opened the way for the development of the new and broadly based "social thought." Sharing the Progressive view that the first step must be the establishment of a "genuine people's government," Ward felt that no lasting reforms could come about until legislators had trained for their work as "social scientists." He felt that every legislator must have a total view of how society should be molded before he could participate in the process. In Ward's view of the legislator

[6]Russell Kirk, *Prospects for Conservatives* (Chicago: Regnery, 1956), p. 115.
[7]Robert L. Heilbroner, *The Worldly Philosophers* (New York: Simon and Schuster, 1953), p. 212.

it is immediately apparent that he reserved for politics a role as a manipulating device designed to control all society: "Modern society is suffering from the very opposite of paternalism — from under-government. . . . The true function of government is not to fetter but to liberate the forces of society; not to diminish but to increase their effectiveness." In Ward we thus find the original germ of an idea which today forms a significant portion of the social planner's rhetoric.

What made Ward and so many of the other intellectuals of the Progressive era so strangely effective was the large portion of truth contained within their allegations. However wrong-headed the total direction of their analyses may have been, they did have their attention on an important point. Something was very wrong with American society. In Ward's words:

> The charge of paternalism is chiefly made by the class that enjoys the largest share of government protection. Those who denounce state interference are the ones who most frequently and successfully invoke it. The cry of laissez-faire mainly goes up from the ones who, if really "let alone" would instantly lose their wealth absorbing power. . . . Nothing is more obvious today than the signal inability of capital and private enterprise to take care of themselves unaided by the state; and while they are incessantly denouncing paternalism — by which they mean the claim of the defenceless laborer and artisan to a share in this lavish state protection — they are all the while besieging legislatures for relief from their own incompetency, and "pleading the baby act" through a trained body of lawyers and lobbyists.[8]

Drawing heavily upon the legal work of Holmes and Brandeis, and the economics of Ely, Commons, and Veblen, Ward brought together much of the new thinking and projected it upon a broad social screen, destined to provide a highly accurate prediction of the course America would take in the present century. Lester Ward is one of the patron saints of the modern American collective ideal.

In an age when the primary proponents of a free and unregulated economic system were unwilling to urge repeal of the numerous benefits which they themselves received from government intervention, it is not difficult to understand why the ideas of Lester Ward won the day in confrontation with the ideas of William Graham Sumner. The American people were choosing not to be free, and they had many good teachers among the very businessmen who had preached freedom to them. The replacement of the individual by society was clearly the coming attraction of the American intellectual.

[8]Henry Steele Commager, *The American Mind* (New Haven: Yale University Press, 1961), p. 210.

Ward wrote in 1893, "The individual has reigned long enough. The day has come for society to take its affairs into its own hands and shape its own destinies."[9] By the turn of the century, the American intellectual had largely developed the rationale which would dominate the Progressive era and set the course for the rest of the twentieth century.

The Muckrakers

It was by the sheerest coincidence that Lincoln Steffen's opening chapter of *The Shame of the Cities* appeared simultaneously with Ida M. Tarbell's *History of the Standard Oil Company* in the pages of *McClure's*. The results were to make publishing history. McClure was never slow to sense an opportunity, and he quickly realized that the American people were hungry for exposés of the existing system. From that time on, *McClure's* published large quantities of what came to be known as "muckraking" articles. The business became so profitable that *Everybody's, Collier's, Cosmopolitan,* and *Pearson's* soon joined in unfettered criticism of American standards and American life. No aspect of America at the turn of the century was spared treatment in this passion for exposé.

If the earlier Populist era had led people to be dissatisfied with their society and to look for villains who could be blamed, the dissatisfaction and the need for villains had become so great by the Progressive era that such attitudes were the dominant passions of the first decade of the twentieth century. The muckraking novel grew to great popularity during the same period, as America's insatiable appetite for villains and exposés spread to the world of fiction. In fact, the muckrakers so interwove fact and fiction that it became difficult to tell where the muckraking novel left off and the muckraking "factual" exposé began. The muckrakers thus played their own substantial role in popularizing the attitudes which the American people already possessed, paving the way for the acceptance of the political solutions outlined by the intellectuals.

The Mugwump as Progressive

While the Populism of the late nineteenth century had been predominantly rural, the ferment of the Progressive era was primarily urban. Another vital difference between Populism and Progressivism centered on the fact that, with Progressivism, for the first time the middle class came forward in large numbers to participate in reform agitation. The average member of the American middle class had been bitterly opposed to the "radicalism" of Populism. The same ideas, couched in a slightly different setting, offered at a slightly later point in time, and labeled Progressivism, were to sweep the middle class off their feet and lead them down essentially

[9]Carson, p. 24.

the same road that the Populists had urged a few years before. With Progressivism, large-scale government intervention in the life of the American citizen came to be viewed not only as necessary, but desirable.

Why this sudden about-face on the part of the American middle class? Why should the ideas so distrusted when presented under Populist auspices suddenly attract such a large following a few years later? One very plausible answer to the question lies in Richard Hofstadter's suggestion that a "status revolution" had occurred, displacing the older, small-town, American business and professional leadership with the new plutocracy. It was this status revolution, rather than economic depravation, which finally convinced middle-class America that the time had come to wage an active fight against the changes which had been occurring in American society:

> Progressivism, at its heart, was an effort to realize familiar and traditional ideals under novel circumstances. . . . the ordinary American's ideas of what political and economic life ought to be like had long since taken form under the conditions of a preponderantly rural society with a broad diffusion of property and power. In that society large aggregates had played a minor role. Corporate businesses were then just emerging, and they had not yet achieved the enormous size and national scope which they acquired during the closing decades of the nineteenth century, when the Progressive generation was still growing up. . . .
>
> While the worst forebodings of the Progressives were not to be realized, one must see with sympathy the view of affairs taken by the men of their generation whose historical consciousness had been formed on the American experience with individual enterprise. The drama of American history had been played out on a continent three thousand miles wide and almost half as long. Great political issues had been fought out over this terrain, great economic risks taken on it, fantastic profits extracted from it. The generation that had not yet passed from the scene had produced and admired, even as it resented and feared, a Carnegie, a Rockefeller, a Hill, a Harriman, a Morgan. America had engendered a national imagination keyed to epic dimensions, a soul unhappy without novelty and daring, raised on the conquest of a continent, the settlement of an immense domain, the creation within the life span of one man of a gigantic system of industry and transportation. Its people had pioneered, improvised, and gambled their way across the continent. And now were its young men to become a nation of employees, at best of administrators, were they to accept a dispensation under which there was nothing but safe investment, to adapt themselves passively to a life without personal enterprise even on a moderate scale? How, then, was the spiritual

bravura of the whole American enterprise to be sustained? And if it could not be sustained, what would become of America? The Progressives were not fatalists; they did not intend quietly to resign themselves to the decline of this great tradition without at least one brave attempt to recapture that bright past in which there had been a future.[10]

The Progressive leaders were thus the logical outgrowth of the Mugwump tradition, with little or no change in the underlying values, but with full recognition of the fact that a new day of enmassment and bigness had arrived which demanded organized bigness in response. The Progressive leadership despaired of regaining the values of an earlier America by clinging to the policies of *laissez-faire*. They, unlike the Mugwumps of an earlier generation, were quite willing to use large-scale government intervention to achieve their ends. We cannot understand Progressivism unless we appreciate the fact that the Progressive leadership consisted largely of a group of men who held to the basic Yankee values of individualism and self-help. It is only in these terms that Progressivism makes sense as a popular political movement. The great irony of Progressivism, of course, lies in the tragic and seemingly foreordained failure of attempted collective solution to essentially individual problems.

Again and again in Progressive rhetoric, there appears the idea of "giving the little man a chance," emphasizing the entrepreneurial hero, the "new entry in the race." For the first fifteen years of the century, every Progressive political leader spoke incessantly of the fact that the genius of America had always depended upon the small enterpriser, upon the very man who was now being driven to the wall by the massive new organizations. As Woodrow Wilson phrased it in *The New Freedom*, ". . . the middle class is being more and more squeezed out by the processes which we have been taught to call processes of prosperity. Its members are sharing prosperity, no doubt; but what alarms me is that they are not *originating* prosperity." There, in the most simple possible terms, is the complaint that the middle classes were no longer assuming their accustomed place in leadership of American society.

The Progressive was caught in the toils of modern technology and corporate industries. He wished to retain the prosperity and benefits stemming from the new form of social organization but was unwilling to accept the gigantic changes which had occurred in life of the individual as the result of that social organization. It is important to understand that the Progressives were not mere fumblers who wished to turn their lives over to government but, on the contrary, were men of real ability who were trying

[10]Richard Hofstadter, *The Age of Reform* (New York: Vintage Books, 1955), pp. 215, 226–227.

desperately to preserve their traditional freedom and responsibility in a society which made that preservation increasingly difficult.

Ultimately, of course, the new middle class which grew up in the twentieth century changed in its basic character as it became increasingly willing to use government intervention to solve its problems. The middle-class Progressive is thus a sort of halfway house between the highly individualistic and independent Mugwump of the 1870s, and the essentially bureaucratic and corporately oriented member of the middle class which had become so common by the 1920s. Before the process initiated by the Progressives was concluded, the American middle class would itself become, together with the intellectuals and the more radical reformers, the chief agency of change in a society moving from individual to bureaucratic and collective values. This change was already becoming apparent during the Progressive era, not only in the large-scale political intervention which the Progressives were willing to encourage, but also in the number of national associations founded during the period to satisfy the lust for organization which the middle class displayed in its occupational and social activities. Professional organizations, small business groups, social organizations, religious organizations, and a host of similar groups came into being in response to the American's newly discovered need to organize for collective protection, association and social life. The growing number of professional associations and formal licensure procedures accepted by the middle class give an indication of the connection between the rise of the "new middle class" and the collective political action which epitomized Progressivism. The Mugwump had discovered that he had to organize if his power was to be felt in a highly organized society. By the time this professional middle-class leadership finished its organization, it was destined to become the primary agency of bureaucratic organization in American society.

The early years of the twentieth century saw large-scale political intervention nearing the "takeoff" point. The reform current now possessed the ideas of the intellectuals, the popular leadership and imagination of the Muckrakers, and the dominant influence and enthusiasm of the American middle class. The big society was about to come of age.

XII

BIGNESS VS. BIGNESS

Industrial growth and combination, it was argued by progressives and reformers on both sides of the Atlantic, must be paralleled by a consolidation of regulatory powers in a centralized national government. Society in the future would have to be based more and more on an explicit subordination of the individual to a collectivist, or nationalized, political and social order.

Arthur A. Ekirch, Jr.,
The Decline of American Liberalism

The American tradition of political life had always been based upon resentment of special privilege and monopoly. We had never approved of closing the avenues to individual advancement. It was natural enough that the American people should become restive as the nineteenth century ended and as they saw their old world of individual enterprise and decentralized society replaced by a highly organized form of life which seemed to leave steadily less and less room for individual opportunity, at least in the old sense of the word. Americans of 1900 shared with most present-day historians the assumption that concentration of economic power was an inevitable feature in the evolution of modern capitalism. Both the friends and foes of capitalism shared this view. Whether or not the process of centralization *was* inevitable is not really the point; Americans *thought* it was inevitable and began to react accordingly.

It is worth remembering that the centralization of political and economic authority in the federal government had also been progressing rather steadily since the time of the Civil War. The American reaction against the centralization which seemed to be occurring within the business community further accelerated this expansion of governmental powers as a means of counterbalancing the economic centralization.

The rising chorus of voices urging the government to "do something" also bred a strident new political type. The nineteenth century had already witnessed the rise of Populist demagogues such as "Pitchfork" Ben Tillman, the Free Silver hysteria, and the general strikes which had swept throughout whole sections of the country with destructive force. These appeals for "action" and sweeping reform had previously been regarded as the extreme position of a minority; but, by 1900, the necessity for widespread and rapid change in American society had become the generally accepted view of the American people. Some cautious observers refused to go along with the new "reform" currents, but they were becoming a smaller and smaller minority:

> One afternoon in 1900 I listened while a young Jewish Socialist was breathing out threatenings and slaughter against the rich. I had asked him just what it was that he proposed to do when he had got them all properly killed off. "We have been oppressed," he said, "and now we shall oppress." I thought he put the matter very well, for I could see no other prospect.
>
> When one brushed aside the reformers' verbiage, the situation was perfectly clear. I was not witnessing a "revolt of the masses" against an alien power; nor yet a war between labour and capital; nor yet a struggle to break up big business; nor yet an attempt to abolish capitalism. What I was looking at was simply a tussle between two groups of mass-men, one large and poor, the other small and rich, and as judged by the standards of a civilised society, neither of them any more meritorious or promising than the other. The object of the tussle was the material gains accruing from control of the State's machinery. It is easier to seize wealth than to produce it; and as long as the State makes the seizure of wealth a matter of legalised privilege, so long will the squabble for that privilege go on. As John Adams had so correctly foreseen, the few more sagacious mass-men will be continually trying to outwit the many who are less sagacious, and the many will in turn be trying to overpower the few by sheer force of numbers.
>
> So I was sceptical about the reformers' projects, and the more they were trumpeted as "democratic," the less good to society I thought they boded.[1]

Naturally enough, since the special privileges to be accorded by the state were the prize in this new contest, the means for attaining that prize were also political. The Muckrakers and Progressives seized upon a public opinion already inflamed and confused by the events of the late nineteenth century and urged that the people make a new life for themselves through the use of politics. If the hero of the nineteenth century had been the businessman, the hero of the dawning era was to be the politician. The "people" were now to achieve their own salvation by means of reclaiming

---

[1]Albert Jay Nock, *The Memoirs of a Superfluous Man* (Chicago: Regnery, 1964), p. 121.

the political machinery of the nation. The short ballot — initiative, referendum, and recall — the direct primary — the direct election of United States Senators: all the electoral "reforms" of the Progressive era were an attempt to make politics responsive to the popular will.

The Progressive was confident that the place of the individual American would once again be secure as soon as these political changes had been brought about. The dominant note of the era was one of confidence. All problems, it was thought, would be overcome once the American voting population saw what was needed and passed the proper laws. The Progressives did not think of themselves as revolutionaries, but believed that the political solution was the means for orderly social change.

The Leaders

In his 1913 Inaugural Address, Woodrow Wilson expressed the dominant sentiment of Progressive America:

> There has been something crude and heartless and unfeeling in our haste to succeed and be great. . . . Our thought has been, "Let every man look out for himself, let every generation look out for itself," while we reared giant machinery which made it impossible that any but those who stood at the levers of control should have a chance to look out for themselves. . . . We have not . . . studied and perfected the means by which government may be put at the service of humanity, in safeguarding the health of the Nation, the health of its men and its women and its children, as well as their rights in the struggle for existence. . . . Society must see to it that it does not itself crush or weaken or damage its own constituent parts. The first duty of law is to keep sound the society it serves.

All the Progressive leaders during the first 15 years of this century shared Wilson's view. Roosevelt, LaFollette, Wilson and the state and local Progressive leaders across the nation, within both the Democratic and Republican parties, believed that enlarged functions of government were necessary to deal with the other enlargements which had already occurred in American society. Bigness was now to be used to fight bigness. The Progressive leadership consistently displayed a willingness to use the new tools which had been handed them by the academic community: economic analysis of politics, a pragmatic approach to problem-solving, and a clear understanding of public opinion and the means for its manipulation. Seen in this light, the differences between Theodore Roosevelt's Square Deal, Woodrow Wilson's New Freedom, and Franklin Roosevelt's subsequent New Deal seem slight when compared with the wide areas of agreement in underlying philosophy.

The theoretician for most of the Theodore Roosevelt program, variously called the Square Deal and the New Nationalism, was Herbert Croly. His theories were summarized in the 1909 publication of *The Promise of American Life*. Croly's book became the primary campaign document for Roosevelt's attempted third-party comeback in 1912. Actually, the promise of American life described Woodrow Wilson's policies in the White House nearly as well as it described Theodore Roosevelt's intentions. As an influential editor of the *New Republic*, Croly supported Wilson and the New Freedom with as much enthusiasm as he had previously supported Theodore Roosevelt and the New Nationalism. For that reason, *The Promise of American Life* is an accurate description of the Progressive state of mind as reflected in all the principal leaders.

The book itself is an attack upon Jeffersonian individualism. Croly suggests that such outmoded individualism be replaced with a more "realistic" philosophy, based upon an acceptance of the idea of national consolidation. Bigness in society was a foregone conclusion for Croly. He asked only that such bigness be extended to political organization. To Croly, it seemed that Hamilton had convincingly won his hundred-year argument with Jefferson. Centralization had to occur, and the sooner the better. The centralization which Croly envisioned was frankly collective. He assumed that nothing short of the paternalism of the corporate state would solve America's problems.

Faith in Bureaucracy

The Progressive movement, which dominated the American scene in the years from the turn of the century to United States entrance into World War I, was not primarily a liberal movement. It is true that the progressives fought for many a liberal cause and exposed many of the evils and inequities of the post–Civil War industrial society. With the help of muckraking journalists and other idealists, the progressives were also able to put into practice a number of reform schemes — particularly in some of the old Populist strongholds in the West. But in contrast to former American efforts at reform, progressivism was based on a new philosophy, partly borrowed from Europe, which emphasized collective action through the instrumentality of the government. In the progressive state of Wisconsin, for example, German influences were powerful, and many of the reformers who supported the LaFollette program had a great admiration for the social legislation of the German states. In the Federal government, and especially in the progressive philosophy of Theodore Roosevelt and his backers, this element of German nationalism and statism was equally strong. However liberal and idealistic such progressivism may have been in Wisconsin on a local grassroots level, on a national scale it came to have a quite different emphasis and ultimate purpose.[2]

The new political theory of the Progressives borrowed most heavily from bureaucratic thought. The ideal was to achieve a professional staff of government workers who presided over the operations of society in an essentially nonpartisan manner. The old distinction separating executive, legislative, and judicial functions were now to be set aside in favor of "the public man," the leader who could take charge of a modern, highly specialized government. Constitutional interferences which stood in the way of this public man were regarded as anachronisms from a previous and less enlightened age.

Governments on all levels were moving in the same direction. The day of executive control was at hand, with the various executives building their own empires of staff personnel. The ties between national, state, and local governments grew ever closer; exchanges of information and cooperation on various projects became the rule.

The central office in this new emphasis of executive power was, of course, the presidency. Sometimes Woodrow Wilson has been regarded as a Jeffersonian defender of limited government who resisted the Hamiltonian extensions of power advocated by Theodore Roosevelt. This is simply not the case:

> Wilson achieved for the presidency far more power than the office had ever held down to that time. The resources subject to his command were incomparably greater than those available during the Civil War. To a much greater extent than President Lincoln, he laid down a legislative program for enactment by Congress. The subordination of Congress to his will was much more in evidence than during any preceding administration. For the period of the war he went a long way toward establishing the relation between the President and Congress which he regarded as permanently desirable. In spite of the temporary and partial revolt against such a relation during a period of years after the end of military hostilities, Wilson paved the way for the powerful administration of Franklin D. Roosevelt.[3]

The underlying assumption of the steadily increasing reliance upon executive power was the belief, shared by most Americans, that, once government was powered by sufficient energy and authority to overcome the

[2]Arthur A. Ekirch, Jr., *The Decline of American Liberalism* (New York: Longmans, Green, 1955), p. 171.
[3]Carl Brent Swisher, *American Constitutional Development* (Cambridge, Mass.: Riverside Press, 1943), p. 661.

"private interests," the processes of decision would be nonpartisan, rational, and for the good of American society as a whole. In this way, the Progressive love affair with executive power was really an attempted escape from private responsibility. As the result of that escape from private responsibility, government moved rapidly in the same centralizing direction being followed in the corporate world. Measure after measure during the Progressive era centralized steadily more power in government. The politicalization of American society was moving at an accelerating pace.

Such a process is always easier to start than to stop. The centralization of political power in Washington, epitomized by the 1913 law empowering government to tax incomes, was now regarded in a new light. If previously the power to tax had been viewed as the power to destroy, the molders of American society who envisioned a bright Progressive future believed that the power to tax now carried with it the power to create, by political means. The attacks on property which have occurred in the name of social planning since the Progressive era are the clearest possible evidence that the individual's rights, most notably his property rights, have not prospered in the hands of central government. One of the great ironies of the Progressive reformers lies in the fact that the more they used political enmassment to defend or restore individual values, the more they generated a total political and social condition leaving steadily less room for the individual. Nonetheless, the governmental response to American problems continued. If bigness was a problem in the private sector, the only solution to the problem was more bigness in the public sector. Or so the Progressives believed.

This dichotomy explains the peculiarly Januslike quality of the Progressive movement. Within both Theodore Roosevelt's New Nationalism and Woodrow Wilson's New Freedom we find the conflicting demand for greatly increased and centralized political power as the means by which a decentralized, traditional, individualistic system might be reinstated and preserved. The tragedy of Progressivism is that these well-intended people were to learn that such ends cannot be achieved through such means. As the state grows bigger, the individual must grow smaller. The Progressives were bound to fail in their attempt to destroy a power monopoly by creating a power monopoly.

In a speech before the New York Press Club during the presidential campaign of 1912, Woodrow Wilson expressed the Progressive goal: "When we resist the concentration of power, we are resisting the powers of death, for concentrated power is what always precedes the destruction of human liberties." A fine sentiment and a correct observation, but Wilson and the other Progressives were doomed to failure because their weapon against the concentration of power was the concentration of power. The Progressives thus became only another portion of the New Order, encouraging the same anti-individualistic enmassment and social centralization which was already moving this country so far from traditional American values.

The Trusts

Nowhere is the dichotomy of Progressivism better illustrated than in the confusion which developed over governmental policy toward big business during the Progressive era. The Progressives seemed unable to decide whether the "inevitable concentration" of big business was desirable or undesirable. They might better have asked themselves whether the growth of big business was indeed inevitable. Instead, fear swept the Progressives off their feet, causing them to assume that some bigness meant all bigness, and that all bigness meant no room for the little man.

While the leadership of American society, and above all the leadership of American business, talked incessantly of the "inevitability" and absolute necessity for the concentration of economic power, the actual concentration was a process which was never completed. It is true that great enmassment occurred within the American business community around the turn of the twentieth century. This was done partially in an effort to achieve efficiency and lower costs, and partially to reinvest the large capital holdings which had come into existence in the period of great growth and development during the late nineteenth century. However, many of the large American corporations were beginning to discover that overcentralization was not profitable to them. In fact, most of the largest American corporations were decentralizing their internal organization by the time the Progressive era was fully underway. Internal decentralization was viewed as a means of solving the very serious organizational problems which overcentralization had begun to cause. Futhermore, the assumption that big business would become so large that new innovators could not enter the field was not being borne out by the facts. The *New York Financier* in June 1900 warned the business community that "The most serious problem that confronts trust combinations today is competition from independent sources. . . . In iron and steel, in paper and in constructive processes of large magnitude the sources of production are being multiplied, with a resultant decrease in profits. . . . When the papers speak of a cessation of operation in certain trust industries, they fail to mention the awakening of new life in independent plants. . . ."[4]

Despite the large number of mergers, and the growth in the absolute size of many corporations, the dominant tendency in the American economy at the beginning of this century was toward growing compe-

---

[4]Gabriel Kolko, *The Triumph of Conservatism* (Chicago: Quadrangle Books, 1967), pp. 29–30.

tition. Competition was unacceptable to many key business and financial interests, and the merger movement was to a large extent a reflection of voluntary, unsuccessful business efforts to bring irresistible competitive trends under control. Although profit was always a consideration, rationalization of the market was frequently a necessary prerequisite for maintaining long-term profits. As new competitors sprang up, and as economic power was diffused throughout an expanding nation, it became apparent to many important businessmen that only the national government could rationalize the economy. Although specific conditions varied from industry to industry, internal problems that could be solved only by political means were the common denominator in those industries whose leaders advocated greater federal regulation. Ironically, contrary to the consensus of historians, it was not the existence of monopoly that caused the federal government to intervene in the economy, but the lack of it.[5]

The picture which emerges is less a society of business giants which swallowed all competitors, than a society of business giants that would have liked to swallow all competitors but had proven unable to do so. While it is true that, in the 10 years between 1895 and 1904, 300 companies a year had been absorbed, after 1905 the number of firms absorbed each year dropped to one-third of that amount. Also, before 1905, the average merger capitalization per year had amounted to nearly $700,000,000. After 1905, the average annual merger capitalization amounted to only $221,000,000. In short, after 1905 there were progressively fewer companies being taken over, and such mergers as were taking place averaged less than one-third the size of previous mergers. American industry was proving to be so hard to swallow that the attempt became steadily less common at the very time when the Progressive movement was moving to "save" American business from the "trusts." As is so often the case with political solutions, the political reaction was occurring after the problem no longer existed. The enormous consolidation which Americans had feared was apparently failing to materialize, but this in no way slowed the Progressive juggernaut.

In American industry rapid technological innovation apparently was coming so fast that it could not be contained within the old firms. Also, some of the more conservative and established industries were unwilling to speculate in the new products and new markets which the technological revolution implied. It seemed that "big business" simply could not keep little business from innovating. The merger movement in American industry had failed significantly in the elimination of smaller firms. Indeed, the

[5] *Ibid.*, pp. 4–5

decentralization which began to take place in even some of the largest firms suggested a concession to the efficiency of smaller competitors.

United States Steel is sometimes cited as the prime example of an industrial giant so large that it crushed all competitors in its path. Yet it seems that competition in the steel industry was neither dead nor dying at the time when the Progressives moved to save the day:

> In 1909 there were eleven firms other than U.S. Steel with at least $25 million in assets engaged in some aspect of the steel industry. Since this is approximately the figure at which peak industrial efficiency was reached, each of these firms was capable of meeting U.S. Steel on most terms. Moreover, in 1909 there were still 208 companies with blast furnaces, a decline of only seven percent since 1899. The number of companies with steel works and rolling mills increased by one over the same period, to 446. The number of firms engaged in making tinplate and ternplate fell from 57 to 31 over the period of 10 years, but the number of wire mills using purchased rods increased from 29 to 56. U.S. Steel increased its total output 40 percent during 1901–1912, thus having a growth rate far lower than any of its older competitors.
>
> If nothing else, the steel industry was competitive before the World War, and the efforts by the House of Morgan to establish control and stability over the steel industry by voluntary, private economic means had failed. Having failed in the realm of economics, the efforts of the United States Steel group were to be shifted to politics.[6]

It appears to be clear beyond reasonable doubt that concentration of monopoly power in American industry was not inevitable. Indeed, concentration of economic power to the point of monopoly was not even possible, not for the generation of American businessmen who lived during the Progressive era. At least those businessmen found monopoly conditions impossible to attain until they turned to the new problem-solving device which the American people themselves placed in their hands: massive new political interventions in the economy. Then, and then only, could competition truly pass from the American scene.

In the first decade of the twentieth century, for all the imperfections of the existing economic system (and they were many), the system would seem to have been far less repressive of the little man than the radical strain of Progressivism presumed. Still, the typically middle-class American had fears which could be exploited. The customary business unit of the nineteenth century was likely to be owned by an individual or by several partners, who were, by means of their personal wealth, the same individuals who

[6] *Ibid.* pp. 38–39.

both owned and controlled the operation. The corporate form of organization, bringing the development of corporate securities and the rise of really large business, saw that control passing from the proprietary classes to a new managerial class. Not too surprisingly, the change was resented. Meanwhile, as business organizations had been growing larger and larger, the individual citizen by comparison had appeared to grow smaller and smaller. The complaint that the little man was cut off from credit and denied a chance to compete had a measure of truth in the new economic order. Even though the claims made against big business and mergers were only half true "and often not necessarily the more important half," the Progressives were able to make good political capital out of the traditional attitude which favored the small entrepreneur.

The resultant image of the "monopolists," who were presumably dominating American society, was often not in tune with the facts, but it caught the imagination of a generation of American politicians, and several subsequent generations of American literary personalities, thus giving its own special direction to American politics in this century:

> Significantly, it was the trusts, dragon's teeth sowed in American individualism, that now came up to haunt the national imagination and that provoked a national effort toward reform. It was monopoly that seemed to have changed American life — a railroad squeezing predatory rates out of small farmers; political bosses imposing their nominees upon the public; state legislatures electing their most powerful members to the United States Senate, that "rich man's club"; steel combines laying down a law of acquiescence or destruction of thousands of small businessmen. It was monopoly — "the curse of bigness," as "the people's attorney," Louis D. Brandeis, called it — that now gave the lie to the traditional American belief that the people enjoyed automatic liberty of economic action in a society of free individuals.[7]

The bigness which supposedly dominated American society was far less complete than such literary historians as the man quoted above have led us to believe. The point is, however, that the American people believed in the myth of bigness and followed the Progressive leaders on a new and dangerous road.

T. R.

The Progressive leaders suffered the same confusion as the typical middle-class American whom they represented. Theodore Roosevelt, for example,

[7]Alfred Kazin, *On Native Grounds* (Garden City, N.Y.: Doubleday, 1956), p. 72.

could never decide whether the trusts were a great source of evil or were the means by which American prosperity had been achieved. Like most Progressives, he was extremely hostile to great centers of corporate authority, even while admiring the size, efficiency and success of their operation. There was a certain magical quality about the word "progress" that led the Progressives to love and hate big business simultaneously.

Though Roosevelt was known as the "trustbuster" in his own time, he accepted the "necessity" of large economic units. For this reason, the final result of Roosevelt's trust policy was less an enforced increase of competition than it was a strengthening of the regulatory role for the federal government. Business did not grow smaller; instead, government grew larger. Roosevelt set the tone for the Progressive era when he echoed the sentiments of Herbert Croly: "A simple and poor society can exist as a democracy on a basis of sheer individualism. But a rich and complex industrial society cannot so exist; for some individuals, and especially those artificial individuals called corporations, become so very big that the ordinary individual . . . cannot deal with them on terms of equality. It therefore becomes necessary for these ordinary individuals to combine in their turn, first in order to act in their collective capacity through that biggest of all combinations called the government, and second, to act also in their own self-defense, through private combinations, such as farmers' associations and trade unions."[8]

Roosevelt made it clear where his heart lay in his frequent cooperation with the major spokesmen of Eastern industry and finance. He was quite willing to manipulate great blocks of special interest power, provided only that government in Washington would be the prime manipulator in that process. It is perhaps an enlightening commentary on the guiding philosophy which Roosevelt followed to recall that his principal intellectual mentor, Herbert Croly, found himself a few years later, with no apparent ideological unease, writing editorials praising Mussolini's corporate state.

Wilson

Any survey course in twentieth-century American history invariably asks the student to compile lists of the differences between Roosevelt's New Nationalism and Wilson's New Freedom. These lists of presumed distinctions have very little connection with reality. In practical terms, almost no real distinction exists, though for obvious political reasons a great deal of fanfare was generated over presumed differences.

In practical terms, none of Woodrow Wilson's appointees did any more to undermine the existing big-business structure than had Roosevelt. Oddly enough, the only President whose Attorney General ever acted significantly

[8]Richard Hofstadter, *The Age of Reform,* (New York: Vintage Books, 1955), pp. 246–247.

against the trusts was the allegedly "conservative" William Howard Taft. What Taft attempted to do was politically impossible, and he soon found himself quite as unpopular in the Republican Party as in the Democratic Party. In the Progressive era, America wanted more bigness, despite the rhetoric to the contrary.

By 1912, Theodore Roosevelt had decided to run as a third-party candidate. In the ensuing election, Wilson and Roosevelt vied with one another in the progressive rhetoric of their campaigns, leaving Taft to run a bad third. In Wilson's campaign speeches, it at first appeared that he took a basically different view of the American corporate structure than Roosevelt. He seemed to be saying that large corporations were *not* inevitable, and that such combinations should have their privileged position destroyed once and for all. In his 1912 campaign, Wilson thus managed to sound even more "progressive" than Roosevelt, ringing all the changes for the small entrepreneur and "America as the land of opportunity":

There is a great deal that needs reconstruction in the United States. I should like to take a census of the businessmen — I mean the rank and file of the businessmen — as to whether they think that business conditions in this country, or rather whether the organization of business in this country, is satisfactory or not. I know what they would say if they dared. If they could vote secretly they would vote overwhelmingly that the present organization of business was meant for the big fellows and was not meant for the little fellows; that it was meant for those who are at the top and was meant to exclude those who are at the bottom; that it was meant to shut out beginners, to prevent new entries in the race, to prevent the building up of competitive enterprises that would interfere with the monopolies which the great trusts have built up.

What this country needs above everything else is a body of laws which will look after the men who are on the make rather than the men who are already made.

Throughout the campaign, Wilson hammered on Theodore Roosevelt's record of cooperation with big business and "the interests" while President. Once elected, Wilson found himself in a situation which made it far easier to emulate Roosevelt's cooperative attitude than to change the direction of the Progressive movement. The young Walter Lippmann published a book in 1914 which increasingly set the tone for trust policy in the new Wilson Administration. *Drift and Mastery* urged that America must grow up from being "a nation of villagers" and master the twentieth-century technique of large-scale organization. The twentieth century, Lippmann urged, was to be the century of the administrator, not the trustbuster. The older America was gone, and the sooner it was forgotten the better.

A number of businessmen agreed with the Roosevelt idea, as brought up to date by Walter Lippmann. By 1912 it seemed that new industries and new technological breakthroughs were providing a world of all too much competition for many businessmen. The answer seemed to lie in consolidation, a consolidation which could be achieved only by political means, or at least with the full support and cooperation of a government regulatory policy which blocked new entrants from entering the field of competition.

Perhaps in response to the need of the established business community, Woodrow Wilson soon found that the partnership between government and business was much closer than any of his 1912 speeches would have indicated. While Wilson had fewer direct contacts with the major representatives of big business than Roosevelt, Wilson's alter ego, Colonel House, soon became the means by which contact was established. The House diaries are filled with references to conferences with Henry Clay Frick, Otto H. Kahn, Felix Warburg, J. P. Morgan and the major corporate and financial controllers of American life, the same men who had been berated for their privileged position by Wilson during the 1912 campaign. Meanwhile, the Wilson years saw a sharp reduction in the number of antitrust suits prosecuted. Before the Wilson terms of office were concluded, he had begun to cultivate the support of business more openly, while issuing various assurances that the wave of "reform" legislation was drawing to a close. A fear of big business had provided one of the principal motive forces for the Progressive movement, but close cooperation between business and government had made it clear that no one really wanted small business. Progressive America seemed to prefer big business and a paralleling big government.

The Businessman as Progressive

The standard interpretations of the Progressive era have generally painted the period as the revolt against "the business interests." Of late, that interpretation has begun to give way in the face of some persistent facts that simply do not fit the thesis. It is now becoming clear that various business interests themselves led the reform movements of the era.

In the first place, middle-class businessmen themselves feared corporate monopoly to such an extent that they were in the forefront of the fight to adopt the various regulatory actions generally associated with Progressivism. Some historians, notably John Chamberlain in his 1931 *Farewell to Reform,* have gone further, insisting that the primary effect of the new regulatory agencies was to give dominant business groups a greater control over their respective economic interests than they had previously enjoyed. The final step in this revisionist view of the Progressive era has been taken by Professor Gabriel Kolko in his 1963 *The Triumph of Conservatism.* Kolko insists that it was the dominant business groups *themselves* who shaped and promoted the so-called "Progressive" reforms as a means of continuing their own dominance. Kolko can advance a great deal of support for this thesis, since a number of major business representatives during the Progressive era gave serious attention to means by which the new government agencies could be turned to the uses of big business, primarily to "rationalize" the economic scene and eliminate "ruinous competition." There can be little doubt that the Intertate Commerce Commission, the Federal Trade Commission and similar regulatory agencies have been used on occasion to do exactly that.

It is business control over politics (and by "business" I mean the major economic interests) rather than political regulation of the economy that is the significant phenomenon of the Progressive era. Such domination was direct and indirect, but significant only insofar as it provided means for achieving a greater end — political capitalsim. *Political capitalism* is the utilization of political outlets to attain conditions of stability, predictability, and security — to attain rationalization — in the economy. *Stability* is the elimination of internecine competition and erratic fluctuations in the economy. *Predictability* is the ability, on the basis of politically stabilized and secured means, to plan future economic action on the basis of fairly calculable expectations. By *security* I mean protection from the political attacks latent in any formally democratic political structure. I do not give to *rationalization* its frequent definition as the improvement of efficiency, output, or internal organization of a company; I mean by the term, rather, the organization of the economy and the larger political and social spheres in a manner that will allow corporations to function in a predictable and secure environment permitting reasonable profits over the long run. My contention . . . is not that all of these objectives were attained by World War I, but that important and significant legislative steps in these directions were taken, and that these steps include most of the distinctive legislative measures of what has commonly been called the Progressive Period.[9]

Politics thus came to be regarded as far more than a necessary evil. Many major businessmen thought of politics as an important process in maintenance of the corporate position. For this reason, a number of businessmen decided to encourage "reform" lest the Populist agitations move the American public in new directions, directions dangerous to the business community. In this new partnership with government, not only would hostile criticism thus be averted, but the older partnership, through which government had provided business with subsidies and special privileges, could be maintained and expanded. In the Progressive era, government thus became

[9]Kolko, p. 3.

an ally rather than a foe. Political regulation of economic affairs proved to be designed in most cases by the very interests presumably to be regulated. Crucial business support can be detected for every single major political regulatory movement of the Progressive era.

Examples of this support are commonplace. Alpheus B. Stickney, President of the Chicago Great Western Railroad, told his fellow businessmen during the Progressive era that only a strong national government could solve America's economic problems. In the same period, Daniel Willard, President of the Baltimore and Ohio Railway, described the railroad as "a semipublic institution" with "semipublic officers." It was the duty and obligation of federal regulation to harmonize conflicting interests within American industry; or so Mr. Willard believed. Meanwhile, George Perkins of the House of Morgan was also preaching the doctrine that businessmen were obligated to the political processes, in return for the wise government regulatory policies which made modern business possible. As the Progressive years advanced, the National Association of Hosiery and Underwear Manufacturers demanded federal legislation to regulate competition within the industry. The Railway Executives Advisory Committee requested ". . . legislation or constitutional changes as will give the national government the unqualified power to regulate all railroads." By the time of the First World War, the voices in America calling loudest for government regulation were those of the same businessmen for whom the regulation was planned.

The message was not entirely lost upon other elements of American society. The farmers, who had led the public outcry against monopolistic business practices, soon found themselves afoul of the antitrust laws, indicating that they had finally come of age as modern businessmen. At the time of the Clayton Anti-Trust Act of 1914, the farmers were insistent that they as well as labor organizations should be specifically exempted from national antitrust laws. It was clear that farm leadership no longer emphasized the struggle against big business organization, preferring to build their own organizations upon the same model.

The Regulated Economy

The close business involvement in Progressive reform soon produced a peculiar situation in American politics. The "reformers" of the Progressive era discovered that, if they wished to be truly effective in instituting their programs, they had to come to terms with the same businessmen and political bosses which the Progressive impetus had presumably set out to reform:

As reformers sought to expand their influence, they found two important avenues open before them. Newly self-conscious businessmen offered one. They alone among the prominent progressive groups had the inherent resources — the critical positions in the local economy, the money, and the prestige — to command some sort of response from the government. Weaker reformers, therefore, tried to attach their causes to these men's ambitions, relying upon their need for expert advice and their general sympathy for systematization and order. The boss provided the second avenue. "Professionally [the boss] desires to play his role [as benefactor] in the fullest sense," wrote the settlement worker Robert A. Woods, "and if public improvement or general welfare be part of the tradition he is among the first to catch and hold it." Capable of recognizing when he was beyond his depth, the boss also depended upon the special skills of the new reformers.[10]

Thus the strange partnerships of the Progressive era formed along new lines, bringing together the new-type politicians, the old-style political bosses, and the businessmen. Politics does indeed make strange bedfellows.

This new partnership of the reformers, the businessmen, and the bosses took a sharply different form than previous reform currents in America. Where the Populists would have destroyed as many of the characteristics of the modern urban, industrial, corporate, centralized America as possible, the new reformers of the Progressive era wished to maintain and further develop the existing system. In Robert Wiebe's words, "The heart of progressivism was the ambition of the new middle class to fulfill its destiny through bureaucratic means."[11]

The goal of the new era was to find a means by which society's movements could be regulated, producing maximum efficiency. This view came to appeal to business, the workingman, the farmer, and above all, to the new breed of government administrator who now found such a willing partnership with the leadership of most American interest groups. It should not be surprising that many of the most enthusiastic Progressives of the first two decades of the twentieth century later saw so much to applaud in Benito Mussolini, the man who made the trains run on time.

The new style of regulation and bureaucracy touched all aspects of American life. Politics did not have to bring bureaucracy to business, since business was already embracing administrative centralization in an increasingly high degree. The regulation which government brought to the American economy was thus only one expression of the planning ideal adopted throughout American society.

[10]Robert H. Wiebe, *The Search for Order* (New York: Hill and Wang, 1968), p. 174.
[11]*Ibid.*, p. 166.

War and Progressivism

It is generally assumed that World War I brought Progressivism to an end, but if Progressivism is seen in its proper light as a great force of centralization and enmassment, World War I then becomes nothing more than a new development in the same trend.

In a more general sense the mobilization of 1917 and 1918 illuminated the degree to which an emerging bureaucratic system had actually ordered American society. When the Wilson Administration set about coordinating the nation for a modern war, a task that a great many here and abroad considered far too complex for the time allowed, the pieces for a pattern seemed to appear by magic. Businessmen who were suddenly faced with the necessity of negotiating by way of economically functional groups formed a nationwide network of trade associations. Almost as quickly, an agricultural elite organized by locality and by crop. The majority of industrial crafts were already unionized. No administration could have commanded these results. Although the needs of war did act catalytically upon the process of organization, the essential fact was that association represented a natural response. Two decades of organizational experimentation, of a deepening commitment to some form of cooperation, lay behind the record of the war years.[12]

In a very real sense, the First World War brought to fruition the close cooperation between government and business which had been sought throughout the Progressive era. The war brought effective price and marketing agreements which achieved the "stability" and consolidation which big business had already been seeking. Thus Progressivism was not killed by the First World War. It merely took a new form and moved on toward the increasing centralization of the 1920s and the New Deal.

In the new partnership, government power and centralization continued at a very rapid pace. Not only did the war bring greater regulatory and administrative powers for the government, it also brought conscription, a concept of governmental power over the individual citizen largely unacceptable in an earlier America, but well suited to the new American state, patterned as it was on the model of Bismarck's corporate state. Meanwhile, the mobilization of public opinion kept pace:

The extraordinary degree of conformity, illustrated by the lack of any real organized resistance to the draft, was backed up by an adroit mixture of propaganda and repression instituted by the administra-

12 *Ibid.*, pp. 293–294

tion. While the silencing of dissenting opinion was made possible
through espionage and sedition legislation, the more positive task of
indoctrination was placed in the hands of the Committee on Public
Information, created by executive order of the President on April 13,
1917. George Creel, a progressive and rather liberal-minded journalist, was appointed as chairman of the committee, which has been
termed by its unofficial historians "America's propaganda ministry
during the World War." In their words, the committee was "charged
with encouraging and then consolidating the revolution of opinion
which changed the United States from antimilitaristic democracy to
an organized war machine."[13]

The newly created propaganda wing mobilized the printing press and the
attitudes of an entire nation, convincing a generation of Americans that
government could achieve all goals. Meanwhile, the War Industry Board,
the War Labor Board, the Food Commission and similar agencies followed
one another in dizzying succession. The railroads were commandeered and
run by government. In fact, the organizational techniques of bureaucratic
and statist control which were pioneered during the Progressive era and the
First World War proved to be one of the primary sources of later interventions and centralizations in American society:

. . . organizational patterns created for war purposes provided the
technical basis for subsequent control of economic life when war
powers could not be relied upon as the constitutional basis. Experience with wartime organization helped to determine the course of
constitutional development, as knowledge of previously used patterns
of control and desires for the achievement of particular results combined to overcome constitutional scruples about the legitimacy of a
given program.
  The following are outstanding examples of the carryover: Former
members of the War Industries Board aided in shaping the National
Recovery Administration of 1933. . . . The War Finance Corporation
established a pattern for the Reconstruction Finance Corporation and
for other government lending agencies. The Fuel Administration provided background for the National Bituminous Coal Commission and
its successor, the Bituminous Coal Division in the Department of the
Interior, as well as for organization in the Interior Department for
control of the oil industry. The Food Administration provided background for subsequent activities of the Department of Agriculture.
The housing agencies of the war period were succeeded, a quarter of

[13]Ekirch, pp. 214–215.

a century later, by other housing agencies in the New Deal period. The director general of railroads had his counterpart in the federal co-ordinator of transportation. The labor boards of the war period provided experience for other labor boards established in later years, including the National Mediation Board set up pursuant to the Railway Labor Act of 1926, and the National Labor Relations Board.[14]

The parallels could be continued almost indefinitely. It seems clear that the primary effect of the First World War was to place the capstone upon Progressive centralization. Far from ending the Progressive era, it accelerated the tendencies already begun.

All the events and personalities of the Progressive era seemed to move American society in the same centralizing direction. The strong planning bent of the American intellectual, the Mugwump assumption that bigness could somehow be used as a weapon against bigness, the close connections between business and Progressivism, the rise of the new politics which featured new social goals and new means to attain those goals, the events of the First World War: All these combined to produce within American society a high degree of centralization and institutional enmassment both public and private, leaving progressively less room for the individual. Once fully launched upon the centralizing road during the Progressive era, America has seemed unable to reverse the process. The crisis of the First World War, the futility of attempting to dictate morality to a nation with the new commandment "Thou shalt not drink," the crisis of depression and the aftermath of economic distress, the great new burst of centralization and social planning of the 1930s, the renewed crisis of the Second World War and the Cold War of the past twenty years: All form part of a continuing pattern of centralized political authority.

In the contest of bigness vs. bigness, bigness always wins.

[14]Swisher, pp. 661–662.

XIII

THE TWENTIES

Less government in business, more business in government!

Warren G. Harding,
Presidential Campaign Slogan

Many historical analysts describe the Twenties as a period of unfettered "free enterprise." Nothing could be more incorrect. The Twenties continued (under other labels) all the trends so far advanced by the Progressive era — bigness was on the march. "Business in government" and "government in business" turned out to be remarkably similar in practice.

Under the direction of Bernard Baruch, the War Industries Board had already largely achieved the administrative control of business. Though the formal wartime agencies were disbanded at the war's end, the techniques of control and consolidation which they had developed remained in existence. Competitors had been quick to learn the advantage of trade association, standardized products, and agreements to share the market. All of these devices became even more attractive when the regulatory agencies of government, presumably designed to encourage competition, became the bureaucratic means whereby existing business could cooperate rather than compete. The war years had paved the way for a partnership between business and government that was closer than anything previously envisioned in American history.

This keener appreciation of public forces provides one index to a remarkable success story, the ability of prosperous businessmen to protect their positions of leadership in America's twentieth-century society in transition. Capitalizing upon a sudden worship of productivity in 1917, businessmen comprised most of the "public men" who directed the national mobilization of World War I. Here was the America of Herbert Croly's dreams, a corporate society led by the federal government, only Bernard Baruch had replaced Theodore

Roosevelt. After paying for the campaign which elected Warren Harding and a Republican Congress, business leaders held the initiative among the heirs of progressivism early in the Twenties.[1]

The role of government as the agency which fostered bigness in private society was becoming ever more clear. For example, although the railroads were returned to private operation, the very act which accomplished that transfer also empowered the Interstate Commerce Commission to encourage railroad mergers. Big government was now openly encouraging big business. Many leaders were anxious to substitute "cooperation" for competition:

> Herbert Hoover, as an engineer and business executive, was greatly impressed by wartime rationalization. It was no quirk of his personality that one of his greatest heroes was Woodrow Wilson and that a generation after he left the White House he should write a book highly laudatory of his wartime chief. Hoover drew back from the kind of economic rule by edict that government had found necessary during the fighting, but he wanted to continue the governmental program of industrial and commercial rationalization. As Secretary of Commerce he did so.[2]

An End to Competition

During the Twenties, the Department of Commerce encouraged the members of trade associations to adopt uniform systems of cost accounting and uniform formulas for estimating bids. While Secretary Hoover encouraged business cooperation, the regulatory commissions also pursued an essentially anticompetitive course. The Federal Trade Commission annual report for 1927 announced a new policy of "helping business to help itself."

The partnership between business and government was encouraged in other ways as well. The Fordney–McCumber Tariff Act of 1922 raised tariffs to all-time highs, at least until the still higher rates of the 1930 Smoot–Hawley tariff. As the result of these and other areas of cooperation between business and government, big business began to grow once again:

> A characteristic of the time was the reappearance of the combination movement. Between 1919 and 1929, nearly 7,000 firms disappeared as a result of mergers; between 1921 and 1928, some 1268 industrial combinations were organized — in iron and steel, oil, nonferrous met-

[1]Robert H. Wiebe, *Businessmen and Reform* (Chicago: Quadrangle Books, 1962), p. 221.
[2]David A. Shannon, *Between The Wars: America, 1919–1941* (Boston: Houghton Mifflin, 1965), p. 40.

als, food manufacture, textiles, and retailing. In this last, by 1929, corporate chains controlled 10 percent of all retail outlets and made 32 percent of all the country's annual retail sales. So significant had great corporations become that one-tenth of the corporations in the country owned more than half of the nation's corporate assets.[3]

While greater and greater sections of the American economy were coming under the control of large corporations, the nature of the corporations was also changing. The bureaucracy which accompanied bigness in government also characterized bigness in corporations. That bureaucracy became increasingly impersonal and anonymous. While business of the nineteenth century had been typified by such strong-willed types as Rockefeller or Carnegie, the new businessman was often a bureaucrat, faceless and obscure. The age of the organization man had fully arrived:

> The value in consolidation and cooperation was recognized from the House of Morgan to the corner drugstore and practiced above all in the hundreds of business organizations. No group prided itself upon rugged individualism more often than the leaders of the NAM. Yet David Parry's definition of socialism — "delegating to one individual or a small group of individuals the management of the interests of many individuals" — neatly summarized the association's history. It was James Van Cleave who stated that every manufacturer in the country was "an organization man," John Kirby who announced that businessmen lived "in an age of organization," and George Pope who called upon manufacturers to "stand together . . . as a class." A Pennsylvania banker, even more enthusiastic, placed association within the laws of history: Man evolved from autocracy to isolated individualism into "the more advanced civilization of the present . . . based upon more altruistic motives . . . and more complete cooperation." Looking about them, few denied an Illinois businessman's conclusion, "Organization is the watchword of progress."[4]

The New Bureaucrats

Management of more and more large firms came to be conducted less by individual personalities than by standardized "management units." The "system" replaced the individual as the guiding factor of business. Meanwhile, government generated its own bureaucracy. During the Twenties, the administrative class came into its own. The "managerial revolution" affected every aspect of American life, and members of the new managerial

---

[3]Louis M. Hacker, *American Capitalism* (Princeton, N.J.: Van Nostrand, 1957), p. 73.
[4]Wiebe, *Businessmen and Reform*, p. 193.

class, whether in government or business, consulted one another and made the collective decisions which moved a machinery increasingly vast and increasingly beyond the control of any individual. People were beginning to discover another fact which would become increasingly clear: The anti-trust laws could not be enforced. Such legislation remained on the books primarily as a relic of an earlier day, though some few still mistakenly believed that such means could attain and support economic individualism. Despite all the rhetoric to the contrary, how could government use its powers against a creature of its own making?

> Government bureaucrats looked to the private groups in their baili-wick as a natural constituency, men with whom they must develop good relations and from whom they expected regular support. These groups reciprocated, looking in turn to the bureaus for essential ser-vices and acting as their lobbies — just as long as the effective power of decision remained in private hands. In the late nineteenth century, the national government had delegated most of its domestic powers to the states, from whence it scattered to a thousand localities. In the twentieth, the national government parcelled an increasing amount of its power to private groups; and these then exercised it through the national government itself.[5]

Bureaucracy, public and private, was now the dominant technique of American society.

Hoover

There was a great deal of truth in the 1928 Republican campaign claim that the GOP had inaugurated "a new era." A new relationship was devel-oping between the American economy and the national government. In his eight years as Secretary of Commerce before he became the Republican party's nominee in the election of 1928, Herbert Hoover had consistently pursued a program of business expansion based upon the assumption that large-scale social and economic planning was both possible and desirable. In his own words, "We are passing from a period of extreme individualistic action into a period of associated activities." During the Twenties, competi-tion had been increasingly replaced by cartelization, trade associations, "standardization," "self-regulation," and "voluntary action." These epito-mized the new partnership between government and business. The bigness which had been disturbing to Americans of the late nineteenth century now paled in comparison with the bigness of the "new era."

While Hoover was making the Department of Commerce a clearinghouse

[5]Robert H. Wiebe, *The Search for Order* (New York: Hill and Wang, 1968), p. 298.

for business information, and while the Federal Trade Commission was becoming a research organization to encourage "cooperation, not competition," the new partnership between government and business served to facilitate the new blend of social engineering which had already entered the American scene during the Progressive era. The labels were changed, but the principal features of the new big business–big government syndrome remained the same. Herbert Hoover envisioned a new variety of mercantilism. Government was now to take an active role in "rationalizing" the business climate. The planned economy was closer than anyone, least of all Hoover, realized.

The Worker, the Farmer, and the Small Businessman

Big business was not alone in its desire for a close working connection with big government. As the new bureaucratic society emerged, it inevitably created new institutions designed for survival in such a society. One of those institutions was the modern trade union. By the 1920s, the trade union was already well launched in its own process of acquiring bigness. Big labor was about to take its place beside big business and big government as an arbiter of social destiny:

> In World War I the federal government took over the railroads and put them under a commissar, namely, Secretary of the Treasury William G. McAdoo. This put the State into the business of dealing with both labor and management and exercising the final right of enforcing a "public" decision on both of them. McAdoo encouraged the organization of nonoperating railway workers to the point where labor got the idea that the power of government could work magic if one could only capture and hold it for keeps. After the war, railroad labor put the new theory to the test; and in 1926 it succeeded in getting the Railway Labor Act through both houses of Congress. This was the "entering wedge"; it made Washington a "third party" to labor disputes, and the struggle was on for the control of the "third party" mechanism.[6]

Meanwhile, the farmer also desired his seat at the table. The 1920s saw the development of an agrarian alliance called the Farm Bloc. By 1924 the Farm Bloc had achieved a large measure of special interest legislation from the federal government, including high tariff barriers for agricultural products, federal regulation of packing houses, grain elevators, and stockyards, specific exemption of agricultural cooperatives from antitrust legislation, and the creation of an entirely new governmental system for rural credit.

[6]John Chamberlain, *The Roots of Capitalism* (Princeton, N. J.: Van Nostrand, 1959), p. 190.

The greatest single achievement of the farm lobby was the parity principle, which established as national political policy the idea that a special interest group in the United States was entitled to a government-guaranteed price level for its products equivalent in purchasing power to what that special interest group had enjoyed during its most prosperous period in modern times. In Richard Hofstadter's words, ". . . it seems hardly questionable that the agricultural bloc thus succeeded in establishing for the commercial farmers a claim upon federal policy that no other single stratum of the population can match."

The small businessman was also quick to adopt the techniques and enthusiasms of the new era. The temper of even the smallest American businessman was dynamic and expansive during the Twenties. The goals of mass production and mass consumption seemed to hold forth the glittering possibility of a prosperity far beyond anything previously witnessed in America. The journalists, preachers, and professors joined with the average middle-class American businessman in singing the praises of the "new era." Anyone who did not wish to rush along to the new utopia was immediately suspect as an enemy of progress.

In all walks of life, the older America and the older American seemed to be vanishing:

> . . . in the past thirty years American middle-class mass culture has triumphed over capitalist and worker alike. The America of 1890, the capstone of the Gilded Age, was a society of increasing differentiation in manners and morals, the area, that is of *visible* distinction and the one that could give rise, as in Europe, to class resentment. It saw the emergence in baroque mansion, elaborate dress, and refined leisure activities of a new high style of life. By the 1920s this style was already gone. Beneath this change was the transformation of entrepreneurial to corporate capitalism, with a corresponding shift in the social type from the self-made man to the smooth, faceless manager. But beyond that it was a change in the very character of society, symbolized in large measure by the adjective which qualified the phrases "mass production" and "mass consumption." Production . . . was no longer geared *primarily* as it had been in the late nineteenth and twentieth centuries, to turning out capital goods (steel, railroad equipment, tools), but to the output of consumers' durable goods (autos, washing machines, radios, etc.). The mass market became the arbiter of taste, and the style of life was leveled. In another dimension of this vast social revolution that has been taking place during the past quarter of a century, professional skill has been replacing property as the chief means of acquiring and wielding power, and the educational system

rather than inheritance has become the chief avenue for social ascent. In short, a new-type, bureaucratic, mass society has been emerging, and, with it, new institutions. . . .[7]

Institutionalized Avarice

In the 1920s, the American began to equate "bigger" with "better." Chamber of Commerce statistics stood as the measurement of "success." Qualitative values began to be lost in quantitative measurements. Sinclair Lewis' *Babbitt* had a great impact as a novel, because there was a ring of truth in his brutal characterization of the values dominating American society. During the Twenties, advertising also took on new meaning. The typical middle-class American now could choose between ignoring the advertised version of what the Jones family was doing, or struggling along under the load of constantly expanding debt which an endless round of automobiles, house furnishings, radios, refrigerators, and washing machines placed upon him:

Since America's economy had become dependent to a large extent upon new consumers' goods industries and the success of these industries depended upon good public relations, it is not surprising that businessmen sought increasing social control. And since their "prosperity" won for them the confidence of a large part of the population, they became more than ever before the fountainheads of American ideas and the arbiters of American morality. Under pressure to put the Nation's savings to work in productive enterprises, American businessmen vigorously pushed their sales of automobiles, radios, and moving pictures. And as rapid urbanization and agricultural discontent weakened traditional agrarian individualism, the perfection of these new devices of communication together with the older newspapers and national magazines broke down local insularity. Metropolis and village, city and country, factory town and suburban park came increasingly under identical business influences. Provincial habits and customs crumbled. Radios, moving pictures, and automobiles opened new interests to Americans everywhere but brought them also into a tighter network of ideas, habits, tastes. Just as local industries had succumbed in competition with national corporations and local stores had succumbed in competition with national chains, so local manners, eccentricities, self-dependence, and self-determination yielded in the twenties to pressures imposed by those seeking national markets for

[7]Daniel Bell, "Socialism: The Dream and the Reality," *The Shaping of Twentieth-Century America*, selected and with commentary by Richard M. Abrams and Lawrence W. Levine (Boston: Little, Brown, 1965), p. 340.

consumers' goods, national consent for business policies, national approbation for business politics. "The business of the United States is business," said Calvin Coolidge, the official oracle of the new era, and most Americans, impressed with the performance of the new business enterprises and indoctrinated with the belief in a magnificent future of ease and plenty, rallied to his slogan.[8]

In the face of the rapidly developing enmassment and materialism of society, the typical American found himself hard put to keep pace. The pressures mounted to "find a place in the group." The innocence of a nation which only a few years before could be mobilized to "make the world safe for democracy" left it ill-prepared to cope with the new social order. What alternative directions were available? Everywhere in American society, it seemed that change was deemed preferable to continuity. The old values were losing ground even faster than before.

The one surety for the individual in a time of such rapid change was the group. All security seemed located in collective solutions. As the result, the group rapidly replaced the individual. Women's clubs, social groups, civic clubs, and a host of similar activities made Americans a nation of joiners. Religious, educational, and medical institutions pooled their assets in an effort to serve group needs by following the pattern of consolidation already developed to a high art in government and business.

The individual also lost status as scientific management became ever more popular throughout American industry. Experience and skill seemed to have steadily less value in the age of the assembly line. As the life of the worker became more mechanized and stereotyped, the life of the urban resident also suffered. It seemed that fewer and fewer Americans could own their own homes. The number of tenants in both urban and rural areas climbed sharply during the 1920s. Every aspect of the individual's life seemed less secure as he was caught amidst the play of special interest groups and gigantic institutions.

Alienation of the Intellectual

The 1920s and the 1930s are customarily described as an era during which America alienated her artist–intellectual class. The intellectuals were at least one-half right in their critical view of American society. It was true that the individual seemed to be losing his grip. But the intellectuals were also one-half wrong. During the Twenties, the problem stemmed not from "big business," as usually stated, but from the union of business *and* government. This partnership in bigness was producing a situation which steadily

[8]Thomas C. Cochran and William Miller, *The Age of Enterprise* (New York: Harper and Brothers, 1961), p. 324.

worsened. Perhaps we should not expect artists to know a great deal about political economy. It should be enough that they sense the problem in human terms, even though they fail to identify the proper cause for the human erosion which occurs. Be that as it may, by the mid-Twenties, some of the more "intellectual" Progressives were losing their faith in the old verities. Political solutions no longer seemed as filled with promise as they had once been.

The new salvation for many intellectuals was discovered in the largely depersonalized view of human nature contained in the works of Sigmund Freud. Sherwood Anderson spoke for a generation of American artists and intellectuals when he wrote, "If there is anything that you do not understand in human life, consult the works of Dr. Freud."

Not all American intellectuals passed through the Freudian phase, but nearly all saw a sharp decline in humane values in the enmassment and materialism of the new era. Such voices of sanity as Irving Babbitt and Joseph Wood Krutch warned that mass values were eroding the dignity of individual personality, and that the price for such erosion was likely to be very high.

On a more popular level, artists and intellectuals as far apart in their basic viewpoint as Ernest Hemingway and H. L. Mencken could be uniformly pessimistic about the Twenties. Phrases such as "the lost generation" and "the wasteland" expressed a contempt for the direction that society was taking and a willingness to stand aside in complete alienation from the social order.

Whatever the source of their alienation from society, the literary intellectuals of the Twenties generally retained their individuality. Yet even here an erosion was occurring as the twentieth century wore on. John Dos Passos epitomized the change between the literature of the 1920s and the 1930s:

A chapter in the moral history of modern American writing does come to an end with Hemingway and the lost generation and nowhere can this be more clearly seen than in the work of John Dos Passos, who rounds out the story of that generation and carries its values into the social novel of the Thirties. For what is so significant about Dos Passos is that though he is a direct link between the postwar decade and the crisis novel of the Depression period, the defeatism of the lost generation has been slowly and subtly transferred by him from persons to society itself. It is society that becomes the hero of his work, society that suffers the impending sense of damnation that the lost-generation individualists had suffered alone before.[9]

[9]Alfred Kazin, *On Native Grounds* (Garden City, N.Y.: Doubleday, 1956), p. 266.

Dos Passos and his trilogy *U.S.A.* are more typically a product of the Thirties than the Twenties. He epitomizes the big change which occurred in American intellectual circles, a change from the lost individual to the lost group. Now it seemed that even alienation could be accomplished only in groups.

The Depression

One of the great ironies of American history lies in the still widely accepted view of the 1929 crash as a "failure of the free market." Until 1929, or so the story goes, America lived in a world of free-wheeling capitalism . . . that is, *until* the system failed and large scale political intervention was necessary to save society. Such an analysis has absolutely no basis in fact. The recession of 1929, which led to the major Depression of 1931, was the clearest possible case of an economic reversal brought about by government intervention in the economy through credit expansion, artificially low interest rates, and artificially high wage rates.

The 1929 crash was primarily due to the inflationary expansion of money and credit. The crash was then enormously aggravated by the government's unwillingness to take its medicine and to allow prices to seek their own levels. Those who caused and aggravated the Depression — the bureaucrats, the "enlightened economists," the politicians and the social engineers — have thus been able to shift blame from their own failings, blaming instead an imaginary "free market" which had not existed for many years in American society. This is a well documented case, spelled out in careful and scholarly detail in Professor Murray Rothbard's *America's Great Depression* and Professor Milton Friedman's monetary history of the United States.

The irony of the matter rests in the fact that the failure of political intervention in the economy in 1929 then became the excuse for the massive political interventions in the economy occurring since that time. The inflationary powers wielded by the Federal Reserve Board, plus the destruction of competition by the Department of Commerce and by government regulatory agencies, combined to generate an unsound expansion which finally had to fall of its own weight. The fall was much more severe and much more prolonged precisely because the very interventions which had caused the problem were continued and expanded during both the Hoover and Roosevelt administrations:

> Hoover's role as founder of a revolutionary program of government planning to combat depression has been unjustly neglected by historians. Franklin D. Roosevelt, in large part, merely elaborated the policies laid down by his predecessor. To scoff at Hoover's tragic failure

to cure the depression as a typical example of *laissez-faire* is drastically to misread the historical record. The Hoover rout must be set down as a failure of government planning and not of the free market.[10]

Yet, precisely because the 1920s in general and the Hoover administration in particular were assumed to be founded upon *laissez-faire* individualistic principles, the way was paved for the American people to give apparently final and absolute psychological rejection to the idea of individual freedom. The depression became the great bogeyman which allowed America to believe that freedom had failed. Americans could now in good conscience embrace the new collective ethic which had already been growing among us for many years. Now there was no guilt involved in an openhearted embrace of the new collective ideals. The New Deal thus saw the completion of an anti-individualistic process long in creation.

[10]Murray N. Rothbard, *America's Great Depression* (Princeton, N.J.: Van Nostrand, 1963), p. 168.

XIV

THE NEW DEAL

I saw that the New Deal was only superficially a reform movement. I had to acknowledge the truth of what its more forthright protagonists, sometimes unwarily, sometimes defiantly, averred: The New Deal was a genuine revolution, whose deepest purpose was not simply reform within existing traditions, but a basic change in the social, and, above all, the power relationships within the nation. It was not a revolution by violence. It was a revolution by bookkeeping and lawmaking. Insofar as it was successful, the power of politics had replaced the power of business. This is the basic power shift of all the revolutions of our time. This shift was the revolution. It was only of incidental interest that the revolution was not complete, that it was made not by tanks and machine guns, but by acts of Congress and decisions of the Supreme Court, or that many of the revolutionists did not know what they were or denied it. But revolution is always an affair of force, whatever forms the force disguises itself in. Whether the revolutionists prefer to call themselves Fabians, who seek power by the inevitability of gradualism, or Bolsheviks, who seek power by the dictatorship of the proletariat, the struggle is for power.

Whittaker Chambers,
Witness

What had been implicit in Progressivism and in the "new era of the Twenties" became explicit in the New Deal. The revolution of American society had arrived. Following the 1929 stock market crash, business leaders reiterated in ever more cheery and confident tones their optimistic pronouncements. But it soon became clear that the American business community placed no real faith in the workings of a free market. Some observers attribute this loss of confidence to the Depression itself. Actually, American businessmen had long since lost confidence in the working of a truly competitive system. The Chambers of Commerce, the trade associations, and the various other "booster" groups had come to emphasize cooperation rather than competition and had become steadily less individualistic and more socialized. Few if any defenders remained who would stand against the tide and speak out for the traditional American order.

The totally dominant assumption of American society was that government must stabilize the economy and level out the business cycle. Herbert Hoover brought all the power of government to bear in encouragement of "voluntary" agreements on the part of the business community to hold wages and prices at an artificially high level. The Reconstruction Finance Corporation, begun during the Hoover years, pioneered in the form of government intervention which would lead to the National Recovery Administration of Franklin Roosevelt. The rout of free-market capitalism was already completed well before Franklin Roosevelt took office:

> Came the New Deal. There was very little conscious theory behind any of the New Deals, whether First, Second, or Third. Between 1933 and the coming of World War II, Roosevelt chopped and changed so often that he frequently appeared to cancel himself. Between his NRA and TNEC phases there was no visible connection; and with such antipodal prophets as General Hugh Johnson (a believer in market limitation) and Thurman Arnold (a trust-buster) clamoring for the President's ear, it often seemed as though the Tower of Babel had been substituted for the Washington Monument. Roosevelt's own metaphorical conception of himself (as the quarterback always willing to change from a passing to a rushing or kicking game) seemed to argue the complete pragmatist. . . . Raymond Moley and Cordell Hull went to the London Economic Conference in 1933 with contradictory plans in their pockets, each fully confident that his own plan had unequivocal White House blessing.[1]

Franklin Roosevelt harbored little, if any, political or economic theory within his makeup. Nothing in his life or pronouncements suggests that his understanding of political questions went beyond the basic issue of winning elections. In that area he was an acknowledged master, quite capable of weaving together antagonistic philosophies and bitterly opposed interest groups (for example, organized labor and the farmer) into a single working complex which could win elections. The intellectuals forming the brain trust which accompanied Roosevelt to Washington provided the ideology which he lacked.

The "big society–big government" syndrome which had been gathering force for 40 years now burst forth in full bloom. Under the aegis of a political chameleon primarily interested in political power, a group of intellectuals who were primarily interested in ideology came to the fore. Together these two forces would remake the face of America.

---

[1]John Chamberlain, *The Roots of Capitalism* (Princeton, N.J.: Van Nostrand, 1959), pp. 195–196.

The Planned Society

One factor which gave the intellectuals such an extended period of time to entrench their authority over American society was that government power had expanded by the time of the New Deal to a magnitude which now promised to defy the fluctuations of the business cycle:

> In the old days, the economy had recovered quickly, after sharp pains, through the agency of bankruptcies: Marginal producers were bought out at forced sales, and their plants and farms set going again on a basis that did not require the servicing of a vast burden of debt.
>
> But from 1933 on, the very notion of bankruptcy was repudiated. The RFC (started by the Republicans) would take care of big corporations in trouble; the farmer's solvency would be guaranteed by AAA; homeowners would find mortgages easy to finance through the federal government; bank depositors would be insured. As for the unemployed, they were to be supported as a matter of equity: As Isabel Paterson has said, if J. P. Morgan were to be put "on the dole" through the RFC, there could be no good moral reason for denying a dole to any man who happened to be out of work.[2]

By 1933 these ideas made good political sense. Such ideas also meant that the Depression was not to be allowed to run its course, thus institutionalizing the Depression involvements of government. Once such a system had been fully accepted by the American people, they could not renege on the agreement without facing the holocaust of a worse depression than any they had previously suffered. In this way, the intellectuals came to power and were guaranteed long-term tenure.

Henry Adams once commented that, despite all the terrible shortcomings of American Congressmen, if the American people were looking for someone to run the country, and compared Congressmen and professors, he for one would still prefer Congressmen. Adams feared the closet philosopher who had an answer to all life's problems contained within his briefcase. He recognized that the underlying assumption of the planned society presupposed that no one knew as much about his own affairs as the planner did about everyone's affairs. Like the earlier age which he represented, Adams thus rejected the underlying assumption of the planned society.

Probably Henry Adams and the typical citizen of an earlier America shared Herbert Spencer's view of the planner who feels qualified to manipulate everyone's affairs, since he:

[2] *Ibid.,* p. 197.

. . . shows us unmistakably that he thinks of the body politic as admitting of being shaped thus or thus at will; and the tacit implication of many Acts of Parliament is that aggregated men, twisted into this or that arrangement, will remain as intended.

It may indeed be said that, even irrespective of this erroneous conception of a society as a plastic mass instead of an organized body, facts forced on his attention hour by hour should make every one sceptical as to the success of this or that proposed way of changing a people's actions. Alike to the citizen and the legislator, home experiences daily supply proofs that the conduct of human beings baulks calculation. He has given up the thought of managing his wife and lets her manage him. Children on whom he has tried now reprimand, now punishment, now suasion, now reward, do not respond satisfactorily to any method; and no expostulations prevent their mother from treating them in ways he thinks mischievous. So, too, his dealings with his servants, whether by reasoning or by scolding, rarely succeed for long; the falling short of attention, or punctuality, or cleanliness, or sobriety, leads to constant changes. Yet, difficult as he finds it to deal with humanity in detail, he is confident of his ability to deal with embodied humanity. Citizens, not one-thousandth of whom he knows, not one-hundredth of whom he ever saw, and the great mass of whom belong to classes having habits and modes of thought of which he has but dim notions, he feels sure will act in ways he foresees, and fulfil ends he wishes. Is that not a marvelous incongruity between premises and conclusion?[3]

The planning mentality in the particular form which came to dominate America had its origins in the Fabian socialism of England during the late nineteenth and early twentieth centuries. In a lecture delivered before the Fabian Society in 1894, Sidney Webb announced, "To suppose that the industrial affairs of a complicated industrial state can be run without strict subordination and discipline, without obedience to orders, and without definite allowances for maintenance, is to dream, not of Socialism but of Anarchism." Webb went on to urge that a new social order must take the place of the dying capitalist system. The new order was to be based "not on competition but cooperation." The workings of a complex industrial state would require subordination and discipline. That discipline would stem from the planning ideal, from the "best minds" available. For the Webbs, this was the London School of Economics. Meanwhile, America was generating its own intellectual class to take the place of Sidney Webb and the faculty of the London School of Economics.

[3]Herbert Spencer, *The Man Versus the State* (London, 1884), p. 365.

America's parallel to the Fabians had already been evidenced during World War I under the leadership of Bernard Baruch and the War Industries Board, and later, under the aegis of Herbert Hoover's Department of Commerce. The "necessary controls" of wartime had quickly evolved into the "voluntary cooperation" of peacetime. All that was now needed was a crisis of sufficient magnitude to demand the permanent adoption of the new planning ideal, in some form politically palatable to the majority of the American people. The Depression provided that crisis, and the New Deal provided that political "solution."

While it is true that the New Deal went much further than many Progressives had earlier desired, and certainly further than Herbert Hoover preferred, the direction was in no wise different than had already been evidenced in the Progressive era and during the 1920s:

The next episode in the history of reform, the New Deal, was itself a product of that overorganized world which had so much troubled the Progressives. The trend toward management, toward bureaucracy, toward bigness everywhere had gone so far that even the efforts of reform itself had to be consistent with it. Moreover, as the New Deal era went on, leadership in reform had to be shared increasingly with an organized working class large enough to make important demands and to wield great political power. The political and moral codes of the immigrant masses of the cities, of the political bosses, of labor leaders, of intellectuals and administrators, now clashed with the old notions of economic morality. Some of the social strata and many of the social types that had seen great merit in the more limited reforms of the Progressive era found themselves in a bewildering new situation and, especially after the passing of the most critical Depression years, grew increasingly offended by the novelties with which they were surrounded. The New Deal, with its pragmatic spirit and its relentless emphasis upon results, seemed to have carried them farther than ever from the kind of society in which economic life was linked to character and to distinctively entrepreneurial freedoms and opportunities.[4]

In Franklin Roosevelt's famous Commonwealth Club speech in San Francisco during September 1932, he traced the rise of the modern political state and insisted that the growing consolidation of vast powers in the hands of a few institutional leaders demanded that the older American ideals must be replaced with the new planning ideal, since individual freedom and economic cooperation no longer could function in the traditional manner.

[4]Richard Hofstadter, *The Age of Reform* (New York: Vintage Books, 1955), pp. 11–12.

Thus it was the New Deal which provided the first instance of a major American political current that broke completely with the national past in urging complete social and economic innovation. The "sociocracy" of Lester Ward had arrived full-blown on the American scene 50 years after it had been predicted. The union of the intellectuals and political power produced reorganization and centralization of virtually every aspect of American life. While the intellectuals remade the American scene, the special interest group tactics of Franklin Roosevelt remade American politics. More than ever before, political power in American life was to be achieved by brokerage of favors. Our politics have yet to recover from that special interest mentality. Americans were no longer Americans, but had become, for political purposes, a member of the farm vote, the labor vote, or some other special interest group.

The Age of Administration

The culmination of the trend toward the empowering of groups came with dramatic swiftness. In the "Hundred Days" following his inauguration in 1933, Franklin D. Roosevelt pushed through Congress bills which presented the country with collectivism as a *fait accompli.* All the steps toward it thus far had been but background and prelude. The central pieces of legislation were the Agricultural Adjustment Act and the National Industrial Recovery Act. By the Agricultural Adjustment Act Congress acknowledged itself as caretaker of the needs of farmers, and proceeded to provide for them by regulation, subsidies, and parity payments. Industries were invited to control themselves by fair trade codes under the NIRA. Labor was provided for by the section of the Act which guaranteed labor's right "to organize and bargain collectively through representatives of their own choosing." A National Labor Board was created to enforce this provision. These actions marked a climax of the empowering of factions, and their aim has been fully pointed out by Rexford G. Tugwell, one of the architects of these acts. "NRA could have been administered so that a great collectivism might gradually have come out of it, so that all the enormous American energies might have been disciplined and channeled into one national effort to establish a secure basis for well-being."[5]

Of course, NRA and AAA were only the two most significant items in a planning potpourri that poured over America. The Civilian Conservation

[5]Clarence B. Carson, *The Fateful Turn* (Irvington, N.Y.: Foundation For Economic Education, 1963), pp. 123–124.

Corps, the Works Progress Administration, and new agency after new agency followed one another in quick succession. The NRA is especially important since it presupposed the deliberate limitations of price competition, and the limitation of the number of firms permitted to do business. The old Hoover idea of stabilized prices by means of trade associations was now carried one step further and made a specific government function. The NRA blue eagle emblem symbolized a noncompetitive market with a fixed number of competitors and fixed prices. It was no coincidence that both the techniques and personnel of Bernard Baruch's War Industries Board found their way into NRA. The same planning mentality which made NRA possible had already been clearly foreshadowed during Progressivism and during the 1920s. While it is true that NRA was another dose of bigness imposed upon American society, it was a dose of bigness advocated by businessmen themselves:

> Under the National Industrial Recovery Act, industries were encouraged to organize themselves as agents of the state. To each of these groups there was then delegated the power to legislate not only for all who were then engaged in that line of business but for all who might wish to engage in it. No clearer, no more naked, illustration could be offered of what is meant by the statement that gradual collectivism means the conferring of privileges upon selected interests. For the right to make laws and to enforce them by fines and imprisonment is the basic attribute of sovereignty, and the delegation of sovereignty to selected interests is exactly what the word "privilege" means. In the case of the NRA privilege was conferred upon certain trade organizations and theoretically at least upon industrial employees also.[6]

Under the slogan of "fair competition," the blue eagle was spread across the country to the strains of band music and the cheers of crowds. The old War Industries Board member who now headed NRA, General Hugh Johnson, within a year had completed more than 400 industrial codes, covering about 90 percent of American business enterprise and approximately 22 million wage earners and salaried employees. More than one observer has pointed out the close parallel which existed between NRA and the corporate fascism of Italy. Both rested primarily upon organized, institutionalized special interest groups, vying for political power and dividing society into their areas of influence.

While business was given its collection of special privileges through NRA and RFC, while the farmers found their place in the corporate state through AAA, organized labor found its own collection of special privileges under

---

[6]Walter Lippmann, *The Good Society* (New York: Grosset and Dunlap, 1943), p. 123.

the Wagner Act and the subsequent actions of the National Labor Relations Board. It seemed that everyone had a spokesman in Washington except the individual American who did not wish to find himself a place within the new institutional giantism. Meanwhile, Franklin Roosevelt's new political coalition, based upon special privilege for the large power blocs, especially the large power bloc represented by the new CIO, found itself invincible in American politics. The planning ideal of the corporate state was fixed with its talons deeply in the back of American society.

Both AAA and NRA were destined to be nullified by the Supreme Court. This nullification had little or no lasting effect upon the advance toward a collectivized America. As business lost its special advantage and seemed about to be cast into political outer darkness, the Roosevelt Administration found a solution even more politically satisfactory in its search for new support. The beginnings of what today is known as the War on Poverty were now stirring. The Roosevelt Administration had discovered the urban masses as the newest and most effective member of the successful political coalition which made possible Harry Hopkins' dictum: "Tax and tax, spend and spend, elect and elect." Social Security and the WPA offered new planning goals.

Other planning goals of special significance during the New Deal's tenure were the Tennessee Valley Authority and the Rural Electrification Administration. Many of the Roosevelt advisors viewed TVA and REA as the models for an exciting new America. Roosevelt himself predicted that America's potential new command over electrical energy could lead to "an industrial and social revolution that may already be underway without our perceiving it."

The Tennessee Valley Authority was intended to serve as a showcase for the positive linkage of electricity, decentralization, and citizen participation in reclamation of the landscape. TVA was not intended merely to generate energy and produce fertilizer. In the words of the President, it was also to grant the Middle South an exemplary way of life: "a social experiment that is the first of its kinds in the world, a corporation clothed with the power of government, but possessed of the flexibility and initiative of private enterprise," "a return to the spirit and vision of the pioneer," which "touches and gives life to all forms of human concern." "If we are successful here," Roosevelt concluded, "we can march on, step by step, in a like development of other great natural, territorial units . . . and distribution and diversification of industry."[7]

---

[7]James W. Carey and John J. Quirk, "The Mythos of the Electronic Revolution," *The American Scholar, 39,* Spring 1970, No. 2, p. 235.

For David Lilienthal and for a generation of planners, TVA represented a new form of collective experiment whereby the problems of American society would be solved in final form. In the rhetoric poured forth on this particular subject, the utopian and totally collective aspect of New Deal planning was especially apparent.

The Intellectual Climate

One of the leading intellectual lights of American society during the 1920s and 1930s describes a reaction which many of the intellectuals of the Depression era seemed to share:

> The next month the slump began, and as conditions grew worse and worse and President Hoover, unable to grasp what had happened, made no effort to deal with the breakdown, a darkness seemed to descend. Yet, to the writers and artists of my generation who had grown up in the Big Business era and had always resented its barbarism, its crowding-out of everything they cared about, these years were not depressing but stimulating. One couldn't help being exhilarated at the sudden unexpected collapse of that stupid gigantic fraud. It gave us a new sense of freedom; and it gave us a new sense of power to find ourselves still carrying on while the bankers, for a change, were taking a beating. With a businessman's President in the White House, who kept telling us, when he told us anything, that the system was perfectly sound, who sent General Douglas MacArthur to burn the camp of the unemployed war veterans who had come to appeal to Washington, we wondered about the survival of republican American institutions; and we became more and more impressed by the achievements of the Soviet Union, which could boast that its industrial and financial problems were carefully studied by the government, and that it was able to avert such crises.[8]

The Thirties thus brought an attempt upon the part of the intellectuals to enlist in the army of the proletariat, beginning a decade of "writers' congresses" and increasingly active political involvement, often with extreme left-wing overtones. The Soviet Union and its planning ideal came to have a strong appeal for the American intellectual. Now the earlier alienation which the intellectual had experienced found its fruition in the uncritical espousal of the Soviet planning alternative.

The literature of the Thirties thus was often composed less of art works than social critiques. American intellectuals were no longer sure of their

[8]Edmund Wilson, "The Literary Consequences of the Crash," *The Shores of Light* (New York: Farrar, Straus, 1952), pp. 498–499.

own ground. They no longer felt in contact with earlier American values. It had been one thing to say, as George Santayana had said a decade before, that "moral materialism and love of quantity" were inconclusive elements in the American character, since Americans had never yet faced their day of reckoning. But now the day of reckoning had come, and the moral materialism and love of quantity had been found wanting. In such a climate the intellectuals looked about for a new set of values, and discovered the planning ideal.

It was this distressed and lost quality in American thought that made possible the successful social novels of the Thirties:

> It was these associations that contributed to the success of *The Grapes of Wrath* and made it the most influential social novel of the period. Though the book was as urgent and as obvious a social tract for its time as *Uncle Tom's Cabin* had been for another, it was also the first novel of its kind to dramatize the inflictions of the crisis without mechanical violence. The bitterness was there, as it should have been, the sense of unspeakable human waste and privation and pain. But in the light of Steinbeck's strong sense of fellowship, his simple indignation at so much suffering, the Joads, while essentially symbolic marionettes, did illuminate something more than the desperation of the time: They became a living and challenging part of the forgotten American procession. Though the characters were essentially stage creations, the book brought the crisis that had severed Americans from their history back into it by recalling what they had lost through it. It gave them a design, a sense of control, where out of other Depression novels they could get only the aimless bombardment of rage.[9]

That "aimless bombardment of rage" plus the acceptance of the planning ideal left much of the literature of the 1930s operating on the highly antiartistic wavelength of Marxist criticism. Though *The Grapes of Wrath* was a cut above such artless art, the low level of Marxist criticism present in much of American literature during the 1930s was on a par with the WPA art decorating the post office walls. The American intellectual had discovered the dispossessed at the same instant when the American politician had discovered them. The new breed of mass-men generated by the enmassment of American society was now to be cared for by the very people who wished to further that enmassment beyond the wildest dreams of previous planners. In the process, American democracy was changed from a government which emphasized the negative limitations placed upon the state, to a new

[9]Alfred Kazin, *On Native Grounds* (Garden City, N.Y.: Doubleday, 1956), p. 308.

concept of government which politicalized the masses and encouraged the pursuit of government benefits by political means. The pressure group antics of the past 30 years are the direct result of that change. Bigness had now come fully into its own.

.The crisis of the Depression continued to the very threshold of the Second World War. There were more people unemployed in 1938 than had been unemployed in 1932. But in the new intellectual climate which dominated American society, all this was forgotten in the new zest for the planning ideal, for big solutions to big problems. The next big problem on the horizon was to be the Second World War, bringing with it a further enlargement of government and an enlargement of institutional America on all levels, dwarfing all previous comparisons. The controls on the life of the individual American, the pressures to which he was subject in his daily existence, continued to grow. By 1945, Americans found themselves living in a new world of truly big government and special interest politics, with the grim spectre of Depression still hovering in the minds of a generation of voters who remembered what had happened to them. Those voters placed the blame upon an imaginary "free market" which had presumably existed in 1929. They looked to a continuation and expansion of government in their lives as the best assurance that hard times would not come again. In postwar America, the stage was set for further escalation of big institutions and big government, with the individual, as usual, finding a smaller and smaller place in the equation.

XV

THE LAST 30 YEARS:
BIGNESS REACHES A CLIMAX

In the past, people saw one big institution as a problem: big business, or big
labor unions, or big government. If only this one monster could be shrunk
or tamed, they felt there would be no problem of power in our society.

But we have begun to see that our modern industrial society is a complex
of tremendously big power centers: big government, big military, big civil
service, big business, big labor — but also giant universities, giant research,
and so on. A half-century ago, we had a society of untold atoms of social
power. Even the federal government, then by far the biggest concentration of
power on our scene, was a very small affair; all federal employees at the turn
of the century would have found space in one of today's Washington office
buildings. Today our society comprises a multitude of very big power centers
in all areas, and we do not yet understand the politics and social order of such
a society.

Peter F. Drucker,
Concept of the Corporation

If Woodrow Wilson and the War Industries Board of 1917 first demonstrated how all society could be organized into great institutional units,
World War II carried the concept much further than before. Allocation of
productive capacities was tightly regulated, through rationing and price
control. The total institutionalization and rationalization of society was
now assumed to be possible, and the events of the Second World War
seemed to lend substance to that possibility.

These trends did not end when the war ended in 1945. The peculiar
phenomenon which we now call the Cold War gave to American society
many features of the garrison state. A state of mobilization and organization, unprecedented in peacetime America, was continued and expanded.
The permanent war economy, featuring ever closer ties between business
and government, led to the development of what its critics today describe
as "the military–industrial complex." The role of the lobbyist and the
influence peddler became greater than ever before in American history. The

lines between public and private institutions became steadily more difficult to discern. National security provided the rationale for encouraging greater and greater bigness, not only in government, but also in business, labor, and every other element of American society.

The new arrangement also achieved some old-fashioned political results, albeit in a new and highly technological form:

> In the United States the space race performed even necessary political functions. The United States had never completely pulled out of the Great Depression, even under the ministrations of the New Deal. World War II had given the economy an enormous boost. The postwar boom underwritten by repressed consumer demand was followed by the Korean war. Post-Sputnik technological rivalry with the Soviet Union insured that the economy could be kept going almost full blast without any major changes in the American economic or social system. Excess economic capacity could be siphoned off without distributing it among those who could not pay; the government would buy it and either blow it up or literally send it into outer space. The aerospace industry was a particular boon to the fast-growing and increasingly politically potent areas — Florida, California, and the Southwest generally. The space race was controlled from Houston, and during the Johnson Administration Texas moved from eleventh to second place among states in value of defense contracts received.[1]

Big Government — Big Business

The connection between government expansion and defense expenditure is self-evident. More than one-half of the total annual budgets since the end of the Second World War have been spent for "defense." When more than 10 percent of the total national income is spent by a single agency, that agency, in this case the Defense Department, is bound to have great influence over the direction of technological development and institutional growth. Whereas prior to World War II most defense expenditure was conducted in government owned facilities, most defense needs today are met by outside, so-called "private" contractors. The business community and the university have taken over government research and development. Meanwhile, government has used its role in this area of research to become the primary source of research funds in all areas, not only in defense and space matters, but in medical and social matters as well. While most of the brain power is thus channeled into big business and big universities to meet government needs, much of the brawn is also under government contract,

[1]Victor C. Ferkiss, *Technological Man: The Myth and the Reality* (New York: George Braziller, 1969), pp. 8–9.

usually in large institutional operations; 95 percent of all jobs in the aircraft and missile industry, 60 percent of all jobs in shipbuilding, and 40 percent of all jobs in communications equipment are directly dependent upon government expenditure.

The result has been the creation of a new and powerful elite, operating in the rarefied upper atmosphere created by the partnership among the giant institutions of government, business, university, and labor. The same figures who hold appointive positions in government are likely to be men who themselves or whose colleagues hold positions at other times in the large research centers of business or the university, and the same men who generate a large amount of political clout in terms of their capacity to determine which areas of expenditure are to be encouraged and which are to be curtailed. The political lives of more than a few United States Senators and Representatives, in areas heavily dependent upon government contracts of various kinds, hang in the balance of such decisions. No doubt C. Wright Mills went too far in his assumption that a new "ruling class" had developed, but there is enough truth to the assertion to give pause to anyone concerned about the future of the American republic. Some observers, notably Professor John Kenneth Galbraith, suggest that the new "technostructure" and government are working together hand and glove, with the Cold War as their excuse. He further opines that the best source for the intelligent criticism necessary to reverse that tendency is what he calls the "educational and scientific estate." Who more than the "educational and scientific estate" is a part of the present-day Establishment, with a well worn rut between the academy, the private foundation, and appointive positions in government? In short, if a problem does exist, we had better look somewhere else for leadership and solution than to those very elements of society who have most profited from the present arrangement.

It is also important to note that the power wielded by the present-day Establishment is not centered exclusively in the Department of Defense. The National Space Agency, the Federal Aviation Agency, the Atomic Energy Commission, and a number of other publicly funded bodies underwriting long-term contracts for technological research and development are equally involved. When the problem is seen in its larger dimensions, it also should be clear that there are few major American corporations which are not involved in this new partnership with government.

How Competitive Is the American Market?

The lack of competition in the awarding of defense contracts demonstrate the extent to which government has come to dominate substantial portions of the marketplace. It is this noncompetitive aspect of modern capitalism which has served as the basis for much of the contemporary Left-wing attack on the free market. What the Left has forgotten in making this attack is that only a close partnership between big government and nonentrepreneurial business, complete with bureaucratic domination of both government and business, could make possible the present lack of competition. Thus we have the peculiar spectacle of the Left wing attacking a version of "free enterprise" which does not exist, while the Right wing defends the same straw man. American business in its present form is not the competitive model that either Left or Right have assumed it to be in their rhetoric.

In fact, the concept of free enterprise simply has no opportunity to work in its present environment. There are too many noncompetitive aspects of the relationship between government and business, too much openly wasteful expenditure, to allow any real competition with the freely flowing cornucopia of government funds which presently exists. The wasteful expenditure which Senator William Proxmire of Wisconsin has been able to discover as Chairman of the House–Senate Subcommittee on Economy in Government had its inception in the defense spending of the Second World War. It seems that the disease, which might be labeled the "cost-plus mentality," is easy to catch and hard to cure. Indeed, a good case might be made to suggest that the cost-plus mentality killed the Packard Motor Car Corporation and a number of other businesses which had major wartime contracts and were never able to return to the sort of efficient operation necessary for competitive business.

While government has steadily reduced the amount of competition present in the market, it has also been something of a monopolist itself. The United States Post Office, the Tennessee Valley Authority, the provision of highway services, are all instances of such a monopoly mentality. Here again the connection between the public sector and the private sector is much closer than might be supposed. The present uneconomic mail rates which compel government to deliver the mail at a rather considerable loss have their origin in the pressures of businessmen who find that they are able to use the subsidized mails for their own advantage. The Tennessee Valley Authority has become closely identified with the electrical goods industries which have grown up around the artificially low prices for electricity charged in connection with that particular "social experiment."

We talk endlessly of protecting the small businessman from "Big Business," but, as usual with government policy, we are offering the wrong solution to the wrong problem. What we have actually been doing is protecting "Big Business" from rising new competitors. We encourage bigness in a variety of ways besides direct defense and research contracts, including the actions of regulatory agencies, tariff policy, and tax policy.

Regulatory Activity

The original intent of the various regulatory agencies was to protect the consumer by encouraging competition among those serving the public. The actual result of such agencies as the FCC, the CAB, the ICC, and similar regulatory commissions has been to retard competition, thus penalizing the consumer. The classic symptoms of monopoly have been (1) an absence of price competition, and (2) an inability for new competitors to enter the marketplace. What could be a more accurate description of a government-regulated industry? The FCC permits the already established giants in the communications field an absolute monopoly of the area by means of government licensure. The Civil Aeronautics Board does precisely the same thing for the airlines industry, and so on throughout American life. Not only are new competitors thus prevented from entering the field, but those noncompetitors privileged to hold government licenses in various areas of the American economy are further privileged by means of government rate-setting policy which removes all price competition:

The regulatory agencies not only prevent those in the transportation industry from competing with each other — they also protect those in the industry from the entry of additional competitors. You cannot get into the trucking business, the airline business, the bus business as you would enter retailing or manufacturing. You must be certified by the CAB if you wish to enter the airline business. The CAB has not certified an additional scheduled airline in continental United States since it began operating in 1938. The ICC will certify an additional common carrier truck company to operate on a given route only if it can be demonstrated that adequate truck service is not available on the route in question. The only major city in which you can start a taxi business simply by applying for a taxi license and demonstrating that you carry the necessary public liability insurance and have safe equipment and drivers is Washington, D.C. All other major cities stop any additional taxi operators from entering the business. They even prevent taxi operators from increasing the size of their fleets. Transportation regulation very effectively protects transportation companies from new competition and produces the exact opposite of the situation which our antimonopoly laws were designed to produce in other industries.[2]

As one economist who has carefully investigated the contemporary scene summarizes the case:

Economic legislation in the transportation field produces the opposite of its intended result just as so much other economic legislation does. The imposition of regulation on the pricing of natural gas in the field,

[2]Yale Brozen, "Is Government the Source of Monopoly?" *The Intercollegiate Review,* Winter 1968–69, p. 71.

which was intended to produce lower prices for consumers, has caused an increase in the field price of gas. Our tariff legislation, which presumably protects high-wage American workers from the competition of low-paid foreigners, actually monopolizes low-paying jobs and prevents Americans from moving into higher-paying jobs. Our minimum wage legislation, which is supposed to eliminate poverty by raising the pay of low-paid workers, is creating more poverty by causing unemployment and by forcing people out of higher-paying jobs into poorly-paid jobs. Our legislation favoring low-income regions such as the Tennessee Valley and Appalachia which is supposed to benefit the poor, is maintaining pockets of poverty and benefiting the highly paid workers in high income. Our agricultural program, presumably designed to help poor farmers, has hurt poor farmers and enriched rich farmers. Our urban renewal programs, which are supposed to benefit the slum dweller, have hurt slum dwellers and small business men and enriched building contractors, landlords, and the most highly paid workers in the country, the members of the building trades unions.[3]

In area after area the effect of government has been the generation of special privilege, the feathering of the nests of the well-to-do at the expense of those less fortunate. The fact that this has been done under humanitarian labels only makes the program more reprehensible.

Tariffs

Tariffs are another conspicuous example of the strangulation of competition by big institutions, using government as a weapon. Since the end of the Second World War, economists in the United States and abroad have paid virtually universal lip service to the principles of free trade. Everyone presumably recognizes that the tariff is a clear-cut instance of government intervention favoring those competitors already in the field, at the expense of the ultimate consumer. Yet international trade has seldom suffered more complete strangulation than that which the new system of protectionism would force upon it. This is true not only in the direct sense of tariffs, but also in the various forms of exchange controls, import licenses, and quotas. Such governmental manipulations of trade, designed to reduce competition, are a conspicuous instance of the partnership between government and some of the big institutions within American society.

The Conglomerate

Recent political rhetoric on Capitol Hill suggested that government is about to move to "protect" American society from a new form of bigness,

[3] *Ibid.,* pp. 73–75.

the conglomerate. In actual fact, the conglomerate is an excellent demonstration of the means by which bigness of the most bureaucratic and nonproductive sort is furthered by the policies of government. Both government monetary policy and government tax policy have achieved this result.

The inflationary monetary policies pursued by Washington for a number of years have generated a larger and larger supply of credit chasing a comparatively static amount of production. The result has been a steady price rise, or, more properly, a steady decrease in the value of money. Large American institutions have been in the position of holding greater and greater amounts of money at a time when that money was steadily depreciating in value. Anyone even remotely attuned to the realities of our age has come to understand that institutional survival is possible only if that money is converted to some other form than cash, thus stopping the depreciation in the value of the holdings. Those with the largest amounts of ready cash have been first into the market for all kinds of property. Those with the largest corporate holdings have been encouraged, indeed driven, by government monetary policy to expand their corporate holdings still further.

Present antimonopoly laws have made it impossible for these corporate holdings to be expanded within the same industries where the money was originally made, necessitating investment in unrelated fields, and producing the peculiar economic phenomenon which we call the conglomerate.

Government tax policy meanwhile achieves the same effect. At a time when roughly one-half of corporate earnings are taxed away to government, and most of the remaining half, paid out in dividends, is then subject to personal income tax, the choice available to the board of directors of the average large corporation is to expand corporate holdings through various investment procedures, or to pay the money out in corporate income tax and dividends. The real choice for the board of directors is to give the money to government, or to expand corporate holdings. For most boards, this is an easy choice to make. Existing tax policy also makes it attractive to buy corporations operating at a loss, since the resultant tax law carryovers can be helpful to the parent corporation. Government monetary and tax policy is encouraging the very operation against which government presumably is now promising to protect us.

Between 1955 and 1967 the effect of government policy has been to increase substantially the assets held by leading corporations. In 1955, 49 percent of the manufacturing assets of this country were owned by those corporations. By 1967 the figure had risen to 59 percent. The 1969 record of corporate acquisitions had risen to a figure 10 times as high as the corporate acquisitions of 1950. Even the largest of American firms have begun to run scared against the possibility of being eaten up by one of the financial creatures created by government monetary and tax policy. In such a climate it is hardly surprising that Americans are painfully aware of the bigness which surrounds them in the business community.

The Wonderful World of Accounting

The key to the productivity of the American economy has always been responsible ownership. And it is precisely this responsible ownership which has come under such heavy attack in the new partnership which has developed between bigness in the public sector and bigness in the private sector. Many of the responsible owners of smaller American businesses find themselves ill prepared to deal with the financial wizards who are using an essentially government-created source of capital to swallow small businesses, while making elaborate promises to the stockholders. The promises commonly associated with conglomerate takeovers usually are based upon the fact that the new form of organizational business, geared to clever accounting practices rather than to productive activity, can show apparently remarkable profits on the balance sheet. These phenomenal rates of growth have less connection with the "sound management" to which they are usually attributed than they do to the processes of dilution whereby large amounts of "water" may be added to the soundly managed balance sheets of the businesses previously owned by smaller, more responsible managers.

Some of the "funny money" accounting procedures encouraged in the present partnership of the public and private sector have utilized such devices as: inflating the assets of a conservatively run company which has been acquired; revising upward the actuarial assumption of interest in a conservatively operated pension plan, thus pouring so-called "actuarial gains" into the acquiring company's income accounts; increasing plant depreciation to double the previous rate and pouring the difference into "profit" on the acquiring company's income statement.

Such practices have become so widespread under the existing monetary and tax policies of government that accountants themselves are now deeply concerned about the ethics of the situation. Certainly some of the chickens came home to roost in 1969–1970, as conglomerates led all other stocks on their race down the Dow Jones average. The situation is far from clear, but it does seem evident at this point that the peculiar American economic phenomena known as the conglomerate could not have come into existence, and cannot endure, without the full cooperation of government under the existing confusion between the private and public sectors.

Big Labor

The strangulation of competition by big institutions, using government as a weapon, takes other forms besides the bigness of bureaucratic, nonentrepreneurial business. Government has a primary role in producing the existing labor union monopoly, whereby 25 percent of America's workers hold special advantage over the remaining 75 percent of the labor force, while also holding tremendous advantage over the American consumer. The special exemptions granted labor date from the Clayton Act of 1914, a product of the Progressive era. It is, however, with the Wagner Act of 1935 and the subsequent creation of the National Labor Relations Board that government has wholeheartedly intervened in labor affairs, creating a monopoly for some at the expense of society as a whole. Nothing in subsequent labor legislation, including the Taft–Hartley Act, has seriously modified that monopoly position:

> A major source of labor monopoly has been government assistance. Licensure provisions, building codes, and the like . . . have been one source. Legislation granting special immunities to labor unions, such as exemption from the antitrust laws, restrictions on union responsibility, the right to appear before special tribunals, and so on, are a second source. Perhaps of equal or greater importance than either is a general climate of opinion and law enforcement applying different standards to actions taken in the course of a labor dispute than to the same actions under other circumstances. If men turn cars over, or destroy property, out of sheer wickedness or in the course of exacting private vengeance, not a hand will be lifted to protect them from the legal consequences. If they commit the same acts in the course of labor dispute, they may well get off scot free. Union actions involving actual or potential physical violence or coercion could hardly take place if it were not for the unspoken acquiescence of the authorities.[4]

The monopoly power of unions has been used not only against the ultimate consumer in a steady round of wage increases totally unrelated to production, but also has been used against businessmen to force acquiescence in union control. The most terrible abuses of big unionism have been directed toward the individual worker, who has often discovered that his particular work skills cannot be used unless he is a union member. Often the union then engages in political activities to which the individual worker might be completely opposed, as well as dictating the terms of the individual's employment. Here is bigness pressing upon the individual in its most raw form.

[4]Milton Friedman, *Capitalism & Freedom* (Chicago: University of Chicago Press, 1964), pp. 130–131.

Bigness in unionism is closely interrelated with bigness in business. So called "industrywide bargaining," guaranteed in effect by the existing labor legislation, not only grants a special position to labor, but it insures that only the larger concerns are capable of meeting such industrywide bargaining on its own terms. In this double pressure of bigness, the worker and the consumer are both caught, encased within a system from which there seems to be no escape. In our highly specialized, highly interdependent economy, in which all of us are consumers, we find ourselves delivered into the hands of forces over which we have little or no control, as in the strikes of air controllers, dock workers, teamsters, or what-have-you. We have come to accept the assumption that a handful of men can bring the entire nation to its knees. It seems that bigness catches all of us in a web from which there is no escape.

Big Education

Nowhere is the bigness resulting from increased politicalization more apparent than in present-day higher education. "Behemoth U." the monster state university of the 1950s and the 1960s, has grown to its present size precisely because it has been the assumption of the present-day political state that any and all comers should be encouraged to go to college and be subsidized in that effort. Other things which make Behemoth U. grow so rapidly are the defense and research contracts whereby the university does the research and development for government and for government-connected industry. The present university complex also has a vested interest in existing tax policy:

> The universities and colleges in the United States . . . have a major interest in maintaining the present tax philosophy; corporate contributions to higher education, for instance, would hardly survive a reform under which the individual shareholder again looked upon the corporation as "his" asset rather than the property of the managers. The managers of the large existing companies, too, are unlikely to view such a change with great enthusiasm, no matter how much they now complain about the "burden of taxation" and oppose any increase in corporation income tax.[5]

Thus bigness is engendered within modern education itself by virtue of its close contact with government. Meanwhile, bigness is engendered within our culture and our society as a whole as the result of the indoctrination process which has grown apace with modern "education." It seems that we

[5]Peter F. Drucker, *The Age of Discontinuity* (New York: Harper and Row, 1968), p. 64.

are determined to treat the students of our school systems, colleges, and universities as raw material for indoctrination, rather than as individuals seeking the tools whereby they can better order their own lives:

> John Dewey was right when he stated that every powerful faith has always made an attempt to reach the mind of youth and those endowed with superior talents. Churches and states, Fascist, Nazi, and Communist dictatorships, monarchies, republics, and theocracies have relied heavily on education in order to impose their own world view on highly impressionable and vulnerable young minds. Since today's educational establishment works in close cooperation with so many private enterprises and state and federal agencies, it is not surprising that it controls the channels of communication.[6]

Thus it seems that the primary purpose of a large portion of modern education is the development of the new labor force for the corporate system. A system financed and furthered by the collective mentality is now called upon to provide the workers who will take their place in the collective system. In the face of such bigness feeding upon bigness, it is not surprising that many of our young finally withdraw in disgust.

The Foundation

The bigness present in government, business, labor, and education is common to other American institutions as well. Certainly the foundations which derive their existence from present taxation policies have a vested interest in maintaining the existing system. The same might be said of the modern churches. Not only are such institutions a perfect example in themselves of the new-style bigness, but they work hand in glove with the other big institutions of present-day society. Many of today's clergymen and most of the new breed of "foundation men" are a perfect example of the new generation of Americans whose values, attitudes, and professional positions stem from maintenance of the existing order. The very enormousness of these foundations, together with their active encouragement of ideological programs pointing toward further entanglement between private and public concerns, surely could not continue in the absence of the present tax exemption situation, which is itself an obvious form of governmental intervention.

Big Cities

Even the physical attributes of our society seem to take on the same aspect of bigness. Our schools, our churches, our cities reflect the same

[6]Thomas Molnar, *The Future of Education* (New York: Fleet Press, 1961), p. 42.

life-style. Urbanization itself is an obvious result of the same trend toward political enmassment. Americans have traditionally suspected those who urged complete divorce from the land and from a capacity for self-reliance. Indeed, many of the agricultural programs of the past 30 and 35 years have presumably been designed to maintain family farming as a way of life in America. Despite this, the effect of the Department of Agriculture and its subsidy program has been to drive more and more small farmers from the land. Today there are less than one-half the number of farms in existence than there were 35 years ago. It seems that the small businessman, the unsophisticated family farmer, simply cannot cope with the accounting procedures and capital accumulations demanded by modern politicalized agriculture. Our attempt to "save the family farm" has resulted in big operations and mass production, in bringing to agriculture the very bigness which we tried to avoid.

And while we have been so busy forcing people from the land, we have simultaneously encouraged the bigness of cities, by means of uneconomic government interventions. These interventions are readily apparent in the public highway systems and other subsidies which have been developed in connection with urban areas. Meanwhile, the attraction of the direct welfare payments available in our major American cities has been a substantial factor in converting the rural poor into an urban proletariat. During the past 30 years, federal subsidies to major American cities have increased a hundredfold. Big government has clearly subsidized the extension of big cities.

Thus bigness in the public sector continues to generate bigness in the private sector, in virtually every aspect of our lives.

XVI

THE LAST 30 YEARS: HOW FREE IS FREE ENTERPRISE?

> Business and government can ill afford to be adversaries. So mutual are our interests, so formidable are our challenges, that our times demand our strengthened alliance. The success of each largely depends upon the other.
>
> James M. Roche,
> "Understanding: The Key to Business-Government Cooperation,"
> *Michigan Business Review.*

Presumably, when the president of one of America's largest corporations publicly states that the success of the contemporary business community depends upon a strengthened alliance with government, he describes the attitude held by at least a major portion of the American business community. Of course, such statements also serve as an obvious demonstration of how far eroded any genuine concept of free enterprise has become. While so-called "Free Enterprise" is usually blamed for our present discontents, the facts of the matter are actually far different, since we do not have, nor have we had for some time in this country, anything approaching "Free Enterprise."

The New Politics

Any capable observer should be able to see that there has been a gradual and mounting circumscription of liberty in America in the twentieth century. It manifests itself in the spreading tentacles of government control and regulation, in the concentration of power in the federal government, in government by presidential decree, in the unchecked rulings of independent commissions, in the proliferating activities of government agencies, in the virtual confiscation of earnings by means of the progressive income tax, and by a diminishing control of their property by owners.[1]

[1]Clarence B. Carson, *The Fateful Turn* (Irvington, N.Y.: Foundation for Economic Education, 1963), p. 71.

The climate of opinion which has produced this state of affairs has its origin in the intellectual fashions of our times. We are all far more dependent upon certain preconceptions than we realize, and these preconceptions usually come about as the result of various catchwords and concepts in current intellectual vogue.

Joseph Schumpeter has emphasized that the intellectuals who originate a "climate of opinion" are generally characterized by their absence of direct responsibility for practical affairs. That lack of direct responsibility, coupled with the inevitable absence of firsthand information as to the actual workings of a given social order, has tended to mark the typical intellectual, the man with the power of the spoken and written word, as a peculiarly inept policy maker who is always in the vanguard of those wishing to make policy.

Until one begins to list all the professions and activities which belong to this class, it is difficult to realize how numerous it is, how the scope for its activities constantly increases in modern society, and how dependent on it we all have become. The class does not consist only of journalists, teachers, ministers, lecturers, publicists, radio commentators, writers of fiction, cartoonists, and artists . . . all of whom may be masters of the technique of conveying ideas but are usually amateurs so far as the substance of what they convey is concerned. The class also includes many professional men and technicians, such as scientists and doctors, who through their habitual intercourse with the printed word become carriers of new ideas outside their own fields and who, because of their expert knowledge on their own subjects, are listened to with respect on most others. There is little that the ordinary man of today learns about events or ideas except through the medium of this class; and outside our special fields of work we are in this respect almost all ordinary men, dependent for our information and instruction on those who make it their job to keep abreast of opinion. It is the intellectuals in this sense who decide what views and opinions are to reach us, which facts are important enough to be told to us and in what form and from what angle they are to be presented. Whether we shall ever learn of the results of the work of the expert and the original thinker depends mainly on their decision.[2]

The major broadcast networks, with a governmentally enforced monopoly of mass communication provided by the FCC, have control over what news and views reach the public. This control of communication, and

[2]Friedrich A. Hayek, "The Intellectuals and Socialism," *University of Chicago Law Review,* Spring 1949, pp. 418–419.

therefore of the climate of opinion, extends to include publishers of many of the most popular magazines and newspapers, the prominent academic chairs in various institutions of higher learning, the movie makers, the most prestigious pulpits, and so on throughout American life. It is not surprising that this monopoly of opinion making should have produced the results it has in the minds of typical Americans. The only surprising portion of the entire operation is the emotional boost which the modern "liberal" has derived from his apparently sincere belief that he is a member of a beleaguered minority, fighting a capitalistic, materialistic power structure. In fact, the liberal Establishment described above has long since become the dominant power structure of American society.

As the interventionist mentality has come to dominate our opinion-molding process, and as intervention has come to dominate American society, the intellectuals of the Left have also undergone a change. We have now gone far beyond the unsophisticated "socialism" of a few decades ago. Today the Left-wing intellectual tends to think in terms of power segments controlling society, each gigantic, each balancing the other segments. No longer is bigness in government the sole area of concentration. Today bigness throughout all social institutions is assumed to be both necessary and desirable. Such a change makes the interventionist position more subtle and more difficult to counteract than the older socialism. No longer does the socialist assume that nationalization is the final answer to all problems. Today he is far more likely to be willing to leave property in private hands so long as he is able to achieve centralized control through the alternative means of large, interlocking segments of power.

Those intellectuals who have led the way in this striving for bigness and the planned society, together with the generations of Americans who have come to accept such a social situation as the only means of solving our problems, have been led to embrace bigness for a variety of reasons, ranging from "social justice" and "economic security" to the "necessity for planning in the modern world." The new faith in an organic view of society has largely had its way. Americans have accepted the collective ideal in the peculiar form of institutional bigness which dominates modern society, when they would never have accepted the same collective ideals advanced in the normal socialist terms.

And while the intellectuals were generating a form of bigness and collective social organization which would be acceptable to the American citizenry, the process of bigness thus engendered was itself producing more intellectuals likely to encourage such a system:

The all-pervasive influence of the intellectuals in contemporary society is still further strengthened by the growing importance of "organization." It is a common but probably mistaken belief that the increase of organization increases the influence of the expert or specialist. This may be true of the expert administrator and organizer, if there are such people, but hardly of the expert in any particular field of knowledge. It is rather the person whose general knowledge is supposed to qualify him to appreciate expert testimony, and to judge between the experts from different fields, whose power is enhanced. The point which is important for us, however, is that the scholar who becomes a university president, the scientist who takes charge of an institute or foundation, the scholar who becomes an editor or the active promoter of an organization serving a particular cause, all rapidly cease to be scholars or experts and become intellectuals in our sense, people who judge all issues not by their specific merits but, in the characteristic manner of intellectuals, solely in the light of certain fashionable general ideas. The number of such institutions which breed intellectuals and increase their number and powers grows every day.[3]

The narrowing of objectives which Hayek describes is an inevitable development of bureaucratic organization. It is to be found not only in big government and big business, but in any form of bigness. The more complex the organization becomes, the more necessary that it renounce all side issues and all limitations in order to perpetuate itself. Thus stabilization becomes the key word. We are no longer interested in production in business, efficiency in government, salvation in religion or victory in military affairs. No, instead let us be assured that "stabilization" will guarantee the continued existence of the power structure which has grown up.

Such institutional enmassment makes a mockery of presumed differences between the "public sector" and the "private sector." Public or private, such bigness seems to have as its primary objective a social control over the life of the individual. We should not be surprised that such vast powers of control are then used to maintain the existing situation, whatever the cost may be to the individuals who are controlled in the process.

Halfway House to Total Control

It is the proudest boast of the modern American social order that America has achieved "a redistribution of wealth which removes all point and purpose from the Marxian critique of Western capitalism." Proclaiming themselves the middle of the road between a decadent, dog-eat-dog capitalist order and the totalitarian Communist experiment which was presumably the only alternative until modern "liberalism" arrived on the scene, the modern proponents of the new bigness in government and in society are

[3]*Ibid.*, pp. 419–420.

likely to attribute all contemporary "progress" to their enlightened leadership. Actually, American "liberalism" in its twentieth-century form, being
the cumulative effect of the reform currents of the past 100 years, is less a
halfway house between capitalism and communism than a halfway house
on the road between individual freedom and total control:

> From this perspective, the inhabitants of the halfway house can be
> called progressives. The progressive believes that the direction of
> civilization is mainly along the lines that it should be and that Ameri-
> can society is essentially sound. He generally deplores unfavorable
> critiques of his civilization and is inclined to the view that their
> propagators are cranks. He supports the central developments of the
> twentieth century: industrialization, automation, mass production,
> mass media of communication, rapid transportation, the compiling of
> data by scientists, internationalism, and the breaking down of region-
> alism and localism. He approves the centralization of authority, ra-
> tionalization of the economy, the homogenization of the population
> (removal of local, racial, religious, or any other group distinguishing
> features), and increases in public services provided by governmental
> agencies. All of these he is apt to associate with progress.[4]

Progress indeed! But we may find ourselves progressing toward a spiritual
collectivization and proletarianization, a concept of mass-man, a degree of
institutional enmassment, that is calculated to destroy the very bases of
social organization, making tradition, continuity, the rule of law, the concept of private property, and above all, the concept of individual human
personality, no longer capable of maintenance in the modern world.

Government by and for Special Interest

The imposition of this total group control is disguised and softened by
the various "special benefits" which the new system offers to those groups
which appear potent enough to provide serious opposition. The welfare
state itself, of course, operates according to this principle, providing heavy
taxes for all, to be followed by selective political redistribution of the wealth.
Not all forms of partnership in the new bigness are so readily apparent as
the connection between welfare state and welfare recipient. More subtle
examples would include the neo-mercantilism which dominates present-day
society:

> Commercial clubs in the cities, industrial commissions in the states,
> and governors' conferences in the regions all [have] joined in sponsor-

[4]Carson, pp. 178–179.

ship of industrial expansion. The story sprawls out to ungovernable proportions, to tax exemptions, police-guaranteed labor discipline, municipal power-plant construction, and on to RFC, TVA, and AEC. . . . From the grass roots putting up shoots before Chamber of Commerce buildings to the Office of the President's Council of Economic Advisers there can be documented the unceasing pressure for public sponsorship of economic growth.[5]

At times it has been difficult to tell whether government is promoting business or business is encouraging government.

The desire for publicly induced business expansion has spilled over to all sorts of other groups as well. We have labor unions, farmers alliances, professional organizations, all ready and willing to use their own bigness and the bigness of government to achieve specialized ends.

The difference between a collectivistic society and an individualistic one can be succinctly stated. Where individual liberty is the goal, the government will exist, in considerable part, to *disarm* collectives. In a collectivist society, government will act to *empower* groups. The shift for America, then, came at those points when governments ceased to disarm groups effectively and began to empower them.[6]

The process of empowering the special interest groups throughout society has carried enmassment to its final conclusion in American life. Today the individual finds fewer and fewer opportunities to act apart from the bigness of government and the bigness of the other institutions within society. Increasingly, government is thought of as the arbiter among great blocs of countervailing power. Presumably, big government will act to see that big labor, big business, big farm organizations, big consumer groups, and big groups of every other conceivable sort will all receive their proper share of special interest treatment. Of course, this notion of equal privileges for each special interest is not a new form of social organization. In Fascist Italy it was called the Corporate State.

The New-Style Businessman

The saddest aspect of the development of the special interest mentality in American life has been that those groups with most to lose, groups from whom leadership might have been expected in the preservation of a more private and independent form of economic and social organization, have

---

[5]Robert A. Lively, "The American System: A Review Article," *The Shaping of Twentieth-Century America,* selected and with commentary by Richard M. Abrams and Lawrence W. Levine (Boston: Little, Brown, 1965), pp. 21–22.
[6]Carson, p. 110.

been quickest to throw away their independence in the rush to become an ally of government. All too many American businessmen fit this description. Why did this happen?

One reason may be the new technology. The extensions of bureaucracy throughout the business community and the extensions of government research contracts have tended to make the interests of more and more large firms closely parallel the interests of government. The space program, nuclear development, and similar programs have tended to create a situation in which only those companies most closely in contact with government could be full participants in the development of the new technology.

Despite the close connection between business and government, for decades the businessman has written articles and made speeches extolling the virtues of free enterprise and tough competition — without fully believing in competition. It is only lately that more and more of America's business leaders are beginning to stress the close ties between government and business which have already existed for so long. Some of our corporate heads, having made this discovery, or at least having come to believe that the American people are ready for such revelations, have been sounding a theme quite different than that espoused by the traditional American businessman:

> Talk about effective cooperation between business and government is giving way to action. Only recently we have begun to join in efforts to alleviate urban and social ills which bedevil our society and contradict our prosperity. Business is training and hiring the hard-core unemployed, helping to give minorities a better economic break. Business, with government, is helping to restore, renew, and rebuild our cities and our countryside. We work together to shape our national policy, and to fulfill our public purpose. And there is much, much more for us to do together.
>
> As the challenges to our nation intensify and multiply, we can expect — and should encourage — business and government to draw even closer together. Both the business community and our country stand to gain if we work together — if we come together, not as adversaries, but as allies.[7]

Increasingly, the connection between big business and big government, brought about amidst the rhetoric of "public goals," is producing a climate of opinion in which something loosely described as "the industrial system" is no longer considered apart from government. All activities of business are

[7]James M. Roche, "Understanding: The Key to Business–Government Cooperation," *Michigan Business Review,* March 1969, p. 7.

assumed to be a matter of public policy. Professor Galbraith has made this abundantly clear in *The New Industrial State:*

> So comprehensive a relationship cannot be denied or ignored indefinitely. Increasingly it will be recognized that the mature corporation, as it develops, becomes part of the larger administrative complex associated with the state. In time the line between the two will disappear. Men will look back in amusement at the pretense that once caused people to refer to General Dynamics and North American and A. T. & T. as *private* business.

The older, entrepreneurial businessman, of the sort who resisted the encroachments of government 35 years ago, has been replaced by the new organization man. His place in the corporate bureaucracy, and his corporation's place within the new industrial complex of big business and big government, are both based upon repudiation of everything that the older entrepreneur represented. The passing of the entrepreneur is due partially to the rise of the new bureaucracy both public and private, but it is also due, as future historians of American business may one day discover, to a deliberate conspiracy between the new-style businessman and the state. Friedrich Hayek's warning that socialism in its radical form was never so dangerous as socialism in its conservative form deserves our careful reconsideration. When the advocates of state power and the advocates of corporate bigness form an alliance, the resultant form, however conservative, is still socialistic.

The New Alliance and How It Feeds upon Bigness

Bigness in one area of society seems to further bigness in other areas. For example, the universities and foundations have come to have a vested interest in the existing state of affairs. The present tax structure strongly encourages corporate contributions to foundations and educational institutions. These "contributions" are really gifts of stockholders' money. The stockholders have little or no control over such a transaction. Not only does this encourage a heavy dependence upon such giants on the part of the university and the foundation, but it also displays the steadily shrinking control which the stockholders have over the large American corporation. Observation of these phenomena is not limited to any single portion of the political spectrum. The extent to which the present corporate tax structure encourages bigness in universities and foundations, plus the accompanying loss of stockholder control over corporate assets, has been noted by observers as widely separated as Milton Friedman and John Kenneth Galbraith.

The same bureaucrats holding positions within the corporate structure are likely to be the close working associates of the bureaucrats in the universities and private foundations supported by the corporations. Both are likely to be in and out of various appointive positions in government, while the foundations and universities make policy studies concerning how business and government should operate their affairs. And so the steady round of mutual support and perpetual congratulation continues. Bureaucracy develops its own bureaucratic class. A decade ago, when Richard LaPiere wrote *The Freudian Ethic,* he pointed out that American business organizations were increasingly bureaucratic in character. He went on to say, "The present leaders are, of course, products of the older and freer enterprise system; and it remains to be seen what their successors, products of bureaucracy and skilled mainly in the arts of bureaucratic routine, will do when they come to assume command." It no longer remains to be seen. The new generation of bureaucrats is behaving exactly as could have been predicted.

The Socialist Switch — Big Business Becomes an Ally

The old antitrust assumption which lay at the heart of most socialist rhetoric is simply no longer enforcible in the modern world. The socialists would find it necessary to regulate the great majority of American business out of existence if the enforcement of "competition" in the old sense were attempted. This is probably all to the good, since American competition has always been essentially a competition in innovation, rather than competition according to the textbook model. This is a point which Joseph Schumpeter has made abundantly clear. Thus the socialists have had to retreat to the concept of "public interest." Today's bureaucrats in both business and government constantly urge action "in the public interest." The socialists, or interventionists of various other descriptions, have found it largely necessary to abandon their assumption that business must be broken up by government. The temptation of an even more enormous power structure, composed of big business *and* big government, has won the day.

One of the great problems of Britain's Labor party has been a failure to find a suitable successor for the Webbs. Britain has never developed socialist theoreticians to replace the earlier generation of anti–big business thinkers. But the doctrinaire liberals of America, who also had earlier advocated big government controls of business, breaking up the trusts, etc., *have* had their successors who could adapt the old ideas to the new age. For example, Professor Galbraith has now come to encourage bigness for its own sake as the wave of the future — in the name of the "public interest," of course:

If the "liberal" before World War II paid any attention to business enterprise, he was "against" it. He certainly had no use for "big business" and seriously doubted that it performed any reputable function. He was, on the whole, convinced that a business could be big only because of monopolistic malpractices. Today, some "liberals" are equally uncritical in their admiration of big business: the "capitalist revolution" has become an overworked slogan. Such distinguished members of the old liberal leadership as David Lilienthal (builder of the TVA) and Adolf Berle (President Roosevelt's original "brain truster" and later his Assistant Secretary of State), now expect from big business all the blessings they formerly expected from government, including the fulfillment of our promises of civil liberties and individual opportunities.[8]

In *Capitalism, Socialism and Democracy,* Joseph Schumpeter predicted the end of the capitalist order, not because capitalism would fail as the most effective producer, but because it would generate a kind of bigness eventually making even capitalism itself impossible.[9]

Schumpeter predicted that the stockholders would finally hold such a negligible position of *real* ownership and control within American business that the roots of capitalism would be strangled. He made the same prediction concerning freedom of contract:

> Freedom of contracting is in the same boat. In its full vitality it meant individual contracting regulated by individual choice between an indefinite number of possibilities. The stereotyped, unindividual, impersonal and bureaucratized contract of today . . . has none of the old features the most important of which become impossible with giant concerns dealing with other giant concerns or impersonal masses of workmen or consumers.[10]

Schumpeter made it abundantly clear what the final result of these processes would be. His words have a prophetic ring today:

> Thus the capitalist process pushes into the background all those institutions, the institutions of property and free contracting in particular, that expressed the needs and ways of the truly "private" economic activity. Where it does not abolish them, as it already has abolished free contracting in the labor market, it attains the same end by shifting the relative importance of existing legal forms — the legal forms pertaining to corporate business for instance as against those pertaining to the partnership or individual firm — or by changing their contents or meanings. The capitalist process, by substituting a mere parcel of

[8]Peter F. Drucker, *Concept of the Corporation* (Boston: Beacon Press, 1960), p. viii.
[9]Joseph A. Schumpeter, *Capitalism, Socialism, and Democracy* (New York: Harper and Brothers, 1950), p. 156.
[10]*Ibid.,* p. 141.

shares for the walls of and the machines in a factory, takes the life out
of the idea of property. It loosens the grip that once was so strong
— the grip in the sense of the legal right and the actual ability to do
as one pleases with one's own; the grip also in the sense that the holder
of the title loses the will to fight, economically, physically, politically,
for "his" factory and his control over it, to die if necessary on its steps.
And this evaporation of what we may term the material substance of
property — its visible and touchable reality — affects not only the
attitude of holders but also that of the workmen and of the public in
general. Dematerialized, defunctionalized, and absentee ownership
does not impress and call forth moral allegiance as the vital form of
property did. Eventually there will be *nobody* left who really cares to
stand for it — nobody within and nobody without the precincts of the
big concerns.[11]

Schumpeter may have been mistaken in his insistence that the process of
eventual collapse was inevitable. I believe that he was. For the present,
however, the course of our present society would suggest that there is a
great deal of truth in the possibility he raised. Nowhere is this erosion of
entrepreneurial capitalism more evident than in the small operator and his
problems. The small entrepreneur continues his struggle for his place in the
sun, even at this late date. Despite the fact that the number and size of giant
firms in the American market continue to increase, the market itself has
grown so much faster than those firms that today there are more small firms
than 30, 40, or 50 years ago. Small business has always been praised as the
seedbed from which a great concern might grow. Actually, this is a little
misleading, since most small firms are not in primary industries. They are
more likely to be in the insurance business, engaged in the operation of a
restaurant, running the corner drugstore, the community bottling plant or
lumber yard. These are not unimportant services, but they are not the sort
of service likely to change a particular small businessman into a giant
operator. Meanwhile, the advantages of close cooperation with the government which are so readily available to the giants of American business are
simply not available to most corner druggists, automobile dealers, or drive-
in movie operators.

The same inability to share in the new partnership between big business
and big government has also plagued the marginal family farmer. Everyone
over 40 years of age will recall that the original intent of the AAA in the
1930s was to "save the family farm." Yet in the last 35 years the number
of farms in the United States has declined by nearly one-half while the size
of the remaining farms has substantially increased. Here again, we are
confronted with the same situation. The small farmer simply cannot com-

pete effectively in a world of bigness in which government help is extended primarily to those farm operators of sufficient size to profit from government programs. Thus bigness encourages bigness, and, by omission, punishes the small operator.

One Yale professor visited a farmer in upstate New York who had been operating a small dairy. The farmer told him of an inspector who had seen a single cattle dropping twenty feet from the small farmer's scrupulously clean barn. The inspector had threatened to blacklist the farmer. As the Yale professor concludes the story, "The farmer remarked that cattle were hub deep in manure in another dairy not far away, only to be shrugged off with the comment, 'That's different. It's a big business.' Many other factors, not so deliberately stupid or malicious, combine to make life impossible for the small rural operation. These include types of subsidy, design of farm machinery, and character of bank credit."[12]

Licensure and the New Guildism

While government has handicapped the small farmer in his fight for survival, what have government and its various uses done to other small operators wishing to enter business? The role of government licensure is specifically worth examining as a partial answer to that question:

> . . . with the twentieth century came a veritable deluge of licensing laws. By 1952 more than 80 separate occupations, exclusive of "owner-business" like restaurants and taxicab companies, had been licensed by state law; and in addition to the state laws there are municipal ordinances in abundance, not to mention the federal statutes that require the licensing of such diverse occupations as radio operators and stockyard commission agents. As long ago as 1938 a single state, North Carolina, had extended its laws to 60 occupations. One may not be surprised to learn that pharmacists, accountants, and dentists have been reached by state laws, as have sanitarians and psychologists, assayers and architects, veterinarians and librarians. But with what joy of discovery does one learn about the licensing of threshing machine operators and dealers in scrap tobacco? What of egg graders and guide-dog trainers, pest controllers and yacht salesmen, tree surgeons and well diggers, tile layers and potato growers? And what of the hypertrichologists who are licensed in Connecticut, where they remove excessive and unsightly hairs with the solemnity appropriate to their high-sounding title?[13]

[12]Paul B. Sears, "Old Nature, Modern Man," *Audubon,* May–June 1968, p. 78.
[13]Walter Gellhorn, *Individual Freedom and Governmental Restraints* (New York: Greenwood Press, 1968), p. 106.

Meanwhile, licensure in connection with "owner-businesses" is also having its effect on the small operator. Taxicab licensure in New York City has now driven the cost of a medallion (the right to drive a taxicab on the streets of New York City) to over $30,000, a fact not likely to encourage the small operator who desires to own and drive his own cab.

And from what source comes the demand for this licensure? From the consumer? No indeed! From those already within the various occupations, those bringing group pressure to bear to advance the monopoly position and special interest of the group. It seems that the "ins" are quite willing to use the bigness of government to insure their own position at the expense of the consumer and of any potential competitor.

The new guildism, already so evident in licensure, is equally in evidence within the existing labor union movement. Here, monopoly power has been granted to 25 percent of the work force. This power to withhold goods and services from the general public, and to withhold the opportunity to pursue a skilled trade from the individual workman, is then used against all comers by the particular form of bigness which we call "organized labor," (it being clearly understood that absolutely no connection exists between "organized labor" and what used to be called "the workingman").

The new guildism in all its forms has certain common characteristics. While the medieval guild member would not have understood what we mean by "the controlled economy," his modern counterpart has a very clear idea of who is being controlled and the forces which do the controlling. The modern guildsman firmly believes that the organizational whole is more than the sum of its individual members. In the new guild framework, the bureaucracies of big government and of big business are again closely paralleled. This bureaucracy is quick to regard its special interest as the final and highest expression of that most abused term, "the American way of life." Here again, the rush toward organizational bigness has paralyzed the previous American genius for allowing the individual to pursue the development of his own skills and his own business enterprises as he sees fit, while allowing the rest of us to judge as consumers whether or not he merits our business. In the new guildism, as in virtually every other walk of American life, the place reserved for the individual becomes steadily more tenuous.

The Fate of the Small Operator

The present bigness of society, acting primarily through government, has still other effects in making it difficult for the small operator to continue in existence. Our present tax policies and the continuing monetary inflation together make capital formation exceedingly difficult for the small operator. Inflation, induced by government, works its havoc upon the common man who is the holder of a savings account, the operator of a small business, the recipient of a pension. The man with larger holdings can more easily protect himself, and indeed often appears to feather his nest in the process. Fortunately, many men of means are also men of integrity, but this in no way lightens the burden for the small independent citizen who cannot keep pace with the inflationary trend of his society.

One of the demonstrations of the peculiar capital market in operation in present-day America is the tendency to tear down sound, functional buildings and existing businesses. It seems that "the pressure is on" only for bigness and newness, a pressure readily apparent in bank credit, in licensure, and in government policies on all levels. Capital is more readily available for large operations than it is for small. Governmental centralization is surely one reason for this tendency. Aldous Huxley long ago commented upon a parallel reason at work in the private sector:

> In applying the results of disinterested scientific research, inventors and technicians have paid more attention to the problem of equipping large concerns with the expensive machinery of mass production and mass distribution than to that of providing individuals or cooperating groups with cheap and simple, but effective, means of production for their own subsistence and for the needs of a local market. The reason for this is that there has been more money in working for the mass producers and mass distributors; and the mass producers and mass distributors have had more money because financiers have seen that there was more profit for them, and more power, in a centralized than in a decentralized system of production.[14]

Tax policy also presses upon the small operator in a variety of ways. The sole owner of a family business is more likely to sell out before his death because of the inheritance tax situation, and because of the complexity of the tax structure, than he is to pass on such problems at his death. Thus the more successful a family business, the more likely that it will not remain in the family. At the same time, the high corporate income tax rate, coupled with the high personal income tax rates on dividends paid by corporations, makes it extremely attractive for corporations to plow earnings into an expansion of corporate holdings rather than into declared dividends. This has a tendency to make the existing corporations larger, while making it steadily more and more difficult for the small operator, since it restricts the formation of a new capital market. Henry Ford might not have been able to raise the capital necessary for the operation he was starting, had he been called upon to do so in our present society.

Thus there is steadily less room for the individual worker and the individ-

---

[14]Aldous Huxley, *Science, Liberty and Peace* (New York: Harper and Brothers, 1946), pp. 12–13.

ual businessman, either inside or outside big business and big labor. The individual worker or the individual employee finds it harder and harder to function as an individual inside the system, and yet the pressures generated by the big society leave him less and less room to function outside the system.

In a nation which used to pride itself upon the opportunity it extended to every small man to go into business for himself, the present pressure of big government has created a great handicap for small business in tax problems, accounting, regulatory activity, and similar involvements. Today the little man must be large enough to hire his own tax man and his own attorney, or he is likely to be snowed under by bureaucratic detail.

We are confronted with a society in which genuine competition is neither desired nor permitted by the existing power structure, a society in which the small operator, be he worker or businessman, must come to terms with big government, big business, and big labor, whether he attempts to remain outside or is absorbed within the system. In effect, we have lost the American capacity to build a successful society around the concept of the freely choosing individual.

Epilogue

Between the political philosophy of the Founding Fathers and the ideology
of the Sears, Roebuck catalogue, there stretches the fascinating — and still
largely untold — story of what happened to the democratic idea in America.

Irving Kristol,
"American Historians and the Democratic Idea."

It may be that the new system of bigness ministers to our every material
need. I doubt it. But even if the prophets of bigness were right about that,
they would still be wrong in their advocacy of such bigness — men have
other needs over and above the merely material. Our present society fails
in a number of ways to meet those needs. Men must have a reason for living.
Thus the alienation described in *The Age of Bewilderment.* Given our
present society, such alienation seems inevitable.

Small wonder men are alienated. The historical connection between our
present problems and government seems almost unmistakable. Government
has been deeply involved in the enmassment of society at virtually all points
along the way for the past 100 years of our history:

1. The development of the nineteenth century plutocracy,
2. which led to the Progressive era,
3. which led directly to the organization and techniques dominating
   the Twenties,
4. which led to the New Deal,
5. which has given us a continuation of the same big government, big
   society ideology ever since.

The examples and illustrations in the previous pages could easily have
been multiplied many times.This glance at a century of American history
was not intended to be exhaustive, but it should have made clear certain
strains of thought and action which have had unmistakable impact upon
our social order. How odd it is today to hear government intervention
recommended as a problem-solving device for our present discontents,
when government has been so deeply implicated in producing the problems!

Government may be the culprit, but it is the culprit in a special way which we usually fail to recognize. It is deeply entangled in our history and our attitudes. So long as we refuse to admit the wide degree of collective involvement which has already occurred in our institutions and our lives, our analysis of what needs to be done will be woefully incomplete. For example, until we come to admit the extent to which bigness has already come upon us, it will be difficult to see clearly that it is the fear of that bigness which has driven the American population to total acceptance of the collectivist mentality as it prevails today, under a variety of labels.

Men reacted in fear of the bigness which was coming upon them by forming together in groups — pressure groups, farm groups, business groups, labor groups — as a means of achieving certain political results designed to protect individuals. Unfortunately, we now have 100 years of hindsight to see that most of these group activities and most of the political results stemming from them furthered the very bigness they were designed to prevent. The result has been continued enmassment, above all in government itself, dwarfing any of the previous enmassments which originally raised our fears:

Sixty years ago, before World War I, the social scene everywhere looked much like the Kansas prairie: The largest thing on the horizon was the individual. Most social tasks were accomplished in and through family-sized units. Even government, no matter how formidable it looked, was really small and cozy. The government of Imperial Germany looked like a colossus to its contemporaries; but an official in the middle ranks could still know personally everyone of importance in every single ministry and department.

The scaling-up in size since then is striking. There is no country in the world today where the entire government establishment of 1910 could not comfortably be housed in the smallest of the new government buildings now going up, with room to spare for a grand-opera house and a skating rink.[1]

The result of this centralization of governmental authority has been a series of centralizations among private institutions. The interaction of these public and private centralizations has produced an enforced social homogenization, breaking down the older forms of family, local, and personal associations which previously characterized American society. Giantism has bred giantism, bureaucracy has bred bureaucracy, until the individual citizen can continue his existence only by finding a place within the various bignesses which confront him. Professor Galbraith promises the individual

[1]Peter F. Drucker, *The Age of Discontinuity* (New York: Harper & Row, 1968), pp. 171–172.

that the enormous institutions of our times will countervail one another's powers. This would seem to be small comfort to the individual, who would presumably be among the giants at their moment of collision.

All the alienations and fears described in *The Age of Bewilderment* seem predictable in an age in which the individual finds himself less and less able to chart his own destiny. The world of the planner and bureaucrat is quick to accommodate such insecurity, and promises steadily more government aid and institutional support for the wavering individual. Thus the growth of government and bigness in our present society has generated the demand for more of the same. Small wonder that David Riesman could describe us as a lonely crowd of "other directed" people!

Meanwhile, the critical disadvantage of the trend toward bureaucracy and bigness throughout American life is that such bureaucracy always brings with it an increasingly noncompetitive system, giving preference to the most unenterprising among us. Thus, as the result of our lost freedom, we will finally lose our prosperity as well. Our society will finally become so "stable" that it will no longer function at all. As symptoms of this creeping "stability" appear among us, they generate still greater demand among our increasingly anti-independent population for more of the regulation and restraint and "organization" which is already causing the trouble.

Even at this admittedly late date, a deeply concerned American citizenry, although no longer sure just what has happened to it, does sense something wrong. As the result, many Americans have become increasingly suspicious of the present direction of our society. Attempts to articulate this uncertain feeling are usually dismissed as "nostalgia" or as "attempts to turn back the clock." There are vague mutterings about the "Eastern Establishment," suspicions that the great "powers that be" are dominating American life. Such talk is not new to American history. The Jacksonians of the 1830s were saying almost exactly the same thing about the Establishment of their time, including the powerful Bank of the United States.

The Americans of the 1830s won their struggle against special privilege and centralized power. What will historians record concerning the Americans of the 1970s?

3

A Reason
for Living

Prologue

Men do not simply stop work to think: "The age is ending." At most, they sometimes catch themselves thinking: "It has all got too big. Life has got too big. Government is too big. The cities are too big. Even the buildings are too big. The problems are too vast. The solutions are too complex, and each solution breeds new complexity."

Whittaker Chambers,
Cold Friday

What has impelled the American people toward collectivism? If the answer can be given in a single phrase, that answer must be: *the triumph of mass society.* We all know that something of the sort is happening to us, although we have little idea what this means for our lives and for the future. By mass society, I do not mean merely large society. Mass society is better understood as a qualitative than a quantitative term. Anonymity seems to be the key descriptive word for the mass society, as its members forfeit a steadily increasing portion of their individuality and personality. No wonder Mr. Anonymous no longer feels master of his destiny, surrounded as he is by massive institutions in which he is obliged to play a stereotyped role. Nor is it surprising that he reacts by turning to democratic government in all its bigness to represent and defend him against other monstrous institutions. Unfortunately, the bigness growing from collective political action has proven to be the most anti-individualistic of all such forces in modern America.

In an age of technological triumph, man finds he is lord of all things, except himself. Despite our wealth of material means and "factual" knowledge, we find ourselves adrift, uneasy and unsatisfied. We experience simultaneous power and insecurity and find the situation intolerable:

There are not a few signs today that in this America of ours, there is wide revolt against the direction that our life has taken. We are no longer sure that we are to achieve social and economic democracy by giving everyone except minors and idiots the vote; that wealth will create a satisfying scale of values for us; that by losing our individuality so that every want can be satisfied under a national brand we shall somehow attain to a higher standard of living. In a word there is a good bit of questioning of democracy as it has developed; an interest in people who have insisted on being themselves and suiting themselves, even at the risk of being called snobs; a questioning of all concepts, including those of failure and success.[1]

Perhaps this growing sense of revolt has come about primarily from the annihilating sense of futility and boredom which epitomizes mass society. Unfortunately, the shrillness of most contemporary social criticism suggests a shallow immaturity of critic and audience alike — all too little investigation of ultimate purpose and meaning in human life.

There are signs that history is either at a dead end or at a major turning point. All history worthy of the name has emphasized human personality and the moral framework within which that personality could operate; but today those values seem to have been rejected, not only by society, but also by most social critics. To put this another way, history has always been concerned with how men dealt with environment and circumstance, man's attempt to relate *himself* to the universe. Take away that concept of self and you take away the human element that makes history. Today we seem to have withdrawn from history. We have been taught that history is irrelevant — presumably because modern man has superseded previous human experience. At least that has been the dominant message during the first 70 years of the twentieth century. Now, we are no longer so sure. . . .

Still, the need persists for personality and for real people, individuals struggling with their environment. The question of individual personality may no longer concern most social critics, but it does concern many men. This may be the reason for the growing interest of the general public in biography and history. This may even explain why the young person who today feels himself so overcome by standardization will avidly devour movies or books whose central character insists upon being a genuine person. Perhaps this explains the cults which have grown up lately surrounding the racketeers and movie stars of a bygone era. At least they were somebody, and almost anybody may seem attractive in a society of nobodies.

Social Protest

Social protest in contemporary America also stems from our capacity to take so many blessings for granted. It seems that men will value freedom or economic well-being only after they have lost it — being all too willing to sell a national birthright for a mess of pottage. Endless promises of

[1]James Truslow Adams, introduction, pp. ix–x of Henry Adams, *The Education of Henry Adams* (New York: Modern Library, 1931).

"progress" leave us disillusioned when labor unions, women's suffrage, universal education, or any of the other societal panaceas fail to produce the expected millennium. This false notion of inevitable "progress" may be the reason why a generation of young people can dismiss the very real accomplishments and improvements of the past 200 years as fake and worthless. To these young people, only the total destruction of established society seems to offer any "solutions." One cannot help wondering what will be "solved" by sweeping away all the institutions and attitudes that have made this the most free and most prosperous people on earth.

I think that great social and educational changes could occur almost immediately if, for instance, we could teach our young people to give up their unreal perfectionism, their demands for perfect human beings, a perfect society, perfect teachers, perfect parents, perfect politicians, perfect marriages, perfect friends, perfect organizations, etc., none of which exist and simply cannot exist — that is, except for transient moments of peak-experience, of perfect fusion, etc. Such expectations we already know, even with our inadequate knowledge, are illusions and, therefore, must inevitably and inexorably breed disillusionment along with attendant disgust, rage, depression, and revenge. The demand for "Nirvana Now!" is itself a major source of evil, I am finding. If you demand a perfect leader or a perfect society, you thereby give up choosing between better and worse. If the imperfect is defined as evil, then everything becomes evil, since everything is imperfect.[2]

Not just the young, but all of us have been exposed to the various forms of contagious utopianism peculiar to our times. Many are infected. Mass communications and the academic community are filled with examples of the belief that future events can be predicted on the basis of past and present trends. Most of us seem to accept the fiction that it is possible to measure mathematically all the values of society and thus "scientifically" determine what society's course of action "must" be. In looking for easy solutions to involved social problems, we are all too willing to attempt a quantification of human nature in order to discover or implement a panacea.

For at least two generations, Americans have sought major social changes, the sooner the better. But today's third generation demands total change and "do it now!" So far, this sweeping away of all institutions and customs is largely confined to the negative: "First destroy the existing order, and then we'll decide where we go from there."

[2]Abraham H. Maslow, *Motivation and Personality* (2nd ed.; New York: Harper and Row, 1970), p. xxii.

Typically, today's youth is "turned off" by the state of society. Is this, then, the beginning of the end, when people have so little faith in the old system that it falls of its own weight? Perhaps — but, oddly enough, such vague "systems" as have been proposed by the young seem to show an even greater reliance upon socialism and collective solutions than those "solutions" advocated within the present system. To the extent that today's young radicals have any plan at all beyond destruction of the existing order, that plan seems to be even more collective and even more mindless than the society against which they rebel. Surely, that way lies destruction.

Social Change

Neither today's young radicals nor their "liberal" parents and grandparents seem to have an accurate idea of the processes involved in social change. Many so-called "conservatives," and nearly all modern "liberals" of the social planning variety, have been on the wrong track. Beneficial social change involves far more than the protest of the young or the social planning of their elders. It hinges on questions largely unrecognized by current political leaders and planners.

One thing is certain: We can never go back. If it were possible to return to the past, we should be disappointed with our personal lives and our public institutions. One cannot go home again, and the nostalgic conservative attempt is doomed to defeat and frustration. Complete satisfaction is not to be found in the position of conservative traditionalists. Hilaire Belloc described himself and similar traditionalists as "sufferers who will probably fail." This may suffice for a tradition of literary criticism or for a code of personal conduct. Indeed, I admit that such a code is very attractive to me personally, but it affords sorry leadership for the American future. The attempt to put ideas or societies in pigeonholes is likely to destroy the very individuality and freedom one would preserve. There is a vital difference between a living tradition and a museum piece.

Still, conservatives have been partially right. Institutions do not originate in a vacuum, nor are they maintained by mere social utility. In another, more optimistic, phrase of Belloc: "Institutions rise from a certain spirit inhabiting Society, a spirit of which they are the product; and they are maintained by men's acceptance of that spirit."[3] Institutions must be a reflection of such a spirit if they are to remain viable.

What are the elements of that spirit? Surely a people whose institutions will survive must possess a sense of history. History teaches men to be aware that they have a history. The liberating discovery that others have lived and died provides a sense of participation in a larger process than our little moment in time, involving us in questions of greater magnitude than the

---

[3]Hilaire Belloc, *The Crisis of Our Civilization* (London: Cassell, 1937), p. 195.

trivia filling most of our books, newspapers, and television screens. How else are we to achieve the continuity which comes from valuing what we already have?

Change goes on, and in one sense we are all revolutionaries . . . certainly the record of the American people reveals great changes and advances. But the revolutionary achievement of America has come because we were willing to hold onto so many values even while we erected new and radically different institutions as an expression of those values. In short, we have been successful in the conduct of our revolutionary social change to precisely the extent that we have been traditionalist in conserving our older ways of feeling and acting. These older ways have centered consistently upon one central value: the dignity of the individual and the insistence that no institutions be allowed to trample that dignity.

Our tradition has opposed social betterment by pushbutton. The American people generally have rejected the idea of any simplistic and sweeping social changes and have not encouraged the central planner. We have tended to believe that no one man can do everything. America's success story demonstrates that until lately we have generally adhered to our original view of individual difference and institutional variety. Perhaps this should be described as the achievement of revolutionary results by conservative means.

Most Americans generally have been more concerned about ordinary, everyday, hardworking life than with any grand social theories. George Santayana once remarked, "The American people have made a philosophy out of not having a philosophy." To me, Santayana's remark has always suggested a nation unconcerned with ideology, a nation not particularly impressed with plans and planners and "intellectuals," a nation of individuals primarily concerned with attending to their own immediate personal affairs in freedom and dignity. Americans traditionally have suspected that not all human problems can be solved by mere expertise. Therefore, in charting our course, we might profitably couple our sense of history with a total unwillingness to accept the jargon of "progress" that urges change for the sake of change. We already suffer from far too many "experts."

Where Do We Go from Here?

The planners and the experts have largely had their way with American society throughout much of the twentieth century. In the process, they have departed from the traditional American patterns and the sense of history that this nation once had. The dislocations and confusions introduced into American institutional life in the twentieth century have become so obvious that no individual can miss their import and threat. We can no longer flee from the responsibility of deciding our destiny, because there is nowhere left to hide, no private sector safe from the intrusions of bigness. The troubles of an enmassed society have come home to roost. And if we are to answer the question, "What does it mean to be an American?" we must regain our sense of history and the insistence upon individual dignity that once characterized the American people.

Today many of us see quite clearly that the world as we knew it, the world worth having, is slipping away from us. The great question is, "How do we stop and reverse that process?" There comes a time amid the confusions and failures of a souring civilization when it no longer suffices merely to identify what is wrong. Men then want to know what is *right*. How do we regain a world in which it is possible for ordinary people to live with propriety and respect and dignity?

This book is an attempt to establish some vital relationships seldom mentioned in contemporary debate of social issues. I see no end to our troubles until such relationships are again recognized. Of course, the identification of business, labor, government, pollution, "the rising standard of living," and indeed all the other institutions, problems, or benefits of present society, as parts of a single interrelated whole may not appeal to most shades of current political opinion. Our age of specialization makes the thought of such interrelationship unpalatable. Most of us have our respective institutional heroes and villains. We prefer to assign praise for achievement to our own version of the institutional "good guys," while attaching blame for all our problems to the "bad guys." For that reason, this book is likely to please neither my friends nor my enemies; but as the incorrigible Emily Dickinson once said, "Truth is so rare, it's delightful to tell it." However unpalatable to present society, establishing the connection between our present discontents and our own failures is the first step toward finding the solid ground upon which a restoration of values may begin.

> In the same way, we have to inform the multitude that restoration comes at a price. Suppose we give them an intimation of the cost through a series of questions. Are you ready, we must ask them, to grant that the law of reward is inflexible and that one cannot, by cunning or through complaints, obtain more than he puts in? Are you prepared to see that comfort may be a seduction and that the fetish of material prosperity will have to be pushed aside in favor of some sterner ideal? Do you see the necessity of accepting duties before you begin to talk of freedoms? These things will be very hard; they will call for deep reformation.[4]

The prerequisite for the frame of mind enabling us to ask such questions and get the right answers is a fresh understanding of the institutions which

---

[4]Richard M. Weaver, *Ideas Have Consequences* (Chicago: University of Chicago Press, 1948), pp. 186–187.

form our society. Such an understanding will not come about through public opinion polls or the efforts of research teams. The answers must be discovered by individuals who have managed to find a platform of bedrock from which they can look at their society and judge who they are and where they are going.

Such understanding comes only to individuals. People need to find their own reason for living, and that means finding their own answers to the questions that really matter. Granted that the enmassment of our present society has produced an age of bewilderment, and granted that the politics of bewilderment have produced that anti-individual enmassment, we are still faced with the fundamental task of restoration: offering the individual the chance to discover his own reason for living.

XVII

POLITICS

I do not pity the misery of a man underplaced: That will right itself presently: But I pity the man overplaced. A certain quantity of power belongs to a certain quantity of faculty. Whoever wants more power than is the legitimate attraction of his faculty, is a politician and must pay for that excess; must truckle for it. This is the whole game of society and the politics of the world.

Ralph Waldo Emerson,
Complete Works

Today's young radicals did not invent "alienation." The problems of individual identity and the alienation which results when that identity is not achieved have been major themes of interest in the Western world for a century. The alienation theme as propounded by any number of thinkers, both Left and Right, has assumed that there is a certain inner quality peculiar to each individual, a quality which he is forced to deny when he attempts to conform to the demands placed upon him by modern society in his role as consumer, voter, worker, or participant in any aspect of modern, large-scale institutional life. That process of coming to terms with institutional bigness has concerned many critics, since it seems to make of the individual citizen a subject, a mere tool, a cog in a machine, within the mass institutions of society.

Men must retain the capacity to choose if they are to remain men. So, freedom remains the highest goal. But is individual freedom possible in a society devoted to enmassment? Is it possible that we are betraying our highest aspirations in our willingness to allow and even encourage superconcentration within society? Libertarians see the enemy as state bigness; the thought leaders of the New Left see the enemy as corporate and institutional bigness; they both may be right. What faces us today is not merely a political problem, not merely an economic problem. The political blends into the economic, and both blend into the moral problem. The hierarchy of values centering on the individual demands and institutional structure which protects the individual's freedom of action and choice. Any alleged "solution" which is offered to our present discontents can have no deeply rooted effect in our present society unless it recognizes that hierarchy of values. Any other kind of problem solving is truly reactionary in the worst possible sense of the word.

How then should we approach the problem? We need more than a series of slogans, more than a series of congressional enactments, more than a series of neat answers and abstract doctrines. The traditional forms of political and social order must be reapplied within the economic and technical conditions of the modern world. This can be done only if we insist upon the hierarchy of values which gives primacy to the dignity of the individual and to the institutional forms guaranteeing that dignity.

Perhaps the best beginning is a willingness to undertake frank criticism, criticism not only of our enemies, but also of our would-be ideological friends. Enmassment presses on the individual *wherever* it appears. We must do more than harken to the customary Left–Right debate; otherwise we find ourselves defending forms which have been emptied of all meaning. The pressures of our times are forcing us toward either new solutions or new failures. The change is inevitable, but the choice is ours.

One of the characters in the concluding volume of the C. S. Lewis space trilogy makes it clear just how necessary it has become that we make our choice for the individual and make that choice soon:

> If you dip into any college, or school, or parish, or family — anything you like — at a given point in its history, you always find that there was a time before that point when there was more elbow room and contrasts weren't quite so sharp; and that there's going to be a time after that point when there is even less room for indecision and choices are even more momentous. Good is always getting better and bad is always getting worse: the possibilities of even apparent neutrality are always diminishing. The whole thing is sorting itself out all the time, coming to a point, getting sharper and harder.[1]

Institutional bigness, stemming from the encroachments of the state, has so permeated all sectors of our society that the distinction between governmental and nongovernmental activity has become increasingly artificial. The "they" to which the Left–liberal academician is hostile turns out to be the same organizational "they" of whom the conservative–libertarian complains. Those people of the Right and the Left who are still thinking, and who have not given themselves over entirely to reaction and emotion, are actually in revolt against the same "Establishment." Any reformation of

[1] C. S. Lewis, *That Hideous Strength* (New York: Macmillan, 1965), p. 283.

present-day society demands as a first step the careful consideration of our political processes and our attitudes toward those processes.

Mass Political Leadership

The nature of political power seems to demand that those who assume the burden of managing human beings should essentially regard their charges as children. The wielder of political power soon begins to talk as though his primary task were to provide new ideas and new institutions as the people can be "made ready" for it. Such assumptions of power are invariably well intended. Power is always courted for good purposes before it is misused for bad. The politician actually believes that he can determine the quality of other men's lives. Of course he cannot. The man who presumes to raise politics to what he regards as his own high moral level generally finds himself dragged down to the lower and steadily lower levels on which men operate in their desire to maintain political power. Perhaps the politician is doomed to failure, no matter how well intended, because, in Aldous Huxley's phrase, "Good is a product of the ethical and spiritual artistry of individuals; it cannot be mass-produced."

In fact, American democratic politics has operated according to Gresham's law. The worst political type generally drives out the best. In America our politicians tend to choose themselves. Some individual decides that he wants to hold political office, and sets about the task of winning the office for himself. Such political types are commonplace in American politics today. And the result is a very poor means for selecting our political leadership. As one psychologist has described the process:

> It's dangerous because it tends to leave the selection of candidates to just exactly those self-seekers, those people who neurotically need power in the sense of power over other people, rather than getting into office the person who is best suited to the job and who may be modest and humble about the matter and would not like to push himself forward . . . the person who seeks for power is the one who is just exactly likely to be the one who shouldn't have it, because he neurotically and compulsively needs power. Such people are apt to use power very badly. . . .[2]

To be fair to our political types, it should perhaps be admitted that the fault is less in the people who come to the job than in the nature of the job itself. Power *cannot* be controlled beyond a central point of centralization. Some of the most terrible crimes of the twentieth century have been com-

---

[2]Abraham H. Maslow, *Eupsychian Management* (Homewood, Ill.: Richard D. Irwin and Dorsey Press, 1965), p. 125.

mitted by men such as Heinrich Himmler, men catapulted by political circumstances into positions of great authority, total nonentities given the power of life and death over whole societies. Where else but in the political arena would such tragedies be possible?

We still see only one side of the equation until we recognize the fact that great concentrations of political power are likely to overcome the ruler as well as the ruled. When political power runs off the end of the chart, completely exceeding any humane scale, the results are likely to be hazardous for everyone involved. For instance, the power of the President of the United States has grown so far beyond the capacities of any man to exercise that power that government by committee, government by appointment, government by whim is frequently the result. In such a system, great authority often rests in the hands of some official never elected by the people and indeed virtually unknown to them.

We need not look so far up the ladder as the Presidency to see the effects of power in people's lives. Consider the changes often wrought in an individual's personality as he moves up the organizational ladder and wields more authority in *any* bureaucracy. The results for all concerned are often disastrous.

Thus government, like other bureaucracies, seems to suffer from trying to do too much and too many things in the lives of men. Again and again we see the same pattern emerging: Organizational interlock frustrates legislative control. The day comes when not even the wielders of power can any longer control power. Meanwhile, nonpolitical institutions suffer as the result. As political power spreads throughout the fabric of society, it becomes "undemocratic" to have backwaters of individual or organizational difference. An imaginary "equality" is extended to the poor, the adolescent, the female. Democracy will no longer tolerate differences between employer and employee, between officer and enlisted men. We are all to be one, part of one great amorphous, politicized group. It is in this fashion that the totalitarian mentality comes to the fore under democratic labels.

All institutions which stand in the way of this process of politicalization must be either swept aside or restructured along politicalized lines. Soon either the existence or the meaning of the church, the university, the military, the law, the medical profession, or any other institutional or professional grouping is swept into the discard. Without the protection of a private institutional umbrella shielding the individual differences which make up personality, the individual is likely to be in deep trouble. When private institutions that once protected him become politicalized, the individual becomes exposed to the direct application of political power in all its social implications.

Today many people, especially the young, see the central problem of our time as a struggle against society's institutions. In one sense, these people are fundamentally wrong, since, in attacking the institution, they are attacking the very heart of the social fabric protecting individual difference.

In another sense today's institutional critics are quite right, because the institutional structure they are attacking is a largely politicized definition of the institution. The fault is less with our present institutional structure than with the political processes that have largely taken control of that structure. Those who advocate political action as a means of dealing with the institutional problems of our age are asking for more of the same medicine which has already sickened our society.

Whether the state takes control of our lives directly, or does it through increasingly politicized institutions, the end result is the same:

> Let us suppose that instead of being slow, extravagant, inefficient, wasteful, unadaptive, stupid, and at least by tendency corrupt, the state changes its character entirely and becomes infinitely wise, good, disinterested, efficient, so that anyone may run to it with any little two-penny problem and have it solved for him at once in the wisest and best way possible. Suppose the state close-herds the individual so far as to forestall every conceivable consequence of his own bad judgment, weakness, incompetence; suppose it confiscates all his energy and resources and employs them much more advantageously all round than he can employ them if left to himself. My question still remains — what sort of person is the individual likely to become under those circumstances?[3]

Political Problem Solving

Today, disenchantment with government has become a well-established fact. This disenchantment cuts across ideological lines. It is probably an inevitable reaction to the love affair with government that has been carried on worldwide in the twentieth century. Twentieth-century men, in this country and elsewhere, have tended to believe that government was both well intended and omnipotent.

Whatever we think of government's intentions, we surely can no longer believe that all problems are subject to political solution. Today's assumption seems to be that programs which are turned over to government are doomed to disaster. The Post Office is a national joke; urban renewal and welfare programs are a public scandal. The typical citizen tends to shrug and say, "What can you expect from the government?" During the past 10 years this shift in attitudes has become obvious.

---

[3]Albert Jay Nock, *Snoring as a Fine Art and Twelve Other Essays* (Rindge, N. H.: Richard R. Smith, 1958), p. 27.

Special interest groups still call upon political power to perform various functions, but it seems that such power is less and less capable of effective action. Even the Communists seem more and more doubtful about central planning. The student radicals in this country regard themselves as a New Left, but many of their criticisms of present big government sound like the Old Right.

Not only our young are discontented with political solutions. The disenchantment of the liberal with the welfare state which he has erected has become painfully evident. Men with such certified liberal credentials as Irving Kristol and Daniel Moynihan simply no longer believe that the political action can solve our present discontents. Nor should it be surprising that such political solutions have failed. Dr. Johnson's remarks on a lady preacher seem apropos: "Such a creature is like a dog walking on his hind legs. We do not expect the thing to be done well but are surprised that it is done at all."

The same thing can be said for modern political problem solving. One reason for this inevitable failure is the bureaucratic incapacity to adapt to changing conditions. It seems that once political rules are written, it becomes almost impossible to change them. Soon such a maze of legislation and rules has grown up that only the administrator with a gift for sidestepping the rules has any hope of getting a job completed. Typically, the most valuable person in a government agency is likely to be not the expert in the particular field but the lawyer who knows the bureaucratic ground rules.

Further, it seems that government can never stop a program once initiated. The result is a total lack of flexibility and creativity, coupled with a bureaucratic unwillingness to assume responsibility. The increasing failures are dismissed with a shrug and reference to "the system." Meanwhile, bureaucratic empire building continues. Only in such politicized functions, whether in government itself or in those institutions taking their tone from government, is it in the interest of an administrator to spend as much money as possible. Inefficiency becomes a key part of the system.

As the politicalization of our economy and our way of life proceeds, the "private sector" becomes steadily less private, and steadily more interested in competing for government largess. Special interest politics comes to dominate the scene. We are all to blame for the resultant change. Today it seems that demands outrun our capacity, political or otherwise, to satisfy those demands. Our cities cry for more money, our policemen are underpaid, our teachers are underpaid; meanwhile, the poor taxpayers are taxed to the hilt. We seem to want more things than we can pay for, personally and socially. We mortgage more and more of the future in the impossible race to keep up with appetite. It seems that the rising standard of living *does* go up with our economy, but at what cost? Do we truly gain in the things that count — in a more human, more fulfilling life? Or are we becoming so breathless in our impossible race with unlimited appetite that we are too harried to enjoy life? Is it possible that we can want so many things that we ruin our lives paying for them?

Failing to gratify these appetites on a personal basis, we are then taught by modern democracy to turn to government, to collective action, to satisfy our goals at the expense of "everyone." Thus Frederic Bastiat's grim definition of the state becomes literally true: "That legal fiction by which everyone attempts to live at the expense of everyone else."

The state, of course, can only continue this hopeless race against appetite, with bankrupcy the certain result, since it has nothing not previously taken from the people. Still, this race will go on without end, to the point of total social collapse, unless the people themselves — the individuals who compose our society — come to understand the problem. Then and then only, when people are not driven by appetite, when they are no more eager to have government take from others than to have government take from themselves, when they value their independence above all else, will we get a free society. Until then, politicians will continue to promise what they cannot deliver — the good life. So long as they are believed, politicalization will continue to centralize, organize, and ultimately pauperize life for us all. As our society pursues this form of special interest politics, we should remember that those politicians whom we are so quick to criticize are nothing but the reflection of *our* attitudes and appetites.

Let us be more specific. As a case in point, consider urban renewal. In the words of Professor Martin Anderson, one of the most thoughtful analysts of the subject:

> I have had the opportunity to talk to a number of community leaders in cities where urban renewal was being considered. During these conversations I was particularly interested in finding out why certain people strongly advocated the program, and I was surprised to find a consistent theme running through their off-the-record statements. They were not seriously concerned with the poor people living in the areas they had tentatively marked for renewal; they were not concerned with any personal financial gain; they were not even very concerned with getting a substantial amount of cash from the rest of the taxpayers via Washington. But they were concerned with *power*.
>
> Again and again — from bankers, politicians, newspaper editors, businessmen, and even religious leaders — I heard statements like these: "Well, I've tried to buy property in that area of town, but the owner won't sell at a reasonable price. Somebody has to *make* him sell at a 'fair' price. Who does he think he is, standing in the way of the whole city?" Or, "We need at least a whole block to do anything worthwhile; we can't fool around trying to buy a lot here and a lot

there. Besides, some old man may feel attached to property that's been in his family for years. We can't wait for him to die. We need the tool of *eminent domain.*"

In today's context, the public interest has become a synonym for declaring that, in the speaker's or writer's opinion, the deliberate, intentional sacrifice of the interest of one group of people is justified by the benefit that accrues to another group of people.[4]

Special interest politics also constitute the reason why a number of other programs do *not* come into being. Legal pressures against pay TV are a significant instance of government-backed cartels in radio and television using the power of government to eliminate competition. On how much higher a level might our programming be if it were directly influenced by market pressures? How much less influential might the present mass communications power structure be if pay television could compete? And yet the reason for this continuing interference is presumably "the public interest."

Unfortunately, it appears true that a group can always be bought, since it is the "interest" of the group which makes it a group. Today all too many trade associations, among them people presumably antistatist and "conservative" in nature, are in the vanguard of special interest politics. It seems that men no longer want a government that will leave them alone. Instead, more and more of our groups want a government they can use. Perhaps there are grounds for Albert Jay Nock's gloomy assertion that "the sole invariable characteristic of the State is the economic exploitation of one class by another."

The same pressures which produce special interest politics make the situation difficult to correct. Any reduction in the benefits accruing to various groups will be fought tooth and nail, with the usual accompaniment of dire predictions of the consequences for the "public interest" and for the economy as a whole. The greed of each group, be it minorities, the aged, business, labor, the education lobby, or what-have-you, blinds the people involved to the fact that they are indeed living in Bastiat's nightmare world where everyone attempts to benefit at the expense of everyone else.

There was a time in America society when an older ethic held sway:

No government has ever operated for long and in all respects in terms of the Protestant ethic; but during most of the nineteenth century the governments of Western Europe and North America came closer to that ideal than any government has before or since. Moreover, it was to a considerable degree the fact that these governments represented

[4]Martin Anderson, *The Fnederal Bulldozer* (New York: McGraw-Hill, 1967), pp. ix, x.

and to some extent operated in terms of the Protestant ethic that made possible the rapid development of industrial technology and the emergence of what is now contemptuously termed the "capitalistic system."[5]

We turned from that ethic of self-responsibility to the new and tempting possibilities of special interest politics. Now, special interest politics has clearly failed. The new politics has been failing because it eliminated and penalized the very character traits which had made the entire capitalistic structure possible in the first place.

In our highly politicized age, the next question sure to be asked is, "Granted that special interest politics has its evils, doesn't politics have a large and proper role in the operation of society? Aren't there problems plaguing our society which demand political solution?"

In fact, we made far too much of "problems" in our present society. Not all problems are necessarily capable of solution. Indeed most of those problems that have been solved have not achieved solution by political means, but rather by the active invention of individuals and institutions operating with enough flexibility and freedom to discover their own solutions.

The great problem today is the structure of politics itself, the total politicalization of our society. From that one great problem have grown the innumerable paralyses, confusions, and dead ends that plague us. For this problem of politicalization and all its various mutations, the collectivist has only one answer. But his one answer of endlessly-increasing political power simply does not work; and behind that single-answer mentality there looms an enormous intellectual vacuum.

Yet, the view of government as "problem solver" persists. Any redirection of people's thinking amounts to an uphill effort. Consider the experience of Professor Martin Anderson, who offered nonpoliticalized solutions to the present urban renewal mess:

In the book I offer the economic system of free enterprise as a viable alternative to the government program, and point out that it would not force people from their homes, that it would not take homes, land, and buildings from people without their consent, nor would it cost a dime of the taxpayer's money. I have since discovered that this alternative is unknown and unthinkable to many people, either because they know so little about modern economic theory or because they have a deep-seated antagonism toward the economics of laissez-faire capitalism. I am insistently pressed for a "positive alternative," which,

[5]Richard LaPiere, *The Freudian Ethic* (New York: Duell, Sloan and Pearce, 1959), p. 246.

to the questioner, invariably means an alternative government program.

One does not *have* to offer any alternative government program for two reasons. First, to presume that any valid alternative *must* be a government program is to take a blatantly unintellectual position. Second, and more importantly, the federal urban renewal program, by itself, is a bad program. It is causing harm, and its very elimination would therefore be an improvement. To suggest that one should not stop harmful government action until one has thought of new government action is absurd. In fact, one of the most efficacious ways to improve the present and future living conditions of all people in the United States would be to repeal the urban renewal program as soon as practicable.[6]

A generation of young scholars like Martin Anderson are beginning the task of documenting what happens when men retreat to the principle of coercion for the organization of their affairs. The promise of the political arena is that problems can be solved by force. Yet the use of that force increasingly limits both the means and ends available to a social order. The resultant conformity does far more to cause problems than solve them.

Decentralized, Nonpolitical Problem Solving

One reason that the politicalized, collective solution still holds such sway in our society, despite its bad performance record, might well be that the same utilitarian philosophy which produced modern liberal interventionism also helped to produce the old nineteenth-century version of laissez-faire capitalism. Men are more than the raw material for some experiment in social engineering, but we also need to remember that men are more than units for efficient industrial organization. Men are first of all individual human beings, and it matters little what variety of centralized grand design we are implementing in their lives. Too many of the critics of modern big government have offered only another variety of dull uniformity in its place.

The old laissez faire failed to provide a rallying point for the opponents of the all-powerful state because it was a social philosophy which tended to view individuals as interchangeable parts rather than unique members of widely varying voluntary associations, groups, and communities. The old laissez faire thus did a great deal to pave the way for the modern superstate, since it undercut the all-important sense of community. Federal responsibilities began to grow in this country when we no longer recognized local and community responsibilities. American democracy at its best was a demonstration of local options and true consensus, a consensus worlds

[6]Anderson, p. viii

apart from the alleged "consensus" that plays such a large role in the vocabulary of present-day mass democracy. The earlier American democracy started with the assumption that the individual was important, because it took all types of individuals to operate an effective social order. In a society not oriented to mass politics, the ordinary, average "common" man had a chance to be creative in his private life, to bring up his own children, to serve his own sense of community. In the last analysis, the answer to the abuses of coercive power and the politicalized regime of modern society is a reinstitution of those voluntary, cooperative activities which grow from the sense of community. The more centers of local and individual cooperation, providing more opportunities for individuals to cooperate in voluntary associations to solve their own problems and achieve their own creativity, the more effective our social regime will be. It is true that times have changed. It is true that we cannot go back to the past. But it is also true that the most effective problem-solving devices which a society can evolve must center on the sense of community and voluntary association that characterized our earlier history. Before we became so highly politicalized, our society had the capacity of flexibility and variety which allowed it to meet new problems as they arose. The modern collectivity is sterile and tied to the status quo.

For several generations, Americans have carried on such a love affair with government that they have failed to see what many of our young people are beginning to see, that the present politicalized institutional framework will no longer meet the needs of our society. Many young people have grasped at least a portion of the truth. They quite properly regard our present institutional framework as fossilized and nonfunctional. Today's youth is increasingly impatient with a generation of liberal academics who preach in the classroom only the same outworn nonanswers of collectivism. It seems then that many of these young people are moving in the right direction; though, with the typical exuberance of youth, they are likely to go too far and thus miss the point entirely. They often fail to distinguish between the present politicalized institutions which becloud our social scene and institutions geared to the individual.

A society in which all institutions were destroyed would soon become so atomized that genuine community could not exist; nor can individualism long endure in the absence of a sense of community. Implicit in the rhetoric of the young revolutionaries is the suggestion that collective solutions will soon fill the institutional void created by their revolution: "All power to the people!" Thus the same young revolutionaries who presumably are so concerned about the antipersonal tendency of our present society finally become highly antipersonal themselves.

Perhaps what we all need, youngsters and older generations alike, is some plain old tolerance. Unlike the catchy slogans and action programs that are likely to accompany politicalized activity, tolerance requires only that we let others be different from ourselves. How easy this sounds, yet how difficult in practice. Perhaps we should talk less about freedom in the abstract, and more about the *application* of such principles in our daily lives, in our institutions, in our society. Then we would be on the way to genuine problem solving. Then the rollback of the politicalized society would begin, once again leaving room for little people, simple virtues, and, above all, individual differences.

I fully realize that what I am suggesting is unpalatable to our present society. Today we want quick, simple, all-encompassing answers. And many are on hand to provide such answers. Most such specific, nine-point programs for saving society have in common the willingness to stratify and further centralize more of the political and economic procedures of our life. The prescription they offer turns out to be another dose of the disease for which they promise a cure. And yet this may not be an entirely lost cause:

> In the enormous bellowing chorus of advertisers singing the praises of centralized mass-producing and mass-distributing industry, and of Left-wing propagandists singing the praises of the omnipotent state, these few isolated voices have some difficulty in making themselves heard. If it were not for the fact that, in the past, apparently negligible movements, originating among individuals without any political power, have yet exercised a prodigious influence over mankind, there would be reason for discouragement. But fortunately it is not impossible that the presently tiny piece of decentralist leaven may end by leavening the whole huge lump of contemporary society.[7]

It is in this hope for decentralization that the real virtue of the free market lies. The market demands surprisingly little conformity from those it serves. The greater the number of activities administered through the marketplace — the fewer the activities which must be manipulated by political decision — the greater the range for individual decision and *voluntary* association. Even if individuals make mistakes, they are not likely to be worse than the government's mistakes. And at least the individual will have the satisfaction of knowing that the mistake he pays for is his own. Incidentally, responsibility for one's mistakes affords the greatest possible incentive for correction. It is this connection between responsibility and authority that breaks down in a politicalized society:

> And how else, when we pause to ponder the matter, can the human race advance except by the emancipation of more and more individu-

[7]Aldous Huxley, *Science, Liberty and Peace* (New York: Harper and Brothers, 1946), p. 57.

als in ever-widening circles of activity? How can new ideas be conceived? How can new relationships, new habits, be formed? Only by increasing freedom to think, to argue, to debate, to make mistakes, to learn from those mistakes, to explore and occasionally to discover, to be adventurous and enterprising, can change be more than the routine of a recurrent pattern . . . the energy of progress originates in the great mass of the people as the more gifted among them are released from constraint and stimulated by intercourse with other free-thinking and free-moving individuals. . . .

Because of the limitations of our understanding and of our power, the dynamics of human capacity follow the rule that the more complex the interests which have to be regulated, the less possible is it to direct them by the coercion of superior authority.[8]

Is this really such a bizarre idea? Or is it just that the idea is at once so new and so old, so obvious and so subtle, that we have been refusing to give it serious consideration? Mark Twain may have been right, you know: "The man with a new idea is a crank until the idea succeeds."

Jefferson or Hamilton?

Any social order always is confronted with the problems of how the productive forces of society are to be organized and operated and who is to have the power of decision. The collective mentality holds that such decisions and organization must be made according to a centrally enforced plan. In following that advice, we have discovered the high price which must be paid for collective decision making: the destruction of the spiritual and personal elements which underlie the social order. Irving Babbitt once remarked that we are living in the Meddle Ages. Reckless interventions of all kinds have produced smothering perversions and inelasticities, a morass form which escape is made all the more difficult by the wide acceptance of politicalized problem solving. Many people see our only choice lying between revolution and reaction, between anarchy and despotism. Paralyzed by such choices, we begin to be frozen into a pattern of total conformity. The latter days of American liberalism have been characterized by an increasing politicalization, no longer undertaken so much in the hope of solving problems as in an effort to retain some control over a steadily deteriorating situation.

One hundred eighty years ago, America's future presumably lay somewhere between the Hamiltonian and the Jeffersonian expectations. The unfolding of events would seem to have fulfilled the Hamiltonian vision. We are materially well to do, we have a strong government and industrial

[8]Walter Lippmann, *The Good Society* (New York: Grosset and Dunlap, 1943), pp. 19–20, 35.

development beyond even Hamilton's wildest dreams. Most Americans have approved this course. It is the common man who enjoys the benefits of commercialism in all its forms. Presumably most Americans would not like to give up their affluence and material possessions. But perhaps we have followed the Hamiltonian vision further than we bargained for. Jefferson may yet have his day.

The centralization which Jefferson so much feared may yet be turned aside. Jefferson was too wily and astute to depend upon the efficacy of mere political devices for decentralization. He seemed to sense what later generations would do to the limited government guarantees of the Constitution. He placed his reliance more upon social than political decentralization. True, Jefferson expected centralization to be resisted by yeoman farmers, a class long departed from the land. But the time may be coming in this country when the absence of individual dignity and voluntary association will press so hard upon the typical American that a new class of leadership will arise, addressing itself to the kind of social decentralization which retains our Hamiltonian goals, so far as we wish them retained, but that also brings with it the best of the Jeffersonian ideal.

Most Americans seem agreed that Hamiltonian ends have long since won the day. The institutional structure of our present society makes that obvious. We want the things our present system provides. It seems equally obvious that the Jeffersonian ends of a rural, totally decentralized America have become historically impossible. My question: Granted that America favors Hamiltonian ends, might not the value of those ends be enhanced if they were achieved by Jeffersonian means?

Isn't it possible that we could keep our vaunted social efficiency, perhaps even enhance it, by allowing decentralization to solve some of the economic and organizational problems which plague us? Further, the resultant personal development and freedom of choice thus achieved by the individual could go a long way toward curing our present spiritual malaise.

A related question has to do with national loyalty and pride. In this decentralized antistatist ideal, is there a place for patriotism? Does the passion for decentralization, the suspicion of political solutions, rule out all possibility of a worthy function for the state? Is there no place for an honest pride in country?

Perhaps Henry David Thoreau, and certainly many of his modern-day votaries, would answer that question in the negative. There is a tendency abroad in the land to assume that loyalty to country, or the granting of sufficient political power to allow the country to defend itself, is an invasion of personal privacy. Of course any genuine freedom for the individual, any hope of maintaining a system of voluntary associations and a sense of community, is premised upon protecting the system as a whole from aggressors who most emphatically do not believe in human freedom. There is more to living in this world as a free man than the adoption of a moral stance. Action is also required. A free society operates with responsibilities as well as rights.

The kind of nihilism that would sweep aside all institutions is far from a new idea. An old and tired myth in any society is the assumption that all problems stem from a small, evil minority. Sometimes the devil has been labeled as a church, sometimes a government, sometimes another institution in society. But to jump to the conclusion that all institutions should therefore be swept away is as invalid and anti-individualistic as the totally politicized view of society. Neither the anarchist nor the collectivist has the sense of community and individually oriented institutions upon which human liberty depends.

Those who find their loyalty to the nation wavering are perhaps suffering from the discovery that the values they have adopted are not worthy of loyalty. Love of country grows out of love for a nation's traditions. Traditionally, Americans have defended and supported their nation because it reflected their values and interests, representing a true sense of community and individual difference, preserving individual opportunity. Such a nation was an extension of our own best values and attitudes. This was a vision of America, a vision of our institutions, a vision of self, that we were willing to defend against all comers. Our latter-day politicalization and the resultant damage it has done to our society are blurring that vision. Unless we can conduct our society and our affairs with pride, we will not be willing to defend our institutions and actions. Fifty years ago, even such a crusty old iconoclast as Albert Jay Nock was saying just that:

> The time has come, in our opinion, to disallow all this and to reaffirm the revolutionary doctrine set forth in the Declaration of Independence, that the Creator has endowed human beings with certain inalienable rights; to give more interest to principles and less to machinery; to think less about acting and organizing and instituting, and more about establishing a culture that will afford a proper foundation for national action. The time has come, in short, for inaugurating a really moral movement instead of protracting the succession of ludicrous and filthy hypocrisies which have so long passed for moral movements. . . . It is all very well to go about establishing justice and human rights, in the time of it; but the first step towards establishing them is to believe in them, and that is the step to be taken now.[9]

America has always prospered in direct ratio to its capacity to develop the individual and free him for constructive action. If America cannot

[9]Albert Jay Nock, *The Freeman Book* (New York: B. W. Huebsch, 1924), pp. 125–126.

undertake this task once again, then it has lost its political genius and will be doomed to impotence. It seems to me that we still have that capacity, the ability to assume the responsibility for being free men. Nothing less will suffice. There comes a time, as such disparate characters as Little Orphan Annie and Robert Louis Stevenson will tell you, when "You cannot run away from weakness, you must sometimes fight it out or perish; and if that be so, why not now, and where do you stand?"

In short, the restoration of a traditional American society does not depend upon finding a way to reorder peoples' lives. Americans are quite capable of doing that for themselves. What needs restoration is an institutional and social order within which people once again may act and choose freely. And this can come whenever we want it.

In the task I've described, I believe there is a rule, a primary rule, for the common people:

I use the expression as the highest measure of praise, as Lincoln noted that God must love the common people; He made so many of them. For, in America, most of us begin on the wrong side of the railroad tracks. The meaning of America, what made it the wonder of history and the hope of mankind, was that we were free not to stay on the wrong side of the railroad tracks. If within us there was something that empowered us to grow, we were free to grow and go where we could. Only, we were not free ever to forget, ever to despise our origins. They were our roots. They made us a nation.[10]

Restoration of the American dream depends upon how well the American people will remember who they are and where they came from and what made them great. Justifiable pride in country, community, voluntary associations, and self is the only effective antidote to the impositions of politicized society.

[10]Whittaker Chambers, *Witness* (Chicago: Regnery, 1952), p. 793.

XVIII

ECONOMICS

More than a hundred years ago Karl Marx predicted, in the Communist Manifesto, that industrialization was bound to create an ever-swelling proletariat which soon or late would topple the whole capitalistic system. In ways not vouchsafed to Marx or, for that matter, Khrushchev, to understand, the U. S. has refuted that prediction, creating, if not a classless, at least a class-fluid society in which the benefits of material progress have been ever more widely shared.

John Davenport,
The U. S. Economy

The American success story in material terms has become the envy of the world. It was founded upon a high degree of safety for private property, plus ample opportunity for individual achievement.

Far more than material concern was involved in the forefathers' insistence upon closely guarded property rights. In Paul Elmer More's phrase, "To the civilized man the *rights of property are more important than the right to life.*" More's point was that a civilized human community is simply not possible without closely guarded property rights. Though all animals have life, only men have the concept of property and the attendant human rights and responsibilities which make civilization possible.

The Founders also realized that property is the necessary condition of economic freedom. They knew that a man without control of his property would inevitably become the tool of those who did exercise that control, whether the controller was another individual or the collectivity. Freedom for the individual was thus thought to be impossible without the individual's control of those extensions of personality which constitute property. No protection of property rights — no freedom; no freedom — no self-responsible and creative citizens; no self-responsible citizens — no lasting civilization. Or so our Founding Fathers believed. Who, taking stock of today's social order, would care to debate the point?

The Free Market

The freedom to pursue one's own goals goes hand in hand with the guarantees of private property. While it is possible to overstate the role of economics in human affairs, it is also possible to understate that role. Men are more than producers and consumers, and it is important to keep that fact always before us. Still, given the irrevocable industrial direction our society has taken, an understanding of economics is essential to anyone who wishes to understand our present social order.

First, we must understand the market and how it works. It is a remarkable regulatory device, when it is allowed to function. Production and consumption are in constant readjustment, moving toward equilibrium. This comes about because consumers are constantly engaged in an election of sorts, casting their ballots for the quantity, quality, variety, and price of goods and services they most prefer. This democracy of the marketplace gives the consumer what he wants, at a price he is willing to pay, and rewards producers to the exact extent that those wants are satisfied.

No political plebiscite has ever rivaled this "rule of the people" which the free market provides. The principle underlying political decision making is *conformity*. One may vote, but, if overruled, must conform to the wishes of the majority. No such limiting factor is present in the decision making of the free market. All transactions are voluntary. The minority need not conform to the majority. The individual is left free to determine his own scale of values.

Another advantage of such flexibility is the capacity of the market to correct its own mistakes. In an enterprise truly dependent upon the market, responsibility directly accompanies action. This is totally unlike the political realm, where responsibility and action are often divorced. The political arena is notorious for its tendency to institutionalize mistakes:

> The generation that was in love with the state 30 and 40 years ago believed fondly that government would be economical. Eliminating the "profit motive" was thought to reduce costs. This was poor economics, to begin with. If there is competition, profit assures accomplishment of a task at the lowest cost. It is a measure and an index of the most economical allocation of resources, that is, of the optimum in terms of costs as well as of results. This is the reason why the Communist countries are all rushing now to reintroduce profitability into their system.[1]

Big Business

The emergence of big business has been a phenomenon of continuing interest throughout the Western world. The social and economic impact of

[1]Peter F. Drucker, *The Age of Discontinuity* (New York: Harper and Row, 1968), p. 230.

the large, integrated concern may be regarded by future historians as the single most important development of American society in the twentieth century. Whatever future historians may have to say on the subject, most of the commentators during the past 40 years have had no doubts about the role of big business: It is presumed to be evil incarnate, a force to be controlled, if not broken, by decisive political action.

A few years ago, the great question was: "Shall we permit big business to exist?" Now, the advocates of big government have largely decided that big business is not only desirable, but necessary, provided only that the economy is properly politicized: that is, provided that a sufficiently close working relationship exists between government and business. The Sherman Act, the Clayton Act and Thurman Arnold notwithstanding, it seems that big business is here to stay.

There *are* a few holdouts. Professor J. K. Galbraith is prone to talk about the domination of the American economy by 500 firms, who set their own prices, provide their own capital, and "manage" consumer demand. Presumably these firms, which Galbraith has labeled the "technostructure," work hand in hand with government in controlling the economy.

In fact, only about 25 percent of all goods and services are produced by the 500 largest industrials. This means, I assume, that 75 percent of our goods and services are *not* produced by "the technostructure." It is also reassuring to recall that in the past 50 years about two-thirds of America's giant concerns have been displaced from their leadership position on the list of this nation's 100 largest concerns. It seems that the top is a very slippery place.

No doubt the Galbraith revelations come as a real shock to the corporate giants of America. Imagine learning that they need no longer go into the capital market to finance their businesses! Imagine their relief upon discovering that the consumer will buy whatever he is told by the corporate giants! In short, Professor Galbraith notwithstanding, the American market is *not* monopolistic or oligopolistic in the sense in which the charge is usually made.

Consumer Control

The standard academic model which assumes oligopoly to be the rule throughout the big business community simply does not correspond to reality. More and more alternatives for the consumer's dollar, offered at lower and lower prices, suggests that increased competition has accompanied the growth of big business. Choices have widened, prices have dropped, capital has flowed to those productive activities most demanded by the consumer. As one GM executive expresses corporate policy: "Our program is finding out what people like, doing more of it; finding out what people don't like, doing less of it."

The result of that policy is the legendary GM giant, a favorite target of the big business critics. It is worth remembering that half a century ago, the counterparts of those who today urge "breaking up" General Motors were urging exactly the same thing concerning the Ford Motor Company, presumably because Ford was so large and had such a hold on the market that no other firm could compete! Apparently neither General Motors nor the American consumer was properly informed that Ford held an indomitable place in the market.

Bigness which is created and maintained *only* by a capacity to provide better service to the public is not only tolerable but also desirable. The consumers are quite capable of applying their own decision-making process in the market. So are investors:

> Leftist folklore holds that corporate directors constitute a self-perpetuating oligarchy, wholly independent of realistic constraints by millions of widely diffused, small shareholders. But if that were so, it is very doubtful that Americans would continue year after year to pour billions of dollars into such a system. The truth is that every shareholder in a U. S. corporation has a restraining influence over his corporate managers exactly commensurate with the size of his holdings. And since the latter precisely reflect the amount of wealth he is willing to risk in the venture, the equation of power and individual responsibility is perfect.[2]

Trouble does enter the largely self-policing marketplace when political control replaces stockholder and consumer control. Ralph Nader's proposals to place political observers on corporate boards is only the latest variation on an old theme — "Big business must be controlled; the consumer must be protected." With business, in the marketplace, the consumer can exercise his own controls, directly and to the precise extent that his interests are involved. Once the process is politicized, such consumer controls are swept aside. How responsive to the market is an appointive political watchdog who has no primary obligation to satisfy consumer demand?

When government remains outside the marketplace, competition is the order of the day for the big business community, precisely because of the consumer demands which the businessman is bound to respect, but the political appointee may safely ignore.

Small Business

The mistaken concern over big business tends to obscure one of the great forces in American society, the small businessman. Small firms employ well over half of the privately-employed labor force of the United States, while producing half of the national dollar volume of sales and revenue. The

[2]Henry G. Manne, "Good for General Motors?" *Barron's,* May 18, 1970.

world of General Motors, U. S. Steel, Texaco, and DuPont operates side by side with the world of small business.

General Motors requires 25,000 supplying firms to run its business; Western Electric has 40,000 suppliers. Marketing also requires the small firm. The giants in petroleum and automobiles have learned to their sorrow that local ownership, with its personal attention, is absolutely necessary for the successful operation of retail outlets. The small businessman needs the big producers, but the big producers also need the small businessman.

There are other areas of the economy where the giants fear to tread. Service businesses favor the small competitor, because he has lower overhead costs. This advantage, plus personal service to the customer, guarantees that the giants will not even try to compete.

Contrary to general opinion, the small operator often is a great deal more efficient than his giant competitor. Some production programs must be large — the automobile firm, for example. But size brings bureaucracy, and bureaucracy brings inefficiency. Not all efficient production takes place in large operations. Bigness can and does stifle new ideas, discourage real growth, and hamstring effective action. The corporate structure reaches such a size that the lines of communication clog with bureaucratic waste.

Some of the largest concerns have discovered the bureaucratic trap of excessive size and have deliberately decentralized, insisting that the various sections of their firm must compete with one another. Many giants have discovered that size may be more a liability than an asset in their competition with smaller firms.

Nor has the big, established concern proven to be a good environment for growth and new ideas:

> In general, though with some important exceptions, the little fellow, whether a small company or the lone "garage inventor," has been more innovative than the large company. To cite one example: Despite all the money that the aluminum companies are spending on research, only one of seven major changes in aluminum processing has come from a major company. The remaining six have largely been the work of individuals or of small companies.[3]

Many other research breakthroughs have come not from the highly touted research and development programs of big business, but from the small operator. A list of those individual breakthroughs would run to thousands of items, including the zipper, plastics, ball point pens, insulin, the jet engine, and air conditioning. True, large concerns further developed these

³Drucker, p. 62.

ideas and made mass production possible. The point is simply that the vital role of the small operator must not be ignored.

Another important role of the small businessman lies in the social function which he performs. The small businessman provides major support to America's 6,000 nonprofit organizations, 320,000 churches, and 100,000 private welfare organizations. These people feel that community service *matters,* not only in charitable terms, but in the daily business contact with their customers. True, these solidly middle-class people are the butt of a thousand jokes originating in the academy and among the "intellectuals," but the small businessman still remains the primary means of resisting the totally enmassed, totally politicized society. The key to that resistance is the sense of community, which functions best, it seems, closest to home.

For all our economic problems, the workings of both big business and the small operator seem well within the American definition of leaving all men free to compete, while doing a rather effective job of satisfying our material needs and wants in the process. Such economic problems as we have, and those problems *are* serious, are not due to a failure of the much-abused free enterprise system, but stem instead from our violation of a cardinal rule of that system: *Keep government out of the marketplace.* The results of that violation threaten to be disastrous.

Special Privilege

The reign of special privilege, granted by government, has disrupted the normal working of the market and created problems of monopoly and oligopoly in contemporary American economic life. If Adam Smith were to return to today's world, he would not be surprised at the results of government entry into the marketplace. After all, the canny old Scot had defined monopoly as a government-granted special privilege in the market. Historically, government regulation has always been the means by which established producers protected themselves from innovating competition.

Despite the mythological struggle between government and big business that dominates our economic folklore, most government intervention in modern America has meant problems especially for the small operator. Taxation is a case in point. The small businessman finds himself in such a complex tax structure that additional clerical help and a CPA are required just to keep him on the right side of the law. The National Federation of Independent Business reports that 30 percent of the clerical business expense of its members is directly due to tax regulations and resultant record-keeping. The small operator is simply not geared to such clerical and accounting operations and finds himself at a disadvantage to the huge concern, with its pool of expensive talent in the form of accountants, bookkeepers, and lawyers.

High taxation bears most heavily on the small businessman and the middle class in yet another way. The very poor and the very rich, with our present complex tax structure and exemption system, carry a small proportion of the tax load. The result is a system pressing by far the hardest upon the traditionally most thrifty elements of society. Thus savings, personal effort, and finally property itself come under attack in a politicalized economic order in which the middle classes are called upon to support the rest of society, but are offered virtually no incentive for doing so.

Meanwhile, present-day politicalization presents the big operator with a very different situation. At a time when the capital market is increasingly limited, when it is difficult for the small operator or the man with a new idea to get the capital to enter business or expand his operation, our present tax laws force the big concerns to retain capital. Double taxation of corporate dividends, once as a corporation profit and again as shareholder income, makes it attractive to retain capital in existing corporations. The result? The big get bigger and the innovator starves for capital.

The larger, established concerns also benefit from government-enforced monopoly in the marketplace. The CAB for airlines, the ICC for railroads and trucking, the FCC for communications, the SEC for brokers, all are examples of government licensure and regulation enforcing a monopoly situation. After all, there are two primary symptoms of monopoly: no new competitors allowed in the market, and no price competition. Under the politicalized regulatory activity now in force, government agencies exclude new competitors and fix prices. Monopoly? You bet!

It is probably true that some of the earlier variations of this government intervention in the market gave rise to the great outcry against monopoly which occurred earlier in this century, although at the time most people never suspected government was the culprit. Still, it should be obvious by now that government regulation is a poor device for correcting a politicalized system of special privilege, when it was the same governmental intervention which initially produced the situation. The concern over monopoly and special privilege evidenced by the American people was altogether appropriate, but it has been directed at the wrong target. Government itself has been the underlying cause of the problem.

Because government has been primarily responsible for special privilege in the market, antitrust legislation presents the peculiar aspect of asking the embezzler to audit his own books. On those occasions when antitrust has been applied, it has always been used as a political weapon, making the market even less responsive to competition. Nothing is done about the privileged positions in the market made possible by government, while a great deal of rhetoric is devoted to "the enemies of the people," the trusts, and similar bogeymen.

Thus the economic case is sometimes presented as the rich against the poor, with government presumably defending the poor. How misleading this is! In fact, most so-called "rich people" seem to prefer the existing politicalized system. Are they merely favoring the "status quo?" Or are they refusing to examine the underlying interventionist rationale which supports the system? Whatever the reason, the well-to-do in America are, as a group, conspicuously *not* oriented to free enterprise.

Perhaps many of the corporate executives and large stockholders have bought the argument that the way to avoid collectivism is through corporatism. The central idea here seems to be the belief that a partnership between government and the existing power structure in the business world will "maintain stability." The result of this imperfect alliance (despite some outspoken dissenters) may bear some resemblance to Galbraith's "technostructure" and the student radicals' "Establishment." Whatever it should be called, it will not work for very long:

> An economic system where each group entrenches itself more and more in a monopolist stronghold, abusing the power of the state for its special purposes, where prices and wages lose their mobility except in an upward direction, where no one wants to adhere to the reliable rules of the market any more, and where consequently nobody knows any longer whether tomorrow a new whim of the legislation will not upset all calculations, an economic system in which everyone wants to live exclusively at the expense of the community and in which the state's budget finally comes to devour half of the national income: a system of this kind is not only bound to become unprofitable and thus bound to intensify the scramble for the reduced total profit, but it will moreover in the end suffer a complete breakdown. This is usually called the crisis of capitalism and is used as an occasion for new and revolutionary interventions which complete the ruin and corruption and finally present us with the inexorable choice of either returning to a reasonable and ethical market system or of plunging into the collectivist adventure.[4]

Other Politicalized Institutions

Not only in business does this situation exist. Special economic privilege, privilege by government, also permeates the labor market. The large and powerful unions of today came into existence as the result of widespread governmental assistance, beginning especially during the 1930s. Presumably unionization was to redress the economic balance, insuring that the

[4]Wilhelm Roepke, *The Social Crisis of Our Time* (Chicago: University of Chicago Press, 1950), p. 130.

individual workingman would receive a measure of security from the vagaries of big business. What we have learned in the past 40 years is that unions are subject to the same effects of politicalization as any other organization of society. The union, enforced on the American workingman by the power of government, has been subject to a giantism and centralization of its own. The result for the workingman has been to penalize efficiency and progress, to reduce individual self-determination, to unleash, in circumstance after circumstance, a wave of brutal and callous disregard for life and property almost without precedent in American history. Here, as elsewhere, room for the individual or for individual values has steadily contracted as politicalized enmassment has expanded.

Special categories of government intervention in labor affairs, not usually considered under this heading, are licensure of professionals, providing many of the evils of monopoly for such groups as medical doctors, and farm subsidy, providing monopoly conditions for some of those engaged in production and distribution of food and fibers. The present shortage of medical care and the sad state of American agricultural production clearly show the results of government intervention in these areas of the economy.

The same problem afflicts other social institutions as well. Between big business and big government, there remains little room for university autonomy. It seems that bigness in one sector encourages bigness in another. In education, as in unionization, bigness has grown as a direct response to bigness in the corporate world and the political world.

As the universities have grown larger and become steadily more politicalized, both teacher and student have suffered a steady deterioration in the quality of the educational process in which they participate. Who would suggest that the quality of higher education has improved during the 1950s and 1960s?

The autonomy of the university has also slipped away in the face of an increasingly politicalized society. Financial connections, the ties that bind, link the university to the legislature and the corporation in tighter chains of subservience than any educator worth his salt would have tolerated two decades ago.

Throughout society we have suffered marked institutional erosion as the direct result of a politicalized economic fabric. The irony of it all is that we then turn to government, the same political agency that produced the situation, for a solution to our deteriorating situation.

To divorce our institutions — our businesses, our labor unions, our medical doctors, our farmers, our universities — from political controls and special interests; to insist that our institutions demonstrate and constantly reemphasize their social utility; in short, to make our institutions again responsive to free market pressures, would be a giant step toward reversing that deteriorating social scene which we face today. Free institutions can perform a service to America that politicalized businesses, unions, doctors, farmers, and universities cannot hope to match.

XIX

TECHNOLOGY

Man rushes first to be saved *by* technology, and then to be saved *from* it. We Americans are front-runners in both races. The United States led the world away from small wheatfields and toward big ones, away from outhouses and toward toilets, away from the virgin forest and toward the pulp mill, away from scarcity and toward abundance, away from few loaves of bread that were nutritious and toward many loaves that are not, away from the peasant and toward the factory worker, away from the child of nature and toward the quiz kid. Now a few Americans want to go, not in the other direction, but toward an intelligent use of their new advantages that permits them to find abundance in their personal lives, lives that have not been processed out of genuineness or fulfillment.

Gerald Sykes,
The Cool Millennium

The history of technological change and the reaction to that change throughout Western civilization reflects the same ambivalence which Mr. Sykes attributes to Americans. As early as 1811, England witnessed the Luddite assault on the machine. However, the laboring man was soon convinced that technological progress was all to the good. Many British intellectuals were less easily convinced. The result has been a century of anti-industrial polemics.

The agrarian background of American society left a residue of anti-industrial mentality among us as well. Yet from the beginning it has seemed clear that the new industrial civilization has been an unstoppable reality. Change has perhaps been inevitable, but is extremely difficult to measure, since the effects of technology reach far beyond mere industrial change. For example, the automobile has done far more than supplant the buggy manufacturers — it has revolutionized the American social scene. Virtually all our institutions have felt the impact.

The technological change which has occurred thus far seems slight when compared with the changes which lie ahead. New technologies are upon us.

Advances in theoretical knowledge — quantum physics, biochemistry, atomic and molecular structure — may soon have far-reaching practical consequences. Major new industries may well be formed. Some of today's largest businesses will either conform to this technological revolution or will cease to exist.

As the pace of technological change accelerates, it becomes steadily more important (and less likely) that the personnel of the new age be well grounded in humanities and some understanding of the social sciences. The result is an increasing tendency to regard all nontechnological values as ineffectual and irrelevant.

This lack of contact between humanism and science, between people-values and technological values, is not a new problem. It has caused many critics over the years to feel that technology has outrun our human values and put us on the road to an anti-utopia. Orwell's *1984* and Huxley's *Brave New World* have been the forerunners of an extended body of literature on the subject:

> Beyond all the differences of emphasis among its attackers, despite the different levels of abstraction and the conflicting motives, premises, and types of evidence offered by the critics of industrial society, a common image emerges. The essence of industrialism is mass production by means of the machine. A machine is a device that performs work through the use of moving parts that exert physical force upon one another in a rigidly organized and regular fashion so as to produce a standardized product. Society itself has become such a machine, an assemblage of standardized moving parts acting on each other by force so as to produce standardized products that in turn become parts of the machine. Man is a cog in the machine, or a product produced by it, or both. He is subject to forces beyond his control, just as are his fellows to whom he has become identical. Gone is freedom, gone is identity. Man is simply a machine, in a society of machines, in a physical environment of machines.[1]

Even allowing for the hysteria and special pleading to which such subjects lend themselves, it seems that some deeply troubling problem keeps surfacing concerning modern technological society.

Not All Change Is Progress

The gospel of material growth may yet prove to be an incomplete and unsatisfactory goal for human existence. An endless round of increasing

[1] Victor C. Ferkiss, *Technological Man: The Myth and the Reality* (New York: George Braziller, 1969), p. 75.

production and consumption may begin to exact too high a price from the quality of life. The GNP, it may be discovered, is only one of a number of measures which can be applied to human affairs.

As the pace of life increases, it does not necessarily follow that a corresponding rise occurs in the quality of that life:

> One can go from New York to Chicago in four hours, and the morning papers of either town can be read in the other at noon, and this is supposed to be a valuable achievement — but why? One goes from a vacuous dishevelling life in New York to a vacuous dishevelling life in Chicago, and the newspapers merely inform one that such is the kind of life lived in both places. I doubt greatly that the sum total of human happiness is increased by increasing facilities for keeping the human body in rapid motion; or that the capacity for enjoyment is enhanced; I should say rather the opposite.[2]

It is well to remember that technology exists for the sake of men, not men for the sake of technology.

The concern voiced by more and more people today is likely to center on such terms of waste, congestion, pollution — all terms related in one fashion or another to the problem of *glut,* terms describing a world in which the traditional problem of "too little" has been replaced by a new problem: *too much.* Surely men should have other things to do with their lives besides *consume;* yet, in our present social order, it is viewed as almost disloyal to suggest that preservation might on occasion be a virtue. Today we junk machines which might be repaired; we destroy sound buildings to erect far inferior "new construction" in their place; we bulldoze neighborhoods to make way for still more freeways. The GNP mentality, the exclusive preoccupation with the economy and with material production which Roepke has labeled "economism," tends to reduce all human affairs to the function of consumption. The effect is to treat man as a statistical appetite and nothing more. Thus advancing technology has simultaneously freed and bound the individual. While freeing him from material *needs,* it has bound him to material *concerns.* Such one-dimensional thinking afflicts many on both ends of the political spectrum.

Though Right and Left often share the diseased imagination associated with economism, they are quick to see faults in the particular version of avarice advocated by their opponents. Each side has its own definition of the Philistines. The Right criticizes government programs designed to expand and gratify social appetites at the expense of the public. Completely overlooking the appeal to collectivized avarice within its own position, the

---

[2]Albert Jay Nock, *Journal of Forgotten Days* (Hinsdale, Ill.: Regnery, 1948), pp. 114–115.

Left counters with an attack upon the urge to consume as stimulated by Madison Avenue. According to the Left, advertising *forces* people to consume.

This idea has great appeal for Americans who love to be told that their material appetites are in reality the fault of the wicked advertisers. This lets us eat our cake without feeling gluttonous. But it remains a basic fact of life that seduction demands a willing subject. If we don't like what our producers and advertisers sell us, we need only stop buying, and results will be prompt. Witness the Edsel.

Granted that people often display bad taste and bad judgment in the nature and quantity of their purchases, the fact remains that transference of that expenditure from the individual to the collectivity is likely only to make matters worse. Organized greed, enforced by coercion, is not an edifying prospect. Still, the politicalization of avarice is likely to occur precisely because we so largely accept consumership as a way of life and a primary value in the "private sector." In the peculiar logic of the times, "If consumership is good, why not collectivize it and do the job on a bigger and better basis?" All "production-for-use" schemes begin with this argument.

Until our social attitudes change, it is unlikely that we can hope for much improvement in our politics. As Whittaker Chambers expressed it, "The West believes that man's destiny is prosperity and an abundance of goods. So does the Politburo." The result on both sides of the Iron Curtain is an increasing substitution of the means of life for life itself, and this is a substitution peculiarly suited to political processes.

When the means and ends of life become confused, the resultant materialism brings special problems all its own. And we have reached such a point in America:

> Having many things seems to create a desire for more things, more clothes, houses, automobiles. Think of the pure horror of our Christmases when our children tear open package after package and, when the floor is heaped with wrappings and presents, say, "Is that all?" And two days after, the smashed and abandoned "things" are added to our national trash pile, and perhaps the child, having got in trouble, explains, "I didn't have anything to do." And he means exactly that — nothing to do, nowhere to go, no direction, no purpose, and worst of all no needs. Wants he has, yes, but for more bright and breakable "things." We are trapped and entangled in things.[3]

There was a time in this country when that was not so. There was a time when our material goals were designed to achieve nonmaterial ends. To the

[3] John Steinbeck, *America and Americans* (New York: Viking Press, 1966), pp. 139–140.

Americans who remembered the cold and hunger of the Old World, the chance to improve one's material holdings was a great blessing, because it provided a chance for human dignity. To the frontiersman or the poor urban worker, improved material status gave a man a chance to become more completely a man. There is nothing "graceful" or "character building" about poverty.

At what point does "prosperity" become mere material glut? Perhaps it is time to recall that man's primary task is to finish God's work, to develop our innermost selves. So long as material affluence furthers that goal, the result is prosperity. When wealth stands in the way of achieving that goal, the result becomes mere glut.

The Use and Abuse of Technology

One of the oft-heard promises of the mass-production technologists is the assertion that increased production will bring increased leisure. The results have not been reassuring:

> Leisure and free activity are not accessible to everybody, and they are conditions in no way connected with the machine. A man who is relieved of work is not thereby capable of leisure; a man who gains time does not thereby gain the capacity to spend this time in free activity, for leisure is not a mere doing-nothing, a state that can be defined negatively. Leisure, to be fruitful, presupposes a spiritual and mental life from which it draws its meaning and its worth. An *otium sine dignitate* ("leisure without dignity") is hollow, empty loafing. Nor is leisure, as many seem to think, a mere intermission in work, a limited time — no, by definition it is unlimited and indivisible, and from it originates all meaningful work. Leisure is the prerequisite of every free thought, every free activity. And this is why only the few are capable of it, since the many, when they have gained time, only kill it.[4]

The "many" to whom Juenger refers are the casualties of mass society, the people who have lost power to direct their own spiritual and mental existence and have become dependent upon mass occupation and mass entertainment to do the job for them.

There was a time when Americans did not need collective organization of their every moment. We knew how to work together to get a job done. Perhaps just as important, we knew how to play. Today many of us have forgotten how, except in some highly organized, specialized sports or some totally nonparticipatory spectator activities.

Technology is a useful servant, but a hard master:

[4]Friedrich Georg Juenger, *The Failure of Technology* (Hinsdale, Ill.: Regnery, 1949), pp. 5–6.

The advantages of the machines are so obvious and so desirable, that we tend to become, small step by small step, seduced into ignoring the price we pay for their unthinking use. The emphasis here is on *unthinking* use, because they all have their good uses. But the most careful thinking and planning is needed to enjoy the good use of any technical contrivance without paying a price for it in human freedom.

If an example were needed, TV is certainly a case in point. Much has been said about the contents of television programs. But my concern here is less with content and much more with what persistent watching does to a child's ability to relate to real people, to become self-activating, to think on the basis of his own life experience instead of in stereotypes out of shows.

Many children, four to six years of age, communicate mainly in terms of their favorite shows and relate much better to the TV screen than to their parents. Some of them seem unable to respond any more to the simple and direct language of their parents because it sounds unimpressive compared to the suave diction and emotionally loaded idiom of TV professionals. True, for such far-reaching consequences, not only the children, but their parents have to spend too much time in front of the set, or talk so little to each other that their adult conversation cannot offset the talking down or overemphatic voices of the programs.[5]

In the last analysis, the problem probably lies less in technology itself than in the uses to which men put that technology. For example, the increasing interdependency produced by modern technology gives great leverage to the force which one social group has available for use against another. The interrelation of our technological order leaves us defenseless in the face of a strike by postal employees, taxi drivers, hospital workers, "public utility" employees, or some other group with technological leverage.

We can also see an example of the effects of technology on the individual by examining his relations with business in the computer age. It seems that computers, once programmed, become deadly opponents. Letters, telephone calls, and indeed any other standard form of communication, may not suffice to correct a billing error, once the impersonal machinery has gone into operation. Versions of the "Nothing can go wrong . . . go wrong . . . go wrong . . ." joke are widespread. Unfortunately for many of the victims of such billing errors, the computerized, impersonal billing operations often also set in motion processes which adversely affect their credit rating. Some such mistakes have tragic and lasting consequences.

In a September 4, 1969, letter to the *New York Times,* Alfred Blooming-

---

[5]Bruno Bettelheim, *The Informed Heart* (New York: Free Press, 1960), p. 12.

dale, Chairman of the Board of Diners Club, described the "progress" of computerized business:

> We have been in the credit card business for 20 years — longer than anyone else — and I can remember the time when if something went wrong with a member's account, I called two little old ladies who rushed to the back of the shop and straightened out the problem in a matter of minutes. Obviously with today's volume of business, the little old ladies are gone and a monster machine has taken their place. This machine is fed periodically with various data and if the input happens to be wrong, God help the human being involved! It triggers off a series of dunning notices, legal letters, telegrams, it warns the collectors to start calling on the phone, and sends a letter of misinformation to everyone concerned. To repair the damage and reprogram the computer with the correct information takes months.
>
> . . . Just how to humanize the computer and the people who work with it is going to be a very big job.
>
> . . . In today's credit card business the small margins do not permit humans to be involved to any great extent in customer public relations. Every two years we stylishly go from one stage of computers to the next, and many good members get helplessly caught in these transition periods.

Mr. Bloomingdale went on to pledge that his firm hoped to humanize the technology of current business practices. But it seems that each new technological advance always moves us further in the opposite direction.

Another aspect of technology which can produce adverse effects on the individual is the pressure toward specialization which inevitably occurs. Technology tends to focus only on function and production, demanding a steadily increasing specialization of function to achieve a steadily increasing production. *Function* is technology's substitute for *purpose. Machines should have function — men should have purpose.* Any "efficiency" achieved by specializing men to the point where they come to have function rather than purpose is the kiss of death for human dignity.

There is only one *man* — abstractions such as economic man, political man, or technological man are likely to produce a fragmentation in human existence that disrupts life, no matter how "efficient" one's function in society may be. Men must be treated as more than interchangeable parts, if technology is to be used and not abused.

While sharply criticizing the dehumanizing effects of modern technology, we must never forget the advances in material well-being and health achieved by the American businessman and modern technology. Our problem is to remember that the goal of increased production is to free men from constraints, a task which technology cannot perform if in the process it binds men down as mere functioning parts of a productive machine. Advancing technology is desirable so long — and only as long — as it helps us in our pursuit of individuality.

We are all ambivalent on this issue. We recognize the conveniences and material comforts of technology. Yet we are prone to dream of the frontier, with its clean air and its individual values. A recent television special featured a raft trip down the Snake River, showing wilderness and simple, outdoor life on every hand. One of the young men making the trip had been stricken with appendicitis during the filming and had been flown out to a hospital for emergency treatment in the nick of time. I wonder how many of the television viewers, who watched the helicopter land, pick up the boy, and zoom off to life-saving treatment in a modern hospital many miles away, speculated upon the probable fate of someone who suffered appendicitis on that same river a century ago. We can all see the scars left by technology, but we tend to take for granted the advantages it provides.

What Do We Want?

Technology *can* provide us with a freer life. Whether it does or not is up to us and to our hierarchy of values. Undoubtedly there are other applications and developments possible for technology besides the current trends. Those developments need not be antithetical to the development of the individual.

Perhaps many of the problems of modern technological society have come about because we have never really thought about the subject. What do we *want* from technology? If we want only more and still more, we'll probably get it, with all the attendant consequences. If we insist upon improved quality in the lives of men, I believe technology can also provide that. The time has come to ask ourselves not merely whether we *can* accomplish certain technological goals, but whether we *should*. Though we cannot go back, we *can* decide how and where we go from here:

> Conservatism must insist that while the will of man is limited in what it can do, it can do enough to make over the face of the world; and that the question that must always be before us is, What shape should the world take, given modern realities? How can technology hope to invalidate conservatism? Freedom, individuality, the sense of community, the sanctity of the family, the supremacy of the conscience, the spiritual view of life — can these verities be transmuted by the advent of tractors and adding machines?[6]

Technology is essentially an exercise in problem solving. It solves the problems, and only those problems, with which it is confronted. Like one

---

[6]William F. Buckley, *Up From Liberalism* (New York: Hillman, 1961), pp. 213–214.

of its modern symbols, the computer, technology does not think for itself. It must be programmed. Until now, that programming has been pointed toward mass production and mass consumption. If technological change were programmed to provide answers to a new set of problems, we might surprise ourselves with the decentralization that could result, leaving far more elbow room for the individual than our present institutional structure affords.

To take industrial production as an example of what might be done:

> . . . it is possible to transform the organization of an industrial plant in such a manner that the work will acquire the meaning, self-determination and rhythm which characterize the working life of the artisan.
>
> Without sacrificing the output rate of industrial production methods, the depersonalizing and mechanizing effects of the old large-scale industrial enterprise, its massiveness, its minute division of labor and its barracklike atmosphere, would have to be replaced by forms which are diametrically opposed to the conveyor belt and the Taylor system.[7]

What's more, such methods work. When workers regain a sense of purpose and satisfaction in their work, more and better work is the direct result.

Not all products need be mass produced. We live in a world which hungers for craftsmanship, quality, taste, and variety. The "personal touch" can afford instant success in many lines of endeavor, even at a higher price than its mass-produced counterpart. Another economic pressure moving us toward more personalized, less mass-oriented organization is the rapid transition of society from *production* to *service* industries. Certainly, if Americans carry out their preferences in the market, turning from collectivized consumption habits to more personalized and specialized taste, we may rest assured that technology will follow suit. The choice is in our hands.

Let Men Live as They Will

If we would allow men to live as they will, we might begin by getting government out of business. If the business combinations now maintained only by government intervention were to pass from the scene, we might approach the goal of a partially decentralized industrial order. This seems especially relevant since current estimates suggest that only about one-third

---

[7]Wilhelm Roepke, *The Social Crisis of Our Time* (Chicago: University of Chicago Press, 1950), p. 220.

of American industrial production need occur in the large units to which we have become accustomed.

An antigovernment stand is not altogether sufficient, however. It begs the question to say "leave men free," when the social order surrounding them is so heavily weighted in one direction that no real choice is offered.

In order to recognize the true antithesis of a collectivist society we must look far beyond economic freedom. We shall find it in a society in which the greatest possible number of people leads a life based on private property and a self-chosen occupation, a life that gives them inward and, as much as possible, outward independence, which enables them to be really free and to consider economic liberty as a matter of course. It is at the same time a form of society whose arbiters are not the proletarians — with or without white collars — not the vassals of a new industrial feudalism and retainers of the state, but men who, thanks to their way of working and living, depend on no one but themselves and do not allow the affairs of the world to touch them; these are to be found among the best types of peasants, artisans, small traders, small and medium-sized businessmen in commerce and industry, members of the free professions and trusty officials and servants of the community. They set the tone not because they are a minority which has usurped power, but because their number will be so great that they will determine the character of society. Whatever one may think of it, no one will dispute that only such a society and not one which is herded together in large cities, giant enterprises, tenements, mass associations, trusts, and monopolies of all kinds, represents the true antithesis of collectivism.[8]

The development of such a leadership community would go far toward the restoration of life on a humane scale. Such men would know that crossing the continent at twice the speed of present planes would not double technological "progress" in that area — not unless it were accompanied by comparable progress in abatement of noise and other pollution.

Imagine how the first airline using nonpolluting jets would bring its case to the public, a public composed of enlightened consumers determined that technology must be men's servant, not their master. The market pressure thus generated would be irresistible for other airlines and manufacturers. Such leadership could redirect technological development away from indiscriminate quantity and toward real quality. We must decide.

In Antoine de Saint-Exupéry's story, *The Little Prince,* the prince meets a merchant:

[8] *Ibid.,* p. 178.

This was a merchant who sold pills that had been invented to quench thirst. You need only swallow one pill a week, and you would feel no need of anything to drink.

"Why are you selling those?" asked the little prince.

"Because they save a tremendous amount of time," said the merchant.

"Computations have been made by experts. With these pills, you save 53 minutes in every week."

"And what do I do with those 53 minutes?"

"Anything you like . . ."

"As for me," said the little prince to himself, "if I had 53 minutes to spend as I liked, I should walk at my leisure toward a spring of fresh water."

The little prince offers each of us some advice which we might profitably consider while making decisions concerning our technological future.

XX

THE ENVIRONMENT

The world today is sick to its thin blood for lack of elemental things, for fire before the hands, for water welling from the earth, for air, for the dear earth itself underfoot.

Henry Beston,
The Outermost House

The area of technological impact of most pressing concern in today's world is our environment. Historians may come to regard the second half of the twentieth century as the period during which science and technology made the greatest strides, while the quality of life on earth most sharply declined. Man-made damage to our environment has become the cause of the hour. It is alleged that one-third of the nation's sewage is dumped into our waterways in untreated form, that industrial waste is the equivalent of the untreated sewage of another 165,000,000 persons, that oil and pesticides are reducing the life forms of our oceans and lakes, that 800,000,000 tons of pollutants enter the air each year — in short, that our air and water are being dirtied to the point where life, human life included, can no longer survive in this world.

Imbalance and disharmony seem to accompany man's increasing divorce from nature. We seem to feel that science, technology, and industrial "progress" have made it unnecessary to live in harmony with the plant and animal life sharing the planet with us. This process has been carried to the point at which we now feel that parcels of land in their natural state must be set aside and protected from "progress." This protection is called "conservation."

The mere fact that protection is required to save bits and pieces of the natural order from the industrial order in itself indicates lack of balance and harmony in the present situation. Wildlife, space, food, plants, landscapes, all now exist at man's sufferance. It is worth noting that the only mammals other than men which have increased in numbers during the past 100 years are rats, animals apparently capable of living on the same terms as men. We have been teaching our young people that science and technology are man's weapons in the battle with nature but have forgotten to mention that men themselves are a part of the natural order and therefore subject to harm from those same weapons. When we oppose ourselves to nature, we should recall that the natural order is more than a passive victim. Nature can fight back with elemental forces that make men less masters of the situation than we would like to think:

> Ambitious men fight, first of all, against nature; they propose to put nature under their heel; this is the dream of scientists burrowing in their cells, and then of the industrial men who beg of their secret knowledge and go out to trouble the earth. But after a certain point this struggle is vain, and we only use ourselves up if we prolong it. Nature wears out man before man can wear out nature; only a city man, a laboratory man, a man cloistered from the normal contacts with the soil, will deny that. It seems wiser to be moderate in our expectations of nature, and respectful; and out of so simple a thing as respect for the physical earth and its teeming life comes a primary joy, which is an inexhaustible source of arts and religions and philosophies.[1]

Does all this sound a bit harsh and hysterical? Let's take a look at our world.

Lost Elbow Room

First of all, it is worth remembering one aspect of our environmental quality that receives less attention than it deserves: the sense of lost elbow room, of the annihilation of space. The sense of annihilated space takes several forms. One form is the world shrinkage of which modern transportation always boasts:

> The truest and most horrible claim made for modern transport is that it "annihilates space." It does. It annihilates one of the most glorious gifts we have been given. It is a vile inflation which lowers the value of distance, so that a modern boy travels 100 miles with less sense of liberation and pilgrimage and adventure than his grandfather got from traveling 10. Of course if a man hates space and wants it to be annihilated, that is another matter. Why not creep into his coffin at once? There is little enough space there.[2]

[1]John Crowe Ransom, "Reconstructed But Unregenerate," *I'll Take My Stand* (New York: Harper [Torchbook], 1962), p. 9.
[2]C. S. Lewis, *Surprised by Joy* (New York: Harcourt, Brace and World, 1955), p. 157.

Another form of decreasing elbow room is epitomized by urban existence itself. Former Secretary of State Dean Acheson writes nostalgically of the golden age of childhood ". . . before the plunge into a motor age and city life swept away the freedom of children and dogs, put them both on leashes and made them the organized prisoners of an adult world."

For one raised in the Rocky Mountains of Colorado, high in a mountain valley surrounded by snow-covered peaks, the matter of environment and space was of vital concern to me long before it became a popular subject. America still has unspoiled wilderness. Most of the ugliness surrounds our urban and industrial centers. But as our factories and housing developments push further into the country, still another form of space annihilation is progressing, ruining for all time what no amount of technological expertise can reconstruct.

The growing numbers of human beings who have grown to adulthood trapped in city corridors or lost in sprawling suburbs have been cheated of an irreplaceable heritage. We do not yet fully comprehend the nature of our loss:

Little if anything is known, however, of the ultimate effect on man of such drastic elimination of the natural stimuli under which he has evolved as a biological being. Air, water, soil, and fire, the rhythms of nature and the variety of living things, are not of interest only as chemical mixtures, physical forces, or biological phenomena; they are the very influences that have shaped human life and thereby created deep human needs that will not change in the foreseeable future. The pathetic weekend exodus to the country or beaches, the fireplaces in overheated city apartments, testify to the persistence in man of biological and emotional hungers that developed during his evolutionary past, and that he cannot outgrow.[3]

Worse yet, this denatured ugliness is no longer confined to our cities, suburbs, and industrial areas. Forty million visitors a year now jam our 32 operative national parks. In the National Forest Service units, 157,000,000 visitor days (one person staying 12 hours), were chalked up in 1969. On busy weekends, thousands are turned away because no campsites are available. Those who are lucky enough to get in find something less than "wilderness." Instead, they discover transistor radios turned up full blast, a horde of campers more jammed together than they normally are in their urban homes, traffic jams, vandalism, and a crime rate in national parks rising at four times the rate for the country as a whole. The experiment of

[3]René Dubos, *So Human an Animal* (New York: Scribner's, 1968), p. 177.

government-provided wilderness areas is deeply in trouble. Both national and state park facilities, offered "free" or at nominal charge to all comers, have again demonstrated that what is everyone's business soon becomes no one's business. The result is a wilderness slum, worse in most cases than the urban–suburban nightmare the people came to escape.

We have begun rationing space here in America, and the unaccustomed feeling has us scared. The big woods, the frontier, the mountains, the prairie have been such a basic aspect of the American Dream that perhaps we are entitled to wonder if there is an American Dream any longer. Certainly our environment is becoming steadily more confining as we annihilate space.

A Sense of Values

The evangels of "progress" tell us that the old American Dream is still there. In fact, we are told that the dream is now available in new and improved form, complete with all the "modern" trimmings. Yet there are losses as well as gains:

> Among the profits and losses of this age of industrial expansion must be counted those inherent in jet transportation, by which the span of a continent has been contracted to less than six hours. Granted that the pressurized cabin affords an indispensable convenience to the executive, who can close a deal in San Francisco on the same day his attorneys draw up the papers in New York, and to the labor leader, who, breakfasting in his split-level home on the outskirts of Detroit can turn up that noon in the cloakrooms of Congress. Yet just as certainly something has been lost along the way — something which those who recall the wonders of clicking westward over the rails of the Union Pacific or the Sante Fe will cherish with more than nostalgia. However time-consuming a three-day-and-night passage across the American continent may be, it is at least a potent reminder of the land from which the seeds of industry have sprouted. Even Premier Khrushchev, not so bright in many ways, got the point on his visit here in 1959. Having paid his disrespect to the White House and pounded his shoe in the United Nations, he headed for the tall corn of Iowa.
>
> For the corn is there in abundance, and beyond it the wheat, and almost everywhere the grazing cattle. And without them there would, of course, be no Cleveland, Dayton, Indianapolis, or Denver — or the executive sitting behind his desk in Rockefeller Center, figuring his next move in Saudi Arabia.[4]

[4]John Davenport, *The U.S. Economy* (Chicago: Regnery [paper], 1965), pp. 63–64.

The wilderness, the farm, the ranch, the small town have all played a vital role in our nation. Some of that crusty, old-style America is still around. Witness the old gentleman who recently commented, "Dollars? I never put too high a price on them. When lumbermen beg me to sell more of my timber, I tell them I'd rather look at the trees than the money."

The rest of us have something to learn from such men. In our world of artificial securities and arrangements which isolate us from nature, we run the risk of believing that our food comes from the grocery store, and our heat comes from the radiator. Such delusions are both stupid and dangerous. Overlooking the natural world, the real world and our relation to it, is always a dangerous business.

Natural surroundings have a way of providing peace to anyone who comes to share and not to change. Probably no one knew this better than Whittaker Chambers, and certainly no one had a better sense of the spiritual shortcomings reflected in our society's environmental crisis:

> In that sense, the farm is our witness. It is a witness against the world. By deliberately choosing this life of hardship and immense satisfaction, we say in effect: The modern world has nothing better than this to give us. Its vision of comfort without effort, pleasure without the pain of creation, life sterilized against even the thought of death, rationalized so that every intrusion of mystery is felt as a betrayal of the mind, life mechanized and standardized — that is not for us. We do not believe that it makes for happiness from day to day. We fear that it means catastrophe in the end. We fear it if only because standardization leads to regimentation, and because the regimentation that men distrust in their politics is a reflection of the regimentation that they welcome unwittingly in their daily living.[5]

The sense of values so well expressed by Whittaker Chambers has a deep and controlling hold upon America. The reverence for nature seems to have its roots in the quest to possess one's own soul and to see the world in perspective. The need for natural surroundings thus expresses a need for God in the lives of men. Perhaps it is necessary to renew one's wonder occasionally. In that way, nature again makes children of us all. This sense of the Ultimate, this sense of wonder, comes to those who love nature for her own sake.

Perhaps, then, the concern for today's environmental crisis is centered less on whether or not men can survive in a polluted world than on whether or not survival itself would have significance any longer in an unnatural, artificial world in which material "progress" has completely triumphed.

[5]Whittaker Chambers, *Witness* (Chicago: Regnery, 1952), p. 517.

One final word to those whose retort to everything we have said in this chapter is the reproach of romanticism. It certainly is romantic, if by that term we understand resistance to the destruction of dignity and poetry and the "unbought graces of life." If this is romanticism, we profess it unreservedly and proudly, and we will not allow ourselves to be intimidated or abashed by these would-be masterminds. We do not want to set the clock back; we want to set it right.[6]

Is Our Situation Really That Bad?

The "environmental crisis" has replaced Johnny's famous inability to read, the "missile gap," and similar temporary alarms as the nation's Number One Threat. Typically for a Number One Threat, prophets of doom have been outdooming each other on the subject of our environment, the current record being a prediction of total disaster within two years.

Actually, there is both good and bad in the developments which we now decry. Scientific and technological advance has improved our environment in many ways. The same pesticides and other chemicals which today are described as life-destroying have also increased the food supply for the world and made us the best-fed people on earth. The crowding of wilderness areas which we so disapprove is due to our greatly increased affluence and free time, developments directly traceable to our present industrial system. Surely food, material well-being, and time to pursue one's own interests are items in a person's life which demand some attention.

Any criticism of the system which fails to take into account both the good and the bad is sheer propaganda. Whether such one-sided analyses are made by the chamber of commerce or by a conservation group, they are still propaganda. It is the *total* life of the individual which must concern us.

Priorities are the key. How much do we value various portions of our lives? All things are characterized by degree. Eccentricity and madness, a drink with friends and a drunken orgy, a caress and a killing blow, all are matters of degree. We must decide what to emphasize.

Unless we keep the question of degree constantly before us, we are likely to do great harm to the same qualities of humanity we are trying to protect. Sometimes our "solutions" are worse than our problems ever were. The Presidential Commission on Population Growth and the American Future is a case in point. We hear a great deal in such circles about "optimum population planning," presumably to achieve "a population level properly suited for environment," but little or nothing is said about the moral question involved. We are so concerned about the quality of peoples' lives that we are willing to place them under a regime of scientific planning, presumably to be enforced by political coercion. If the plan is not to be enforced,

[6]Wilhelm Roepke, *A Humane Economy* (Chicago: Regnery, 1960), p. 88.

why do the planning? If the plan is to be enforced in peoples' lives, divorcing them from their own plans and choices, why waste further rhetoric on such phrases as "the quality of personal life?" Such phrases have no place in the feed-lot or the broiler house.

Neither does it help to select scapegoats:

> It doesn't need the confusion produced by attacking the power companies that are burning fuels efficiently so that thousands of other industrial plants won't have to burn them inefficiently.
>
> And recognize that if really good electric batteries are developed, and good electric cars become available — the power plants will immediately be the Number One Producers of Pollution. They'll be burning the fuel to produce the electricity stored in your pollution-free automobile. Then people can *really* scream about those awful power plants.[7]

Who's To Blame?

The problem of environmental quality is deeply rooted in billions of small decisions, decisions each of us make many times each day. The solution to almost any environmental problem can be achieved *at a price*. The question is how many of us are willing to pay how high a price for those solutions. Many of us balk at the increased costs involved, preferring to talk loosely about the "necessity" of political action to solve the problem.

Unfortunately, government shows utterly no sign of being able to deal with such problems effectively. In fact, government itself is a notorious polluter. Those so concerned about the ecology of San Francisco Bay should realize that the United States Navy daily dumps in the bay raw sewage in amounts comparable to a town of 4,500. The Corps of Engineers, while maintaining ship channels in the bay, routinely dumps "dredge spoilings" into the bay and the surrounding marshlands.

More devastating are the environmental side effects accompanying federal programs of other sorts:

> The interstate highway program is a classic example of the environmental problems a major program can spawn . . . its purpose is clear-cut — build highways. "And," one council staffer notes, "we sure as hell built them."
>
> But the unanticipated environmental damages — immediate and long-range — have been serious. Highways plowed through parks, split neighborhoods, obliterated scenic areas. The program bred an elite corps of professionals that now lobbies for new projects before

---

[7]John W. Campbell, "Red Tide," *Analog*, June 1970, p. 178.

old ones are finished. Suburban development followed the freeways
and the low suburban population densities, in turn, now pose serious
obstacles to economically viable mass transit systems. No one quite
foresaw, says one Federal official, that the program would "lead to the
ultimate dependence upon the automobile by nearly every family in
the country."[8]

This is a serious charge, considering that the automobile is America's
number one source of pollution!

Other examples of government as direct or indirect polluter confront us
on every hand. The supplementary generators of TVA get their coal from
strip and auger mining on the Cumberland plateau, in a process which
leaves pollution and ugliness in its wake. Federal tax and regulatory policies
also take their toll of the environment:

> Accelerated depreciation and redepreciation provisions, for example,
> surely encourage . . . a whole breed of entrepreneurs who throw up
> shoddy real estate developments, take a quick writeoff, sell the prop-
> erty at a nice profit and move on. And the oil import quota system
> limits the ability of domestic oil companies to import the low-sulphur
> oil needed to help reduce air pollution. . . .
>
> Old automobile hulks litter the landscape, yet one economic barrier
> to reconverting them to usable steel is ICC-approved freight rates.
> Railroad freight rates on scrap are substantially higher than the
> freight rates on ore. . . .[9]

The United States Government owns 34 percent of the acreage in this
nation. Each year, federally financed highway, airport, and reservoir projects change the face of nearly 600,000 rural acres. The Council on Environmental Quality reports that federal grasslands are badly overgrazed, that
national forests (often managed exclusively with an eye toward lumber and
pulp operations) are suffering the loss of various native wildlife species, that
federal financing of predator control programs is driving other species
toward extinction. And now it is proposed that we turn to government to
save our ecological balance!

Government also hurts our environment in less obvious ways. Minimum
wage legislation renders unfeasible any form of labor-intensive industry.
The present "throw-away" culture is the result. It costs too much to handle
glass milk bottles, pop bottles, and thousands of other returnable packaging
items. As recently as 15 years ago, waste paper processing was still economi-

[8] *Wall Street Journal,* September 23, 1970, p. 1.
[9] *Ibid.*

cally feasible. Over 60 percent of the waste was recycled, compared with 10 to 15 percent today. The manual sorting required to collect, separate, and salvage the reusable plastic, glass, aluminum, and paper has been largely priced out of the market by government, with waste and litter as the direct result.

Government on all levels becomes involved in our deteriorating environment. If we're concerned about "too many people," perhaps we should recall that by far the most rapidly expanding segment of the population is that portion receiving a subsidy for irresponsible procreation. The more illegitimate children, the less parental responsibility, the higher the government subsidy. Any sign of parental responsibility — as, for example, a father in the home — leads to reduced income for the people involved.

Available on every hand are examples of local and state governments causing the very problems of which they most complain. In New York City, the only industries failing to meet the new anticontamination requirements are the city-owned water and power facilities. Municipal incinerators and inadequate sewage treatment plants pollute the air and water from coast to coast. The State of Illinois maintains a law on the books requiring Illinois public institutions to use Illinois coal. Since most of that coal is soft, the result is to specify by law that state institutions must pollute.

And it is to government, I repeat, that we now turn to save us from pollution and environmental decay!

What Can Be Done?

If government cannot do the job of protecting our environment, what options remain open to us? A good point of departure is the reassertion of a basic fact: Decent water, decent air, privacy and the other environmental factors which so concern us are all instances in which private property rights can be applied. Much of our present environmental decay stems from an unwillingness of our present society to protect property rights. As usual, what is everyone's business quickly becomes no one's business. When rivers, lakes, roadways, and parks are "public," which of us will take care of them? Don't say government — the demonstrated case against government-as-conservator is too clear. What is less clear is the fact that government has been as remiss in protecting property rights as in protecting the environment. In fact, the two governmental failures go hand in hand.

Government preempts ownership of over one-third of the land in the United States, and then leases or otherwise grants use of that land to various individuals and groups. The absence of individual ownership, the absence of property rights, produces an irresponsible attitude toward use of the property involved.

Campers and tourists, granted use of national parks at little or no cost, have made a nightmare of many wilderness areas.

Lumber companies lease forest land from the government and, lacking the responsibility of long-term ownership, have no motivation to consider preservation of forest resources.

Industries located along rivers they cannot own have no motivation to preserve the quality of the water. In fact, the company's costs are lowered by using the river as a dumping ground.

Government does not grant ownership of ocean fisheries to commercial fishermen. The fishermen have little occasion to preserve long-term fishing conditions. In fact, the more they capitalize upon short-term use of the fishing waters, the greater their profit.

Why are we surprised when our wilderness becomes a slum, our forests stripped, our streams polluted, our fisheries exhausted? In the absence of property rights, the results will always be the same.

Clean water and clean air are property rights. A government which fails to protect such rights finally ceases to have positive social function. How does it happen that common-law defense of property rights, the most basic of guarantees for centuries, has not been applied? In a word, because governmental policy, duly reflected in the courts, has not been oriented toward protection of private property. Our dominant social philosophy has contrasted "property rights" with "human rights," as though the property right could ever be anything but a most basic human right. The result has been a decline in the very "human rights" so much discussed, including a decline in the right to clean water and clean air. Let the courts begin enforcement of property rights, let government get out of the business of interfering with property rights, and many of our present environmental discontents will pass away.

If those who invade a property right are called upon to bear the full cost of that invasion, most such invasions will promptly cease. Pollution control technology is already available, but it is expensive. Who should bear those additional costs? Justice demands that consumers who use the service necessitating those increased costs should pay accordingly.

Let the customers of a polluting paper mill pay the additional product costs for cleaning up the water. What if the increased cost makes the paper too expensive? If those who use the product do not wish to pay the full costs of production, then production should cease. Stringent enforcement of property rights can return to us the control of our environment.

Control of the environment will not return to us so long as we continue in our present vein of politicalized thinking. Things will not improve so long as we believe that someone else should pay for our mess. If environmental pollution is allowed to continue under its present politicalized auspices, there will be virtually no economic incentive to develop the technology to deal with the problem.

Actually, potential profits are there to be made in the technology of

environmental protection. As the tired old political approach to the problem totters along toward total failure, new technologies are already developing. Consider the waste disposal problem of our major cities.

Landfill dumps are fast disappearing. Already New York City dumps are
so far from town that waste disposal costs have doubled. Waste can no
longer be burned since only 30 percent of today's trash is combustible in
this age of "no-deposit, no-return" containers. Politicians no longer know
what to do with the stuff, except talk about it.

Sensing a profit, American industry is on its way to solving the problem.
General Electric, Monsanto, and General Motors are experimenting with
shredding equipment:

> What comes out of the giant shredding machine is something called
> "sterifill." It is odorless and completely decontaminated, and has the
> consistency of peat moss. Anything can go into it — the parts of an
> old Chevrolet, a discarded telephone pole, the bones from last Sun-
> day's leg of lamb, the liquid sludge from sewage disposal plants.
>
> When the shredder has done its job it produces a useful compost
> material that can be put back on the land as fertilizer, roadside con-
> touring, landfill of any type. Mr. Macaluso [a trash removal contrac-
> tor in New York City] speaks of a "total concept" of waste disposal;
> the shredder leaves nothing that is unusable toward the end of re-
> storing to the earth what man takes away from the earth.
>
> Mr. Macaluso insists there is nothing Utopian about the shredding
> proposition. If New York does not come to some variant of it in the
> next few years, the city will have to be deserted. It will cost less to
> transport shredded waste, which is 30 times more dense than the
> average household rubbish, than it now costs to put the leftover
> product of incinerators into trucks or barges for dumping in swamp
> areas or 10 or 20 miles out to sea.
>
> The time is coming when the coal cars that bring fuel from the strip
> mines to urban power plants will be loaded with shredded wastes for
> their return trips to West Virginia or Pennsylvania. The wastes will
> be dumped into stripped areas to restore them to useful fertility. The
> poisoned Hackensack, N. J., meadows, now useless for anything, even
> for "wetland" incubation of marine life, can be made over into odor-
> less and decontaminated building, park and garden space.[10]

This is only one example of the potentialities involved. Industrial Services
of America, a Louisville, Kentucky, firm operates refuse removal systems
for industrial plants and municipalities, first plucking all materials of value

[10]John Chamberlain, "Saving Our Environment at a Profit," *Human Events,* June 6, 1970.

from the waste and then converting the residue to sanitized landfill. The firm cleans up the mess and makes a nice profit in the process.

Similarly, about 75 auto-shredding machines are now in use around the country, engaged in the profitable business of converting old automobiles into valuable scrap metals, while simultaneously helping to clean up the accumulation of the 10,000,000 cars and trucks which reach the end of the line each year.

The notion of making environment protection systems partly self-liquidating has occurred to others. Babcock & Wilson and Esso Research & Engineering have launched a $7 million joint effort to develop an air pollution control system for power plants which will capture emissions from oil- or coal-burning boilers and convert them into marketable sulphur. Rotodyne Manufacturing Corp. is developing a sewage disposal system (it's at the pilot plant stage) which, in theory, will pay for itself through recovery of water and industrial chemicals. Abraham Zion, who took control of Rotodyne six months ago, is a fanatic on the subject of recycling waste material. "Why," he demands, "should we go to Labrador for iron ore and to Ghana for bauxite when we have such an abundance of those minerals right here in our own junk piles?" Technology — whether his own or another's — someday will reclaim them. In the process it also will go a long way toward improving the landscape.[11]

The market pressures for a "smogless car" are also building. A great deal of research is going into the subject. Two designers promise delivery in the near future: William Lear of Reno, developer of the Lear Jet, and the General Steam Corporation of Newport Beach, California. Competitors are springing up across the nation.

Residents of many states will see fume-free cars in operation and will be able to judge for themselves the appeal of quiet, odorless motoring. The examples will be provided by local service fleets of gas and electric companies. These cars will use a natural gas fuel system initiated by Pacific Lighting and Service in Southern California. The natural gas is stored in an auxiliary tank in the car separate from and in addition to the conventional gasoline tank. A flick of a switch transfers the fuel feed line from the gasoline tank to the auxiliary and back again. Natural gas is already used to carry visitors around Disneyland. . . .[12]

[11]"Outside the Mainstream," *Barron's*, April 13, 1970, pp. 1, 8.
[12]"Green Light for the Smogless Car," *Saturday Review*, December 6, 1969, p. 86.

Good environmental control and good business go together, so long as the property right and the profit motive are allowed to function. The profit motive functions in indirect ways as well. The Coors Brewery of Golden, Colorado, America's fourth largest beer producer, has been paying cash for return of its aluminum beer cans. Not only do the civic groups receiving the cash payments appreciate the arrangement, but the company reaps a great deal of goodwill with its program. One additional benefit: By the end of 1970, it is estimated that the company will have salvaged some 92,-000,000 beer cans which otherwise might be cluttering the landscape.

Granted that the private property, free market concept can go a long way toward defeating pollution and cleaning up the environment, and could go even farther if we stopped interfering politically, what about the problem of preserving wilderness and privacy? Does the market have any answers in this area?

American business is recognizing that goodwill and good profit go hand in hand. The result has been a renewed defense of wilderness, wildlife, and privacy. A fine example has been the Standard Oil of New Jersey campaign to prove that oil production and refining can be carried on without harm to wilderness or the privacy of others. Consider a sample or two from Esso's current goodwill campaign:

King Ranch is a hunk of pure Americana under the huge Texas sky. It is a lot of things in a large place. And they all get on remarkably well together.

There are 30,000 cattle and 28 oil and gas fields; 2,000 miles of fencing and 1,000 miles of buried pipeline; over 300 windmills and the world's largest natural gas plant. . . . There are schools and stores and fire stations; 500 cowboys; 2,000 cow ponies. A training track for race horses. And 500 miles of private road. Yet there is more wildlife on the ranch today than ever before in its history.

We, at Jersey, believe this last fact proves something about our affiliate, Humble Oil & Refining Company. Good housekeeping.

They have been drilling for oil and gas on the ranch for 45 years. If running an oil field were the noisy, messy business some people think it is, how come wild geese, wild turkey and bobwhite quail elect to stay and multiply by the thousand?

If pipeline and gas plants pollute the water, how come deer, nilgai, and javelinas guzzle it? And thrive.

One more point about this precious water. The King Ranch gas plant uses thousands of gallons an hour for cooling purposes. When this water is returned to the ponds and creeks, the cattle drink it.

These include the famous Santa Gertrudis, the first breed of cattle developed in the Western Hemisphere. They are now bred in forty-eight foreign countries. Quite an export.

Would the owners of King Ranch expose these rich, red beauties to anything less than good water? Not on your life.[13]

Imagine a tiny green hump of an island in a Louisiana swamp. Its total area is less than five square miles.

Put 200 houses on it and 700 people. Add one of America's largest rock salt mines, the Tabasco sauce factory and over 100 oil wells. And what have you got? Overcrowding?

Quite the opposite. Avery Island seems almost undiscovered. A place for the painter and poet.

Its bird sanctuary sits in a 200-acre garden. Here you find irises from Siberia. Grapefruits from Cochin. Evergreens from Tibet. Bamboo from China. Lotuses from the Nile. Soap trees from India. Daisies from Africa's Mountains of the Moon. And the world's most complete collection of camellias.

The sanctuary itself is a sight for any sore-eyed conservationist. It was established 26 years ago by Mr. Edward A. McIlhenny, a member of the family that has owned the island for 152 years. It had one purpose. To save the snowy egret from extinction.

Known as Bird City, the sanctuary started with only seven egrets. Now, over 100,000 nest around its man-made lake every year. To see these alabaster birds sharing their Eden with herons, ducks, coots, swans, cormorants, turtles, deer, and alligators is almost a primeval experience. It seems to put the clock back to the beginning.

And wherever you wander on this peaceful island, you have to look hard to spot the oil wells. Many are hidden by grandfatherly oak trees bearded with Spanish moss. Others are screened by banks of azalea and rhododendron. To Jersey's affiliate, Humble Oil & Refining Company, this respect for environment is only right and proper.

The oil industry provides Louisiana with one-third of its total revenue. But even this contribution would be a poor excuse for defiling beauty or disturbing wildlife.

Amen say the egrets.[14]

The market could solve the wilderness and privacy problem in another way as well, by putting a market price on space. Wilderness property is being offered on a condominium basis to those who are tired of being turned

---

[13]"Coexistence on the King Ranch," Standard Oil of New Jersey press release.
[14]"This bird sanctuary is an oil field," Standard Oil of New Jersey press release.

away from overcrowded national parks. The condominium campsite is catching on rapidly. The buyer is offered private, clean camping space, with such utility hookups as he prefers and is willing to pay for, plus joint ownership in the common wilderness area and the recreational facilities provided. When the owner is not using his private spot himself, the space may be rented to others. In many cases, the developers will perform the rental service themselves for one-half the fee.

The virtue of such private developments is that *responsibility* accompanies ownership. The areas are clean, quiet, and *private*. Nor is the price tag oriented toward the wealthy. The market demand which has developed for such privacy and wilderness had made possible developments offering facilities at very modest prices. The idea has caught on so well that private condominiums are springing up all across the country. Even in the area of wilderness, a frank and full application of private property concepts can work wonders.

In the area of our environment, our primary concern is the achievement of life on a human scale. The market can do many things in enabling us to achieve that goal, but the principal thing to remember is that *we,* our preferences, our values, *are the market.* We decide the conditions of our future environment 1,000 times a day. Thus the real source of pollution is the consumer. If we wish to use the products produced by pollution sources, then *we* are the polluters. The corporation is only our intermediary in the transaction.

If we make it profitable to pollute, pollution will continue. On the other hand, if we take property rights back from government and insist that responsibility and opportunity must go hand in hand, we can go a long way toward stopping the deterioration of our environment. The present capacities of a partially free market to do just that should give us the courage to go the rest of the way toward full property rights and a truly free market.

Masters of Our Fate

Contrary to what our protest marchers are likely to shout, we cannot improve our environment by stifling change. The clock will turn backward for no man. Neither can we solve our environmental problems by merely talking about them while still accepting the present social values.

No important change in our standards is ever achieved without a reorientation of our loyalties, tastes, and convictions. Until we do some thinking about the quality of our life, thinking which effects an inner change, no really effective changes are likely to occur in the social values which will be the final determinant of our environment.

History confirms present-day observations in demonstrating that man can become adjusted, socially and biologically, to ways of life and environments that have hardly anything in common with those in which civilization emerged and evolved. He can survive, multiply, and create material wealth in an overcrowded, monotonous, and completely polluted environment, provided he surrenders his individual rights, accepts certain forms of physical degradation, and does not mind emotional atrophy.[15]

This is not a discussion for or against scientific and technical research, but it is an appeal to examine the *direction* of that research. Of course we all want a better material life, but at what cost? While we must be left free to decide, thus implying the viability of market processes (there being no other valid way of deciding), we might remember that our present structure of materialism, which so assaults our environment, may be doing more to dehumanize us than to further our goals and solve our problems. My only point is that no alternative to our present discontents exists, except the free market and private property — *but* even the free market is no alternative unless the people living and making their choices in that market rise to the occasion with choices worthy of free men, men appreciative of the meaning and substance of America's environmental heritage.

[15]Dubos, p. 175

XXI

THE CITY

[The American] . . . is aggressively individual, and yet he swarms and goes to hive in the noise and discomfort of his tenements and close-packed cities. Once when enemies roamed the open, there was a reason for thronging in caves and castle courtyards, but with these dangers removed, he is drawn to packed subways, crowded streets, howling traffic and penal quarters in apartment houses. And in America this human tendency seems to be increasing; the small towns grow smaller so that men and women can breathe poisoned air and walk fearfully through streets where violence does not even wait for darkness. We are afraid to be alone and afraid to be together. What has happened to us? Something deep and controlling and necessary.

John Steinbeck,
"America, Where Are You?"

Seven of every 10 Americans, some 140,000,000 people, make their home on one percent of the land. Most demographic projections anticipate a steadily advancing trend toward still further urbanization. One urban planner predicts an agglomeration of 50 million to 100 million people in what he terms the "East Coast New York region." This enmassment is presumably to occur within the next 50 years, by which time, the estimate continues, 95 percent of America's population will be urban. Such predictions are based partially on assumptions of a greatly increased population, a subject likely to produce fallacies and hysterical projections. However that may be, such predictions are also often based upon a sociological value judgment: Urbanization of American life is presumed to be desirable in itself, the logical outcome of technological and social "progress."

For many people the hurried and harried life of the city has not seemed the place to achieve the maximum serenity and harmony of life. A frequent literary theme of such dissenters has been to inquire of the American people, in the haunting question of *I'll Take My Stand,* "What are you losing that you once possessed? Are you quite sure that you want to discard it entirely?"

Such critics form a part of an old and distinguished tradition. Plato,

Aristotle, Cicero, and Montesquieu, in common with the entire body of classical political philosophy, have doubted that "the good life" could be led in an urban setting.

The Case Against the City

The "cities" which most such critics had in mind were a far cry from the urban civilization of our times. City problems have been on the scene for thousands of years, but the problems of present urban civilization represent a quantum jump in the nature and magnitude of those problems.

To cite everyone's favorite example of urban decay, consider the plight of New York City. Despite a municipal budget of nearly $7,000,000,000 a year, its citizens can scarcely breathe the air, its homes are robbed with near regularity, its pedestrians are not safe after dark and steadily less safe in broad daylight, its jails are filled, its courts years behind in settling criminal cases, its police can scarcely defend themselves. With over a million people already on relief in New York City, over 20,000 new cases are being added each month. If New York City welfare recipients were to launch out on their own, *by themselves* they would constitute the eighth largest city in America.

The problems of the city are not limited to the poor. In the eloquent words of René Dubos, a distinguished scientist:

I live in mid-Manhattan and, like most of my contemporaries, experience a love–hate relationship with technological civilization. The whole world is accessible to me, but the unobstructed view from my 26th floor windows reveals only a confusion of concrete and steel bathed in a dirty light; smog is a euphemism for the mud that constantly befouls the sky and blots out its blueness. Night and day, the roar of the city provides an unstructured background for the shrieking world news endlessly transmitted by the radio.

Everything I eat, drink, and use comes from far away, or at least from an unknown somewhere. It has been treated chemically, controlled electronically, and handled by countless anonymous devices before reaching me. New York could not survive a week if accident or sabotage should interrupt the water supply during the summer or the electric current midwinter. My life depends on a technology that I do not really understand, and on social forces that are beyond my control. While I am aware of the dangers this dependence implies, I accept them as a matter of expediency. I spend my days in the midst of noise, dirt, ugliness, and absurdity, in order to have easier access to well-equipped laboratories, libraries, museums, and to a few sophisticated colleagues whose material existence is as absurd as mine.[1]

[1]René Dubos, *So Human an Animal* (New York: Scribner's, 1968), pp. 216—217.

At least René Dubos has a choice. Many lifelong urban poor do not have a choice. The people most injured by the quality of present-day urban existence are those who have no standard of comparison, those who have always lived that way. Otherwise, why would most people ever stay in the city? The most spectacular increases in population are occurring where living conditions are most crowded, polluted, and inhumane:

> Modern man can adjust to environmental pollution, intense crowding, deficient or excessive diet, as well as to monotonous and ugly surroundings. Furthermore, biologically undesirable conditions do not necessarily constitute a handicap for economic growth. Great wealth is being produced by men working under extreme nervous tension amidst the infernal noise of high-power equipment, telephones, and typewriters, in atmospheres contaminated with chemical fumes or in crowded offices clouded with tobacco smoke.
>
> . . . Murky skies, ill-smelling air, noisy streets, vulgar design, uncouth behavior are accepted without protest and indeed remain unnoticed by those who have experienced these conditions from early life on. Paradoxically, the most frightening aspect of human life is that man can become adapted to almost anything, even to conditions that will inevitably destroy the very values that have given mankind its uniqueness.[2]

Surely environment and life-style have a significant place in determining the attitudes and values of our own and subsequent generations. If so, then what can we expect from a generation of men who have come to accept "a mild civic nausea" as the normal burden of their existence? What chance does a child have for normal development in today's urban environment? Studies undertaken at Massachusetts Institute of Technology would seem to indicate that adult mental health has a close, working connection with pleasant childhood memories, memories which for most well-balanced adults are usually related to natural, outdoor surroundings, involving grass, trees, light, fresh air, running streams. What of a generation who have no inkling of such things? What of those who are so packed together that they no longer think of themselves as part of a larger process? Such lost souls of urban humanity are likely to think little of their own personalities, and think not at all of the others around them. Bernard Iddings Bell, in his prophetic little book, *Crowd Culture,* describes the result:

> The late W. N. Guthrie used to say there was no civilized man or woman in New York City who had not been civilized somewhere else, in a small town on the plains, in the ghetto in Warsaw, on a southern

[2] *Ibid.,* pp. 161, 102–103.

plantation, somewhere like that. New York, he maintained, could
civilize nobody for, while in that megalopolis there is opportunity to
express oneself all over the map, there is next to no neighborhood
opinion to exercise correction. There are, in fact, no neighborhoods,
only frequently migrating human units, anarchs, so lonely that they
will gladly follow any demagogic quack who pretends to be friendly.
This was exaggeration, but not greatly so. With us the *mores* are [no]
longer determined by mutual consent among friends. They are built
up mechanically and anonymously; and because they are what they
are, they no longer help as of yore. We still more or less obey statute
law; we pay little heed to unwritten customs of mutual dignity, or even
of decency.

. . . In such a situation it is not unnatural that individuals should
live more and more each for self, with less and less consideration for
the comfort, even for the safety, of the people next door or the family
over the way. One does not know their names. Why bother to learn?
They will soon be moving, or one will move oneself. After years of
this there remains in America little regard for the rights of others to
privacy or peace. Let the radio blast. Let the children yell. Throw the
rubbish where you will. The sanctity of property, either communal or
personal, becomes nobody's proper concern.[3]

Perhaps men cannot order their affairs according to traditional social
patterns demanding mutual respect and confidence unless they first learn
to have respect and confidence in themselves. And there is little to inspire
either respect or confidence in the individual or his surroundings, in the
current pattern of life lived by many people in urban America. Of course
there are obvious exceptions to the above rule, but the great mass of men
upon whom urban society presently presses are not so fortunate as to be
exceptional.

Nor are the suburbs any sure answer to the problem. Population density
may be less, the desire for quiet and greenery may be at least partially
satisfied, and some of the village atmosphere of a traditional past may seem
to be recaptured. But such suburban differences often prove superficial. In
practice, many so-called suburbs are little more than the satellite cities of
some urban center. Few would regard the communities comprising Greater
Los Angeles as an escape from anything, except perhaps an escape from the
frying pan into the fire.

The suburbanite also finds himself breathing the same air, drinking the
same water, and fighting the same traffic as his urban brother. As people

---

[3]Bernard Iddings Bell, *Crowd Culture* (Chicago: Regnery, [Gateway Edition], 1956), pp.
21–22.

flee the problems of the city, they create their own cities and their own problems. Crime, taxes, congestion, and traffic are all rising at far faster rates in the suburbs than in the central cities. It seems that there are steadily fewer places to hide from urban woes.

The Case for the City

Fortunately for this nation, there is a good deal more to the matter than the critics of urban life are usually willing to admit. Historically, the city has held out promise to those seeking prosperity, glamour, liveliness, opportunity. Dreams in all shapes and sizes have usually accompanied migrations to the city.

The result has been a crossroads where people of different backgrounds and capacities could congregate, asking new questions and discovering new answers, producing artistic, literary, scientific and social advance. The city has often represented the common life, providing men with a sense of community. It has functioned also as a cultural, religious, and economic center.

But today community has become congestion. Opportunity has slipped away, leaving alienation and unrest. The city, once a haven, has become a place from which to escape. What has been happening? How has the traditional role of the city so completely changed? What has corrupted this important institutional form? As elsewhere in our society, the problem is less the institutional form itself than those of us whose shift in values has changed that form.

Who's To Blame?

Our ideas about the city are as unsettled as today's cities themselves. We seem unable to devise machinery for handling the great masses of people brought together in urban civilization. Though we are highly exercised about urban problems, we are paralyzed in thought and action when it comes to doing anything about those problems. Most of the enormous centralized solutions which are proposed sound very like the disease they are purported to cure.

Perhaps the inability to address ourselves to the problems of urban civilization stems from our refusal to recognize the fundamental failure of one of the most cherished assumptions of modern America. In short, perhaps we can't do anything about the urban mass because we suspect that the mass may be our most conspicuous instance of modern material "progress," one of the great gods of America in the twentieth century.

We accept a high level of filth, ugliness, tension, and inconvenience, not because anyone prefers the dirty or the ugly, but because our communities want to possess what we define as material "prosperity." The flow of goods necessary to make us feel "prosperous" has caused us to emphasize productivity, even at a cost in human significance.

Does this sound abstract and absurd? No more abstract and absurd than the values dominating our present urban civilization, values which permit us to accept unbelievably poor conditions because we believe ourselves to be "prosperous":

> Countless incidents in the life of urban dwellers illustrate how we overlook the dangers that result from our temporary adjustments to undesirable situations.
>
> On a hot and humid Friday during midsummer, I landed at Kennedy Airport early in the afternoon. The taxicab that was taking me home was soon caught in a traffic jam, which gave the driver an opportunity to express his views on the state of the world. Noting my foreign accent, he assumed that I was unacquainted with the United States and proceeded to enlighten me on the superiorities of American life. "You probably are surprised by this heavy traffic so early on Friday afternoon," he remarked, as the cab stood still in the sultry air saturated with gasoline fumes. "The reason there are so many people on the road at this hour is that we have plenty of leisure in this country and all of us can afford an automobile." As we removed our coats and mopped our brows, he added forcefully, "In the United States we all live like kings."[4]

Meanwhile, the incessant propaganda of every chamber of commerce in the country is to attract more industry, more government money for more freeways, more and still more of all those things we call "progress"; until, presumably, the day will come when all the country is stalled somewhere on a freeway, with all of us "living like kings." We cannot hope to do anything about the discontents of our urban civilization until we at least recognize that many of our problems stem from the fact that most of us want more and more of what has already made us sick.

New Explanations of Old Problems

Such analysts as Jane Jacobs and Ed Banfield, the brightest of guiding lights today urging reexamination of our underlying assumptions concerning the city, have been pointing out that we are the culprits of the urban situation in other ways as well. Professor Banfield's new book, *The Unheavenly City*, and Mrs. Jacobs' two books have a special impact, not only because they tell us something we need to hear about our cities, but also because they are written by figures thoroughly acceptable to the "Establish-

[4]Dubos, pp. 163–164.

ment." They are not cranks and have no record as dissenters. The result may well be a fresh look at urban problems, a look commanding widespread respect.

Among the causes of our urban discontents, we should include the side effects from other, apparently unrelated events. For example, a substantial proportion of the present urban welfare group which is such a large problem in the inner city today has been made up of southern Negroes, who were first driven from the land by minimum wage legislation and by federal farm subsidy favoring larger operators, and then attracted to northern cities by the currently dominant welfarist philosophy.

Government has been involved in city problems in other ways as well. Public transit and taxi licensure in the cities has reduced competition and aggravated transportation difficulties. The federal "freeway" system has forced all Americans to subsidize highway construction into big cities. The result? More and more roads, more and more traffic, suburban developments greater and greater distances from the city, more and more congestion in the city, caused by the cars of people whom we have bribed to drive to the city on a highway system provided at "public expense." A side effect of subsidizing the auto traffic which strangles our cities has been to retard development of an efficient, low-cost mass transit system for urban areas. When railroads are in the death grip of government-backed unions and the rigid rate schedules of the ICC, what hope is there for competition with the automobile, especially when the automobile driver receives a whopping subsidy? Meanwhile the cities strangle in auto traffic and the fumes of pollution.

Professor Banfield has also pointed out some of the ways in which government has been creating its own class of urban poor, guaranteeing unemployment through minimum wage legislation (which has the effect of pricing unskilled labor out of the market). The unskilled poor are then further penalized by the existing government-backed labor union monopoly, which in many cases denies work in skilled trades to the worker on the bottom of the economic pyramid. It is not coincidental that the worker thus deprived of a job often proves to be a Negro.

Denied a job or access to the skills whereby he might acquire a job, the victim of urban poverty then often finds that his home is bulldozed by an urban renewal program. Since urban renewal tears down more dwelling units than it builds, and since the average rental costs of the housing erected on urban renewal sites is far above the poor's ability to pay (1965's *average* rental on urban renewal sites was $235 a month, hardly a rental calculated to solve the housing problems of poor people!), the result is that the poor are forced into other lower-income neighborhoods. The increased population pressure tends to reduce the new neighborhoods to slums, while driving up the price of housing because of increased demand. Thus the urban poor are required to pay more for slum housing, while the city finds itself with steadily more slums.

From the view of the urban poor, it must be hard to see beneficial effects from such government programs. On humanitarian grounds, we do our poor man out of a job, deny him access to the skills whereby he might get a job, tear down his housing, and force him into more expensive, less satisfactory accommodations. Small wonder our slum dwellers are resentful! One scarcely need delineate the effects of such policies upon city life as a whole.

Despite the sad results of political "solutions" in other areas, we continue to believe that we can institute and enforce political planning in the city:

> There is a wistful myth that if only we had enough money to spend — the figure is usually put at a hundred billion dollars — we could wipe out all our slums in ten years, reverse decay in the great, dull, gray belts that were yesterday's and day-before-yesterday's suburbs, anchor the wandering middle class and its wandering tax money, and perhaps even solve the traffic problem.
>
> But look what we have built with the first several billions: low-income projects that become worse centers of delinquency, vandalism and general social hopelessness than the slums they were supposed to replace. Middle-income housing projects which are truly marvels of dullness and regimentation, sealed against any buoyancy or vitality of city life. Luxury housing projects that mitigate their inanity, or try to, with a vapid vulgarity. Cultural centers that are unable to support a good bookstore. Civic centers that are avoided by everyone but bums, who have fewer choices of loitering place than others. Commercial centers that are lackluster imitations of standardized suburban chain store shopping. Promenades that go from noplace to nowhere and have no promenaders. Expressways that eviscerate great cities. This is not the rebuilding of cities. This is the sacking of cities.[5]

At the same time, the "neighborhood-killing" effect that accompanies welfare and urban renewal projects drives small businessmen and growth capital from what *used* to be good neighborhoods:

> Meantime, all the art and science of city planning are helpless to stem decay — and the spiritlessness that precedes decay — in ever more massive swatches of cities. Nor can this decay be laid, reassuringly,

[5]Jane Jacobs, *The Death and Life of Great American Cities* (New York: Vintage Books), p. 4.

to lack of opportunity to apply the arts of planning. It seems to matter little whether they are applied or not. Consider the Morningside Heights area in New York City. According to planning theory it should not be in trouble at all, for it enjoys a great abundance of parkland, campus, playground and other open spaces. It has plenty of grass. It occupies high and pleasant ground with magnificent river views. It is a famous educational center with splendid institutions — Columbia University, Union Theological Seminary, the Juilliard School of Music, and half a dozen others of eminent respectability. It is the beneficiary of good hospitals and churches. It has no industries. Its streets are zoned in the main against "incompatible uses" intruding into the preserves for solidly constructed, roomy, middle- and upper-class apartments. Yet by the early 1950s Morningside Heights was becoming a slum so swiftly, the surly kind of slum in which people fear to walk the streets, that the situation posed a crisis for the institutions. They and the planning arms of the city government got together, applied more planning theory, wiped out the most run-down part of the area and built in its stead a middle-income cooperative project complete with shopping center, and a public housing project, all interspersed with air, light, sunshine, and landscaping. This was hailed as a great demonstration in city saving.

After that, Morningside Heights went downhill even faster.

Nor is this an unfair or irrelevant example. In city after city, precisely the wrong areas, in the light of planning theory, are decaying.[6]

A New Concept of the City?

It should be clear to all but the most hapless politico that other, nonpoliticalized solutions to our urban problems are required. Decentralization may prove to be the answer, at least for many people. Most Americans, even at this late date, do not live in large metropolitan centers. In the years ahead, the number of those who do not prefer the big city is likely to grow even larger. If we are to become "a nation of cities," perhaps our preferences should produce a nation of relatively small and middle-size communities, avoiding many of the problems now plaguing us.

Market pressures could do wonders in solving our problems, *if* we allowed them to function. For example, the Negroes who have so largely been denied a full role in American life, precisely because of the very governmental interventions designed to "help" them, could use a free hand to good advantage in infusing our inner cities with new purpose and vigor. All we

[6] *Ibid.*, pp. 5–6.

need to do is stop blocking their path to upward mobility by trying to use political means to freeze our urban centers in previously accepted, white middle-class patterns. The Negro is inheriting the inner city anyway — why not see what he can do with it? Let the individual, black or white, cooperate voluntarily. Let men decide their own wages, achieve their own skills, choose their own homes and exercise their own responsibilities, without interference. The desire for prosperity and decency is not limited to white people.

Meanwhile, the longings for quiet and privacy which have already started the white, middle-class exodus from the cities will probably continue. The market value for decentralization is going up and will continue to rise, especially if we stop subsidizing centralization, through such schemes as freeways.

For others, the city will continue to have a real function. Just as some people prefer space, others prefer crowds. "Overcrowding" is a highly relative condition. Those for whom the diversity, growth, and vitality of the city is attractive would make a profitable market for those wishing to cater to the diverse tastes which compose a free city. In the absence of restraints and "planning," the city could again play its traditional role as the center of civilization and community.

In places where zoning and government interferences do not block the way, capital is already becoming available for such new departures. Houston, Texas, the only large American city not crippled by zoning, was the scene of a recent announcement of a proposed 32 square block, $1.5 billion mini-city, financed entirely by private capital. The new development has attracted private capital because it proposes to give Houston what the market wants, not what the central planner dictates. As the result, there's a scent of profit in the air that promises results, for Houston and for the developers. Such a development is poles apart from the usual centrally planned urban development which seldom attracts private capital in sufficient quantity, because of the oppressive restrictions involved.

Technological Answers?

The market pressures which are generated by freedom from central planning could also do wonders in providing technological answers to urban problems. The giant modern city has outgrown technology because our concept of the city has been tied to the view that the city is essentially a political unit, subject to political control. If the urban center comes once again to be primarily a cooperative venture of men unrestrained by government in pursuit of their various peaceful satisfactions and decisions, the result could be a burst of technological advance, *at a profit*, resolving present problems in waste disposal, transportation, housing, clean air, clean water, and clean environment.

Faith in People?

The heart of the present urban crisis is not technology. The heart of this problem, or any of our problems, is people. The city of humane proportions will be peopled with individuals who value themselves. In city after city, the job of reformation has already begun, centering on a sense of individual responsibility to do something about one's own neighborhood. In New York City, "Operation One Better Block" has over 300 neighborhood groups concerned with discharging their own responsibilities on their own streets. Mrs. Mattie Coney of Indianapolis and her husband Elmo have provided real leadership in Negro slum neighborhoods in a similar program. Mrs. Coney knows that the job can be done by no one else. She has repeatedly turned down government money, realizing that it is the dead hand of government which has already done so much harm.

In all these prospective solutions to city problems — technological advance, population shifts, an end to obstructive government efforts to "help" — the idea has been implicit that market action would solve many problems if given the chance. Again and again I must add that "the market" is nothing more nor less than the framework within which people make their own choices and set their own values, while allowing others to do the same. Most of the harm in our present system stems from our collective unwillingness to allow others to make those choices for themselves. The city, like a person's life, is shaped in the last analysis by the way people feel about themselves.

Regionalism

An afterword is in order on this discussion of the city and how its problems might be solved. While the city will no doubt be an enormously improved institution in a society which leaves men free to choose, some individuals may still prefer the freedom of a less centralized pattern of life. It is important that their freedom of choice also be protected.

Actually, there is more room to move than recent "population explosion" hysterics would imply. We suffer a population implosion in the United States. Our problem is less "more people" than it is "centralized people." Our people have drained together into the artificial world of the present politicized city. The result is that the wide open spaces are more wide open than they have been for many years. In the United States deer, bear, and beaver are returning to areas from which they have long been extinct. The end of our nonurban world has not yet come.

This fact raises interesting possibilities for our national future. T. S. Eliot, in his *Notes Towards the Definition of Culture,* emphasized the concept of "regionalism" as a proper social goal. Regionalism, as Eliot defined it, was a concept of local cultural autonomy insisting that it was both desirable and possible to have numerous cultures and subcultures within one social and economic order. The idea could offer Americans a degree of cultural autonomy which we might achieve in no other way. If we were to put politics back in its strictly limited place, if our urban civilization were on a truly self-sustaining and vital basis, to what uses might this great American land be put by men who preferred their own life-styles to what the city had to offer?

Such cultural autonomy could be achieved by men in a truly free society, be it in the urban center, in the smaller community, or in total isolation:

A third friend of mine . . . is a farmer with a face like leather, who owns either 80 or 100 acres of stony ground, on which, by much exertion, he raises potatoes and beans and cucumbers, and keeps a few cows. Intensely independent in character, he resents any endeavor to convert him into another sort of man than the being he is by nature and circumstance. He wants to live as his father lived before him, and to bring up his children in his own steps. He is well enough satisfied with the cabin that always has been his home. He knows that it is highly imprudent to disturb a thing that is at rest; he has a suspicion of most change, although he understands that society, like the soil, can grow sterile from lack of cultivation. But he is convinced that certain moral axioms never can be cast aside with impunity, and that a mysterious continuity guides the destinies of men, as surely as the seasons follow their cycle. A hater of centralization, a lover of old habits and old stories, in his little community he stands out with some success against the ascendancy of the mass-mind and against the threatened conversion of society into a mere state-supervised economic operation, rather than a way of living.[7]

The reader may insist that not many would prefer such a way of life as an alternative to modern consumer capitalism. I am not so sure. But even if only one man had such a preference, the greatest glory of a free society would be a political, economic, and social system in which that one man could maintain his cultural independence.

The same necessity for individual choice applies to both city and country. Let the country stay countrified! Let the city be as varied and alive as the people who live there. It is the dull hand of planning and enforced conformity that does the harm.

[7]Russell Kirk, *Prospects for Conservatives* (Chicago: Regnery, 1956), pp. 21–22.

XXII

PSYCHOLOGICAL VALUES

It is time we asked ourselves exactly what we are lumping together in mass organizations and what constitutes the nature of the individual human being, i.e., of the real man and not the statistical man.

C. G. Jung,
The Undiscovered Self

Men derive their reasons for living from their creativity. Our need to create, to fulfill our purposes in life, is much misunderstood. Often we mistake "creativity" for some mysterious quality possessed only by artists, geniuses, and the like. When we mislabel creativity in such fashion, we sell ourselves short. Creativity is present in any job we do — not for pay, or fame, or gratitude — but for the sheer joy of doing that job. Those who understand the zest which comes from doing a job well, whether a teacher in a class-room, a mother making a bed, or a boy painting a fence, are all creative. The world's work is as much a creative undertaking as each of us makes it.

Some men are more original than the rest of us. Such human beings at their best produce the great music, art, philosophy, and science. And when such original beings achieve their own brand of creation, the achievement always proves to be a highly individual undertaking. Groups can expand and apply original ideas; they cannot create them. The same gift which supplies our creativity also supplies our individuality, by insuring that one quality cannot exist without the other. In the absence of the chance to choose and perform useful work, the chance to be creative, men cannot long remain individuals. In the absence of the chance to be an individual, creative impulse does not long endure.

Despite the highly individual nature of creation, it is far from a random, hit-or-miss proposition. Arthur Eddington once made the casual remark that a monkey, hitting the keys of a typewriter at random, would sooner or later produce all the plays and poetry of Shakespeare. This is the kind of scientistic assumption of random probabilities which presumably renders obsolete the whole idea of unique and peculiarly individual creativity. It is the sort of statement to which our age is much addicted. It is also a statement without any foundation in fact. Random processes, performed by monkey or computer, are not creative.

Taking as his example the sonnet beginning, "Shall I compare thee to a summer's day / Thou are more lovely and more temperate. . . ," one sceptical mathematician, Dr. Jacob Bronowski, senior fellow of the Salk Institute for Biological Studies in San Diego, has calculated the probabilities of either monkey or computer producing Shakespeare at random:

> It is a thousand million years before the monkey comes to print once, in the right order, the letters of the first three words as far as the "e" in "compare". It would therefore be 25 thousand million years before he correctly hit a sequence which went on to the next letter, "t". But the universe is not 25 thousand million years old. It's only between 15 and 20 thousand million years old, and life is only between four and five billion years old. So the answer is that Shakespeare couldn't happen. In the universe as it is, picking at random, you can't get beyond the first three words "Shall I compare" in the time it has taken from the beginning of the universe until now.
>
> Now, if you substituted a computer for the monkey, I calculated that the most powerful computer, typing one letter at random every millionth of a second from the beginning of time until now, could conceivably have reached the letter "u" in "summer."
>
> That really shows that by random processes you could never have written any poetry yet.

Yet a great deal of poetry has been written by those unique beings, men. Surely something besides random process has been at work:

> Art and the process of nature consist of solving problems that cannot be rightly formulated until they are actually solved and then you know what the problem was.
>
> This is what distinguishes life from the computer. You see why my monkeys or computers didn't type very well? They were just programmed for random numbers. But if I had programmed them for the Shakespeare sonnet, then I would also have had to give them the plan. But of course, there is no point in having a computer write a poem for me which I have already written.
>
> The whole point about evolution and invention and creation is that it follows a program that has not been written.

"Creative man" implies a Creator, One who set in motion a process giving meaning to our acts of free will. The result — creativity, a unique process peculiar to the individual human being. Apparently the creative act demands a connection between the individual and the transcendent reality of the universe. Apparently the achievement of what we call "personality" is really the capacity of the individual to draw strength simultaneously from this world and the next. Certainly something of the sort is a recurring theme in Western literature.

This linkage between creative human personality and a transcendent order does not demand an other-worldly quality in the individual. Surely Goethe's observation to Schopenhauer holds true: "If you will enjoy the value of your own personality, you must enjoy the value of the world." He might have said: If you would be creative, you must first be in tune with Creation.

What our literary men have continued to tell us over the centuries, in one of the greatest human themes ever developed, is that the achievement of personality and the development of creativity demand an individual's recognition of his unique potentialities and responsibilities. This is the first step in the task of living, a task which only the individual can hope to accomplish by and for himself. The job requires self-knowledge, staying power, and hard work, and is never complete, at least not in this life.

Men must discover their own reason for living. "Security" and "equality," the shibboleths of our age, are not to be bought or given by any man. They must be earned anew by each of us. They do not come as the result of a material condition, but through achievement of a state of mind.

So long as men had little or nothing in material terms, it was possible to assume that "when we have thus and so, we shall be happy." Yet the addition of innumerable material "thus and so's" does not seem to have brought happiness to many people. Men, at least some men, are beginning to look about them for some more genuine source of happiness, some more convincing reason for living. Can happiness ever be found except in living life in consonance with God's plan, in tune with the natural order, in line with human nature?

Self-Actualization

Human nature being what it is, work and accomplishment seem an inescapable prerequisite for such happiness. Just as each creative act plays its part in creation's final form, the act of *being* human is contained within the constant process of *becoming.* We actualize ourselves by means of the time, energy, and effort we give to the tasks faced in living our daily lives.

The power to do what needs doing comes from within us. The exercise of that power, like the exercise of any faculty, gives us more power, more capacity, more of what the world calls "character," to deal with the next challenge which will inevitably arise. Life is filled with a seemingly endless string of such challenges. Successful living consists of rising to the occasion.

We find our successes in response to different challenges. The challenges of some are likely to be far more prosaic than others, but we are all born with capacities to meet challenge; the use and development of those capacities offer us our greatest chance for happiness. This is the practical, commonsense message of the workaday world. It is also the most profound message of Western religions: "If you would be happy, overcome your *self,* grow, master the inner weaknesses which otherwise will master you."

To phrase this message in psychological terms: It is the resolution of problems which brings integration of personality. The reason for living can be stated in various ways, but it always seems to involve trying for something. The "something" is far less important than the "trying," because it seems to be successful effort which achieves the integration of self, producing personality:

> It seems a threshold fact that personality is some kind of integration. The individual whom we regard as having authentic personality appears to possess a center, and everything that he does is in relation to this. When such a person performs an act, no part of his being seems uninvolved; what happens on the outer circumference is duly controlled by the integrating center. We sense, sometimes with a feeling of envy, that this individual is a unitary being and thus "in possession of himself." Of course, there are poorly integrated or disintegrated "personalities," but these we classify as unformed or degenerate just because they fall short in this property. The true personality is a psychic unity, preserving its identity and giving a sort of thematic continuity to the acts of the individual.[1]

One of the most perceptive of modern psychologists was Professor Abraham Maslow of Brandeis University. Maslow's highly descriptive term for the possessor of the integrated personality was the "self-actualizing person":

> Another meaning of autonomy is self-decision, self-government, being an active, responsible, self-disciplined, deciding agent rather than a pawn, or helplessly "determined" by others, being strong rather than weak. My subjects make up their own minds, come to their own decisions, are self-starters, are responsible for themselves and their own destinies. It is a subtle quality, difficult to describe in words, and yet profoundly important. They taught me to see as profoundly sick, abnormal, or weak what I had always taken for granted as humanly normal; namely that too many people do not make up their own

[1]Richard M. Weaver, "Individuality and Modernity," *Essays on Individuality,* ed. Felix Morley (New York: American Book–Stratford Press, 1958), pp. 63–64.

minds, but have their minds made up for them by salesmen, advertisers, parents, propagandists, TV, newspapers, and so on. They are pawns to be moved by others rather than self-moving, self-determining individuals. Therefore they are apt to feel helpless, weak, and totally determined; they are prey for predators, flabby whiners rather than self-determining, responsible persons. What this nonresponsibility means for self-choice politics and economics is of course obvious; it is catastrophic. Democratic self-choice society must have self-movers, self-deciders, self-choosers who make up their own minds, free agents, free-willers.[2]

The importance of Maslow's observation is immediately apparent for our present society. All too many of us and most of our social institutions distrust and penalize the self-actualizers among us.

Most of what passes for psychology today seems to deny the primacy of the individual, the vital integrating sense of I AM I. We spend most of our time studying the behavior of those lacking this feeling of personal identity, studying the deviations rather than the norm:

It becomes more and more clear that the study of crippled, stunted, immature, and unhealthy specimens can yield only a cripple psychology and a cripple philosophy. The study of self-actualizing people must be the basis for a more universal science of psychology.[3]

It is time for a new emphasis upon the study of freedom and the study of free men. "As a man thinketh, so is he," and lately we have had a rather low opinion of ourselves.

If we should accept Maslow's self-actualizer as our standard, one important step would already have been taken from the cloudy and largely negative view of human personality causing so many of our institutional problems. Men are more than impotent reactors — they are active, responsible agents! The goal for such men is not "adjustment" to a sick institutional world. Our proper goal is adjustment of that institutional world to the personality and needs of men at their best.

The Restoration of Personality

How is such a goal achieved?

The restoration of the dignity of work would be a good beginning. A man who is happy with his work and life is not a likely candidate for the many

[2]Abraham H. Maslow, *Motivation and Personality* (2nd ed.; New York: Harper and Row, 1970), p. 161.
[3]*Ibid.*, p. 180.

discontents to which modern man falls prey. A reawakening of professional pride, of the joys of craftsmanship, rather than preoccupation with the shortest possible working hours and the largest possible paycheck, would go a long way to relieve the boredom and impotence that plague us.

The reemphasis of status would also help to make us whole men once again. The status of personal property, the status of the self-reliant man, the status of the man with a purpose in the community, would go far to restore many of us to dignity in our own eyes:

> . . . every person needs to have a sense of his place, or what is often called a sense of belonging. A sure knowledge of status, I think, confers this more than does anything else. Much of the subconscious anxiety and feeling of lostness from which many people suffer today results from this broadscale attempt to do away with status, which is like doing away with home. Home is the place where our status is known and duly respected. Change for its own sake, and function as the sole criterion, have brought about a condition of mobility such that many people no longer feel that they have a place, physical or spiritual. I am inclined to think that pure function or activity, without a backdrop of status, is meaningless.[4]

One vital way of restoring status, especially to young people, would be a reduction of our institutions to a size in which individuals come again to know what purpose they play in their little platoon. There exists no better example of such an institutional need than on the monster campuses of higher education, in which teachers and students no longer have any real idea of their traditional role and have turned to politicalized mob action as a substitute for true education.

It is sometimes charged that a return to status, with its accompanying reliance upon the dignity of work and the necessity of self-help, would turn us from concern for our fellowmen. On the contrary, the only genuine means of helping one another would be the reinstitution of individual responsibility, status and purpose. A good beginning for those who sincerely wish to help their neighbor is a desire to give of self, instead of attempting the impossible task of enforcing a "fair" division of other people's property.

A restoration of personality which drew upon renewed status, dignity, and capacity for the individual would provide the greatest of gifts: a chance to grow. Growth takes place in privacy, in the inner reaches of personality where the depth and mystery of the individual's heart and soul hold sway. It is there, in that innermost reality, that creativity, growth, and happiness

[4]Weaver, "Individuality and Modernity," pp. 71–72.

originate. Our institutions must be so structured as to permit such development, else they become worse than meaningless:

> Happiness and contentment, equability of soul and meaningfulness of life — these can be experienced only by the individual and not by a State, which, on the one hand, is nothing but a convention of independent individuals and, on the other, continually threatens to paralyze and suppress the individual.[5]

Maturity implies ability to walk alone, and with that ability and the process of struggle which makes it possible, men find themselves. When we interfere with the process, no matter how humanitarian our intention, the results are disastrous. A reason for living cannot be provided by institutional bigness or by more material goods. Like all elements of personality, a reason for living must come from within.

[5]C. G. Jung, *The Undiscovered Self* (New York: New American Library, 1964), p. 124.

XXIII

CULTURAL VALUES

The American, it is true, is often haunted, in the midst of all his surface activity, with a vague sense that, after all, his life may be deficient in depth and dignity. . . .

Irving Babbitt,
Literature and the American College

Perhaps it is this vague sense of deficiency which causes so many of us to become other-directed, abdicating our judgments and tastes to group decision. Having thus lost dignity and purpose, today's young radical and his middle-class parents often have little idea who they are or where they are going. In the process, the sense of community, participation, identity, and direction seems to escape us.

There is no shortage of contemporary cultural critics who are more than willing to bring this identity crisis to our attention. Certainly many things are badly out of phase in our present culture, but American society is far from dead. We have deep spiritual roots founded upon recognition of the scope and complexity of human nature. We have a deep sense of personal and social responsibility. We need to bring these qualities to the surface once again through restitution of an institutional structure which values purpose, diversity, continuity, family, genuine leadership, and the need for individual choice. We need an institutional structure that allows men to believe in themselves.

Need for Purpose

Our present cultural confusions leave us none too sure who and what we are, because we lack the sense of values and purpose which could give us direction:

Why are we on this verge of moral and hence nervous collapse? . . . I believe it is because we have reached the end of a road and have no new path to take, no duty to carry out, and no purpose to fulfill. The primary purpose of mankind has always been to survive in a natural world which has not invariably been friendly to us. In our written, remembered, and sensed history, there has always been more work to do than we could do. Our needs were greater than their possible fulfillment. Our dreams were so improbable that we moved their reality into heaven. Our ailments, our agonies, and our sorrows were so many and so grievous that we accepted them either as inevitable or as punishments for our manufactured sins.

What happened to us came quickly and quietly, came from many directions and was the more dangerous because it wore the face of good. Almost unlimited new power took the place of straining muscles and bent backs. Machinery took the heavy burden from our shoulders. Medicine and hygiene cut down infant mortality almost to the vanishing point, and at the same time extended our life span. Automation began to replace our workers. Where once the majority of our people worked the land, machines, chemistry, and a precious few produced more food than we needed or could possibly use. Leisure, which once had been the property of heaven, came to us before we knew what to do with it, and all these good things falling on us unprepared constitute calamity.[1]

All of us need to *do* something on our own as a first step toward doing something with our lives. Today even our amusements are purchased ready-made. We watch others compete rather than competing ourselves. We listen to music rather than make music. We rush from unsatisfying and impersonal jobs to unsatisfying and impersonal vacations. Many of us have forgotten how to play and forgotten how to work.

Men prefer to feel important, useful, proud, respected; and these feelings come about in situations which provide meaningful work and play. The stronger our sense of participation in business, family, or community affairs, and the more we give of ourselves, the greater the likelihood such work and play will have real meaning for us. This works with children as well as adults:

In the homes that made America a strong and happy nation there were many things to be done. There was fuel to cut; as soon as a youngster was able to handle a little ax he helped to chop wood and carry it in and pile it up in the cellar or the woodhouse. He lent a hand cutting ice in the winter and clearing away the snow. He assisted in the cultivation of the garden and in the care of the household animals.

[1]John Steinbeck, *America and Americans* (New York: Viking Press, 1966), pp. 140–141.

There was cooking to be done and cleaning and mending. Father and mother and children cooperating, the family came to know and respect and love one another in an educative fashion. That sort of thing has today become artificial and dispensable. Where to keep cows and pigs and chickens if one wants them? Why keep them if butchering is more economical when mass-handled and milk is something that comes in a sanitary bottle and eggs are done up in neat cartons? Where can one have a garden in Megalopolis? Automatic devices do most of the housework. Gone from the home are those crafts the sharing of which was the best part of family life and the most effective device for character development. Children no longer feel that the home is *their* home, that they are contributing or can contribute anything much to its support and welfare.[2]

To be successful, a culture must allow each generation the chance to re-create *within itself* a reason for living. Institutional enmassment has largely denied that chance to our present generations — both those who are denied all chance for self-help by a beneficent big government, and those who are denied a sense of accomplishment, challenge, and individuality by a social structure so enormous that little room remains for the expression of personality.

Need for Cultural Diversity

The best hope of reordering the social structure in such fashion as to restore the individual's sense of purpose lies in decentralization as a means of achieving the greatest possible cultural diversity. Such diversity, allowing and indeed necessitating the flowering of numerous subcultures within which the individual could work, play, cooperate with others, and help mold his institutions to his needs *on his scale,* would again clarify the relation of the individual to himself and to his society.

The individual has the best chance in a society which permits and even encourages many different centers of authority, inffluence, opinion, taste, and accomplishment. These things grow out of associations freely entered into by persons of common necessity, interest, or geographical habitat.[3]

However offensive such notions might be to our present mass-oriented cultural framework, those free associations of individuals could center on

[2]Bernard Iddings Bell, *Crisis in Education* (New York: Whittlesey House, 1949), pp. 91–92.
[3]Richard M. Weaver, "Individuality and Modernity," *Essays on Individuality,* ed. Felix Morley (New York: American Book–Stratford Press, 1958), p. 80.

class, locality, custom, community, on any autonomous group or combination of groups which attracted the individual. Loyalty to a particular group is less important in itself than the principle of loyalty for its own sake. Men need to identify with the world around them, and loyalty to our little platoon in life provides that identity.

The free society, since it offers the widest possible cultural diversity, holds real hope for restoration of America and its individual values, so long as we remember that the free society itself can remain operative only if its citizens preserve and cultivate those loyalties to their roots which permit the social order to function. Occupational orders and autonomous groups both serve such a function:

> . . . a number of orders, with distinct functions and responsibilities, is a benefit to society, rather than a violation of free institutions. The ministry of religion is an order; the body of scholars and teachers is an order; a guild or union of skilled craftsmen is an order; the multitude of small farmers, taken collectively, is an order; the profession of medicine, or of law, is an order; the management of industry is an order; the class of shopkeepers is an order. When men recognize their membership in a decent and responsible order, when they are not mere flies of a summer, then that sense of membership and duty is reflected in a respect for law and for social decency . . . the sense of order, of honorable membership, is a great force for good, and ought to be encouraged. . . .
>
> The autonomous groups . . . are church, family, guild or union, local community, school and university, all the complex of voluntary associations which combine freedom with love, and satisfy man's need for companionship at the same time they provide for his security. These free instruments for the welfare of men bring a psychological satisfaction, a sense of membership, that the mass-state cannot possibly supply.[4]

"Loyalty begins with what is near," Richard Weaver wrote. And from that loyalty grows a sound social order.

Need for Continuity

Continuity is required in a culture's values and institutions, because men's loyalties will not attach to what is always changing. When change becomes too rapid and too frequent, a people's cultural memory becomes impaired. Yesterday seems distant and unimportant. Today becomes only a way station to the future. Tomorrow generates hopes which become

[4]Russell Kirk, *Prospects for Conservatives* (Chicago: Regnery, 1956), pp. 206, 142.

desires. When the past becomes irrelevant, cultural values also become irrelevant, except for one all-consuming value: change for its own sake. Throughout history the necessity for continuity has been demonstrated again and again. One of the certain hallmarks of an inferior culture has been an antihistorical attitude, an addiction to present-mindedness.

In our present culture, we are starved for history, especially history based upon highly individualistic epics and eras. Witness the continuing appeal of the western frontier in TV and movies. However corrupted such representations may become, the significance of the frontier tradition gives clear evidence of the need for continuity. Somehow even the most "modern" of us are beginning to suspect that a society which does not pass along its beliefs to succeeding generations is soon likely to have no beliefs at all.

Need for Family

The family has always been one of the institutions whose responsibility it is to pass the beliefs of a society from generation to generation and thus maintain cultural continuity:

> Young persons do not acquire in school, to any considerable extent, the sense of continuity and the veneration for the eternal contract which makes possible willing obedience to social order; children acquire this sense from their parents and other elders, and from their gradual introduction to religion, if they obtain any; the process is illative rather than deliberate. Now let us suppose that parents cease to impart such instruction, or come to regard tradition as superstition; suppose that young people never become acquainted with the church — what happens to tradition? Why, its empire is destroyed, and the young join the crowd of the other-directed whom Mr. David Riesman describes.[5]

The daily family life of the common people is important to the cultural order in another way as well. As Carlyle once suggested, ". . . the happiest hours of mankind are inscribed on the blank pages of history." I believe Carlyle was telling us that the unrecorded daily lives of the little people are of far greater importance than the rise and fall of governments and the machinations of the power brokers. The true measure of a culture lies in the quality of the life lived within that culture. And there exists no better measure of life, for young and old, in work and play, in moral and educational pursuits, than the family and the integration of human personality which it provides at its best.

In a word, the family is culturally significant because it is the conservator

⁵ *Ibid.*, pp. 278–279.

of private, individual needs and responsibilities which the collectivity cannot hope to protect. Above all other institutions, the family should serve as the custodian of the spirit and manners of a people. To the extent that we have allowed this vital institution to degenerate into a process of mere procreation, feeding, and housing, we have betrayed our children and ourselves.

Need for Genuine Education

One of the most vital functions of the family is the education of children. However astonishing the idea may be to our present society, education *is* a family function. No school can hope to serve in any greater capacity than as an extension of parental responsibility. Our present highly politicalized, compulsory educational system is a significant failure in that regard. The present publicly financed educational bureaucracy aggressively asserts its "social" educational goals and denies the primary parental responsibility. The result has not only undercut the family function, but has set in motion a standardized, enmassed educational operation wonderfully adept at the making of mass-men.

The mass-men being churned out on all levels of present education are not likely to have much exposure to the cultural and moral traditions which make a lasting social order possible. We seem to spend more and more money on "education," though we have progressively lost sight of proper educational goals.

Big education and its sad effects on modern youth have already been described in some detail in a number of books, including my own *Education in America.* Simply stated, those effects are in two general categories: a philosophic decline which denies underlying values of lasting significance, and a social decline which stems from a sweeping denial of individual personality.

The resultant collapse of educational standards on the elementary and secondary levels is a cause for concern in most American communities today. Of equal concern, and far more likely to make the headlines, is the situation in higher education. Institutional enmassment and vast expenditure of public funds for higher education have swept all standards and values before them, in the fervent belief that the solution to all problems lies in providing a college "education" for everyone, regardless of interest or ability. The results are seldom educational. The age of the enormous and impersonal survey class and IBM card "processing" is very much with us.

Of even greater danger for our culture is the fact that we have subsidized a large class of "intellectuals" who reject the values upon which this culture is based. Don't go to today's university campus if you wish to hear kind words devoted to such mundane values as the family, the individual, honor, thrift, patriotism, or similar traditions.

We have pushed our children through 12 years in a totally formless educational structure, leaving them without values or sense of direction. Meanwhile, we have subsidized the creation of a generation of intellectuals who totally reject the values of our society. Finally, we have also subsidized an environment in higher education which brings these potentially explosive forces together. The predictable result has been the creation of an "adversary culture" in our midst.

The results have been ugly, on campus after campus, but a word of warning is in order. However reprehensible our present college and university community may have become as the result of institutional enmassment, we must beware the tendency to use political power in correcting the situation. The autonomous university community has usually been a seat of traditional values and a haven for the individual against church and king. At its best it can again be such a haven against the assaults of democratic politicalization. In fact, our present discontents on the university campus are largely due to the extent to which we have accepted political authority (financing, standards, controls, values) in an institutional area where that authority does not belong.

The point of all education and the point of any social institution or organizational form is to give people the opportunity to be more fully themselves, *at their best.* Our present education structure on all levels simply does not live up to that obligation. Privatism is the answer. Government must be divorced from education. Genuine education and government education are contradictions in terms. The values, standards and individual emphasis necessary for genuine education are simply not possible in politicalized schools. As more and more people realize this, a move toward privately financed, privately controlled elementary and secondary education is rapidly growing.

Meanwhile, even on the largest most completely enmassed campuses of higher education, autonomous groups of professors, men concerned with the task of educating, are beginning the restructuring of the university along educative rather than political lines. Whether these men will be successful working within the present educational structure remains to be seen. Whether the job of education can be done by restructuring the present institutions of higher education, or whether true men of learning will move to new institutional forms, there *is* a minority of students on hand who wish to learn, and a minority of professors who wish to teach. They will find each other, politics notwithstanding.

Need for an Elite

A properly functioning educational system can provide the leadership necessary for society's continuing operation. The self-imposed discipline of culture, which is the end product of a sound educational system, will produce a minority whose standards and capacities far exceed the levels reached by the rest of us. From that minority will come the leadership which is an absolute necessity for any society.

It will be immediately objected by many in our mass-conscious age that what I am suggesting is an elite, a return to the dark days when the rich or the "well-born" controlled affairs. I do suggest the necessity of an elite, though not the kind that most democrats have in mind.

Many things have moved our culture from emphasis upon the highly endowed, morally upright individual, capable of real leadership, toward the mass-man concept of ourselves and our society. We are so "present oriented" that we no longer accept the idea of self-discipline and self-restraint upon which all real leadership depends.

Perhaps the future-oriented, disciplined personality types whom psychologist Abraham Maslow described as "self-actualizing" form the leadership community from which will spring a cultural renaissance founded upon individual personality. Perhaps what we most need today is a growing body of individuals who possess *inner* freedom and who do not derive their primary values from the mass-oriented culture around them. Such men, possessors of tolerance, taste, and informed opinion, could work wonders. The essence of such a leadership elite could permeate society:

> The great ones of the race have been invariably and contagiously men and women who did their own thinking, who respected tradition and reinterpreted it and built upon the past. . . .
>
> In a democratic society an elite can justify itself if, and only if, it helps the Common Man to perceive what the good life is, what the democratic life may become. By such an elite the Common Man can be assisted, though with difficulty, to become more than a well-paid hewer of wood and drawer of water and tender of machines, more than a mere producer and consumer of goods, more than an ant in a mechanized and collectivized anthill. . . .[6]

We underrate the power of the self-actualizing individual to help in molding the opinions and the taste of those whom his life touches. The possibilities under the leadership of such an elite are beyond measure.

Need for Individual Choice

The question for our times is less "Are these goals desirable?" than "Are these goals possible?" Are cultural diversity, responsible individualism, a leadership community of taste and standards, genuine education, and the

---

[6]Bernard Iddings Bell, *Crowd Culture* (Chicago: Regnery [Gateway Edition], 1956), pp. 105, 96–97.

other goals of an effective culture possible in our present society? Given the current state of affairs, the future seems dark at times. Consider the state of mass communications. Here we see stunning technological achievements reduced to broadcasting on the lower levels of mass uniformity. Most of our programming denies the very existence of variety, diversity, and taste.

As in so many other areas, the fundamental cause of this culturally destructive situation has been our unwillingness to allow development of individual choice and a free market.

One specific measure taken by the FCC has perhaps done more than any other single thing to stifle diversity and enshrine mediocrity. That is its refusal to authorize subscription or pay television. The FCC has ruled that we may not spend our money to see programs we wish to see. We must accept the programs that are provided as a by-product of advertising. We cannot, even if we wish to, pay to suppress the advertising, except by contributing to and watching an educational television station.

To understand how this measure has such a far-reaching effect in enshrining mediocrity in television and radio, let us consider what the effect would be of applying the same rule in a comparable area to which it is not now applied. Suppose it were legislated that reading matter could not be sold but must be given away, that all newspapers must be like the "throwaways" now often given out, that all magazines must be available without charge, financed only by the revenue from the advertising they contain or by a subsidy from a church, foundation, or other organization, and similarly that any books published must be financed in the same way and distributed without charge to readers. It takes no great act of the imagination to see the results: Those books and magazines that appeal to relatively small groups with specialized tastes would disappear. Few if any advertisers would deem it worthwhile to pay for the publication of avant-garde poetry in order to be able to insert pages extolling the virtue of Gleem or Dreem or Steem. Far better to put those pages in a Western that millions would pick up and read avidly. The book publishing industry would become like television—a wasteland of Westerns, mysteries, and popular romances, with an occasional serious work appealing to a limited audience sponsored by a firm trying to improve its public image. . . .[7]

Of course, to propose the free market as a solution to present cultural disorders is to be laughed out of court. But it is the alternative to the free

[7]Milton Friedman, "The Market v. the Bureaucrat," *National Review*, May 19, 1970.

market which presents a truly ironic picture. Why do we persist in believing that popular taste can be revolutionized by government intervention? Surely by now the weight of evidence to the contrary is too large to be overlooked any longer.

The virtue of the free market need not be primarily economic. It is true that a free society produces more goods, but it is more important that a free society produces better men. Leaving people free to make their own choices demands social cooperation and enlightened self-interest, qualities likely to have far-reaching cultural effects.

"To thine own self be true and it must follow, as the night the day, thou canst not then be false to any man," Shakespeare's oft-quoted advice is usually interpreted on the level of personal integrity. Why not raise that advice to a synergistic level, applying it to the restoration of a truly moral society:

> Every one of us incurs a greater debt to some other than he can ever repay. God meant it so, I think, to teach us our solidarity. If you are in debt to me, I do not realize it; but the sense of it will move you to pass the gift along to many another with big interest. I am in debt to many people — so very many.[8]

Such a view of a free society under moral obligation to generations long dead and generations yet unborn should suggest to us that the answers to our present discontents do not lie in more control over men's lives. The real answers lie in a different direction. All the diatribes against the "free market" as the presumptive cause of poor taste, materialism, and selfishness really tell us nothing about the free market and a great deal about ourselves. If we don't like the choices we are making, let's not further curtail the capacity to choose. Instead, let's expand the area of choice as a first step toward improving the quality of our choices — *there is no other way.*

It is in the culture of a society, not its consumption, that the choices of lasting importance are made. And it is in cultural terms that the argument for individual freedom must be advanced:

> Of what avail is any amount of well-being if, at the same time, we steadily render the world more vulgar, uglier, noisier, and drearier, and if men lose the moral and spiritual foundations of their existence? Man simply does not live by radio, automobiles, and refrigerators alone, but by the whole unpurchasable world beyond the market and turnover figures, the world of dignity, beauty, poetry, grace, chivalry,

---

[8]Francis J. Nock, (ed.), *Selected Letters of Albert Jay Nock* (Caldwell, Idaho: Caxton Printers, 1962), p. 20.

love, and friendship, the world of community, variety of life, freedom, and fullness of personality. Circumstances which debar man from such a life or make it difficult for him stand irrevocably convicted, for they destroy the essence of his nature.[9]

We must not, indeed cannot, *force* a change in people's lives and standards, but proper education and example, stemming precisely from an *absence of force* (private education; private responsibility; smaller, more private units in all phases of life) could bring about a lasting change in cultural values. It is here that a true leadership elite comes into play.

No people can ever become a great people by exchanging their individuality, but only by developing and encouraging it. We must build on our own foundation of character, temperament, and inherited traits. We must not repudiate but develop. We must seek out and appreciate our own distinctive traits, our own traditions, our deep-rooted tendencies, and read our destiny in their interpretation.[10]

Need for Literary Values

One area of leadership demands special attention if we are to regain our cultural bearings: We must discover and encourage a literary elite to illuminate the road which needs to be traveled.

Most American literature of the twentieth century has been so alienated from this culture as to provide little constructive cultural leadership. Sherwood Anderson, Theodore Dreiser, Van Wyck Brooks, Sinclair Lewis and the rest have told us a great deal about what is wrong with our culture (and, indeed, much *has* been wrong), but have provided very little sense of what values and attitudes are worthy of emulation.

Most recent literary production has not shown improvement. Mindless sex and violence, couched in a setting of nonvalues, are the literary order of the day:

... there is something positively absurd in the spectacle of prosperous suburban fathers flocking to see — and evidently enjoying — *The Graduate*, or of prosperous, chic, suburban mothers unconcernedly humming "Mrs. Robinson" to themselves as they cheerfully drive off to do their duties as den mothers. This peculiar schizophrenia, suffusing itself through the bourgeois masses of our urban society, may be fun while it lasts. . . .[11]

[9]Roepke, *A Humane Economy* (Chicago: Regnery, 1960), p. 89.
[10]*The Life and Speeches of Charles Brantley Aycock* as quoted in Richard M. Weaver, *The Southern Tradition at Bay* (New Rochelle, N.Y.: Arlington House, 1968), p. 377.
[11]Irving Kristol, "Urban Civilization and Its Discontents," *Commentary*, July 1970.

"This peculiar schizophrenia," however much "fun" it may be, shows no sign of abatement. The novel, movies and television continue on their morbid and mindless path. The antihero of contemporary literature is a spectacle of self-doubt and self-hatred, displaying impotence, incapacity and nonvalues at every turn. A demonstration of the individual who is guided by the knowledge and habit of honesty, courage, and integrity, who has values and who therefore values himself, is sadly lacking on the literary scene, with a very few honorable exceptions. The reality of the individual has been lost, and the cultural price of that loss is enormous:

When this reality, the one and only power that checks and disciplines man from within, vanishes because belief in it is slackening, the social domain falls prey to passions. The ensuing vacuum is filled by the gas of emotion. Everyone proclaims what best suits his interest, his whims, his intellectual manias. To escape the void and the perplexities of his own soul, a man will rush to join any party standard that is being carried through the streets.[12]

Good art, like the good life, depends upon a proper attitude toward the world around us. Self-discovery of that proper attitude can be achieved by each of us in the pages of a book, provided the book was written by a man who had kept his values intact, and whose gifts of imagination and insight allowed him to share those values with us:

Barring the advent of an illumination by some fateful personality, the task falls upon poets, artists, intellectuals, upon workers in the timeless. We must again harken to these unacknowledged legislators of mankind. They alone can impress us with some splendid image of man in a morally designed world, ennobled by a conception of the transcendent. They will have to abandon, and I am sure they will be ready to abandon, the tortured imaginings of our vexed decades.[13]

The men capable of providing such leadership will be those who first of all have come to grips with their own lives. The artist who can be such a leader must first be a whole person, even if the effort involved in that task limits the time and energy he has left for his art. He must be a man who has come to understand that, "The sane would do no good if they made themselves mad to help madmen." Only such a man, a man unwilling to compromise either the standards of his work or the standards of his personal life, can provide the necessary literary leadership.

[12]José Ortega y Gasset, *Concord and Liberty* (New York: Norton, 1946), p. 20.
[13]Weaver, *The Southern Tradition at Bay*, p. 392.

Until now, the great paradox of the present-day struggle of ideas has been that those who favor room-to-move, quiet, family, and a highly individualistic way of life have themselves been required to depart from such a way of life in order to carry on the fight for their values in the crowded and hectic centers of influence where society's attitudes are being molded. This may no longer be true. The literary leadership I describe will be coming increasingly from those who have withdrawn from the present cultural milieu and rediscovered their own values. Then and only then will they become the literary leaders we need.

The conservative/libertarian position especially suffers at present from the dearth of such leadership. Political economists we have aplenty — whom of comparable rank do we have in literary pursuits? There are some few, but how pitifully few. Few indeed can present the case for human personality and the values on which it rests in the *mythic* terms that can capture not merely the minds, but the imagination of men. Some realities must be *felt* to be communicated. Such realities are thus best expressed in mythic terms. The mythic erosion our society has suffered during the present century has therefore tended to divorce us from reality and from ourselves.

Lest the unfamiliar use of the word "myth" mislead the reader, let me cite Russell Kirk's definitions:

> Myth, fable, allegory, and parable are not falsehoods; on the contrary, they are means of penetrating to the truth by appealing to the moral imagination. . . . A myth is a poetic representation of hidden reality. . . . [F]able, allegory, and a parable are coming into their own once more; and as it was in the beginning, their purpose is ethical, rousing the moral imagination of a people. . . .[14]

Thus, what I refer to as "myth" should more properly be described as fable, allegory, and parable, though all literature of high moral purpose, literature containing the power to catch the imaginations and fire the souls of men, is included in my use of the term. John Bunyan's *Pilgrim's Progress* is a classic example of such literature. More recently, C. S. Lewis, Ray Bradbury, J. R. R. Tolkien, and a few others have also shown us the way to a restoration of our values. Men must believe in events and causes larger than their daily lives if they are fully to believe in themselves. When we fail to order our lives in terms of that larger picture, self-disinheritance is the result.

We can stop disinheriting ourselves by discovering and encouraging a

---

[14]Russell Kirk, *Enemies of the Permanent Things* (New Rochelle, N. Y.: Arlington House, 1969), pp. 111–112.

literature which appeals to the sense of mystery surrounding our lives, a literature which touches the joys and sorrows, the hopes and fears, involved in being a human personality. Our salvation then may be largely in terms of developing new forms to deal with new problems (or new manifestations of old problems), but these forms will have validity only if those of us living in society have a deep appreciation for the ideal of human life and individual personality which makes the whole effort worthwhile. Ideals are never achieved; they are only approximated. Thus the really basic salvation will by mythic in nature, as the genuine salvations for men must always be.

In our scientistic age, we underrate myth. But its possibilities for redemption are enormous. Its hold upon us is more than we know. The lure of the American West, with its room-to-move, its action, its code of honor, has never left the national consciousness. The Mythic American, in all his individuality, his courage, his indomitable capacity to overcome all problems, demands reconstruction for ourselves and our posterity.

Perhaps what I am saying is that the battle for human freedom and dignity must be won in men's souls as well as their minds. The weapons for such a victory must be mythic in nature. I do not discount the uses of the mind in the job of political, economic and social education which lies ahead, but I speculate that the development of a literature which fully expresses and challenges the American character at its best will prove the ultimate weapon in freeing the souls of men. It is in the field of literature that we have most completely abandoned the field to the enemy, leaving a few embattled partisans to stand alone. And it is high time that we joined the fray.

Concluding Thoughts

The formative element in any culture is the view people have of themselves. We must find our own reasons for living. Are people to be fully themselves, moving in a cultural order encouraging variety and individual personality? The answer is in our hands.

I do not pretend to know all the answers, or even all the questions. It *does* seem self-evident that the American people are out of touch with themselves and are losing the peace of mind which used to characterize our culture. What they are losing is something more than small towns, peace and quiet, and leisure — they are losing what made them great. Rather, the greatness of the American people is being taken from them.

I do know that the American people could stop that loss if once they made up their minds to do so. The determination to be different, to be ourselves, is still operating. If left to our traditional diversity, we *can* discover the right answers to the fundamental question: How do we live on a truly human, truly individual scale in the new and rapidly changing world which is now coming upon us?

XXIV

MORAL VALUES

I suggested that we take a good straight look at what the pattern of living has become in the mid–twentieth-century America, at why our way of life is in danger of debacle, at how it is increasingly difficult for anyone with sensitivity to human possibilities to live in such a civilization as ours simply, honestly, bravely, satisfyingly. I arrived at a conclusion, in which I hope a good many of my readers share, that our present difficulties are so great and so basic as to demand nothing short of revolution, not so much political revolution or economic revolution as moral revolution, a revolution in estimate and pursuit of values.

Bernard Iddings Bell,
Crowd Culture

A great deal of what has been said in these pages must seem little more than a collection of vague suggestions. How are we to achieve these goals, allowing the individual to emphasize the psychological and cultural values which make the good society possible? I must confess that I do not know. I do know that such goals can be achieved only by people who feel that they *ought* to be achieved. The word *ought,* applied in social concerns, implies the prevalence of men accustomed to thinking in moral terms. Only for the moral man does the word *ought* have any real significance.

Perhaps, then, I have been asking for a moral renaissance as the solution to our problems. This may seem an imprecise solution to our present discontents, but there is no other solution.

A number of penetrating thinkers, men not easily taken in by the intellectual fads of their age, have recognized that a time of crisis is fast approaching in the Western world, a crisis in which we must either redefine the purpose of our civilization, or cease to have any purpose for continued existence. Whittaker Chambers warned that we could lose the Cold War even while "winning," if in the process we came to embrace the same materialistic, collective goals and methods of our opponents. Ortega stated the same problem in another way, warning that Western men no longer place their faith in the truths by which society formerly was ordered. Both men stressed the moral nature of the crisis, reminding us that the controlling factor in human affairs is the body of philosophic assumptions which men accept as their basic premise in life.

To be sure, there are other aspects to the problem, in addition to the factors of institutional enmassment stressed in this book. We suffer from a number of intellectual fads peculiar to modern America: for example, the behaviorist dogma, the ritual belief in "equality," and the easy acceptance of unlimited majoritarianism. These ideas have not been discussed in these pages, partially because it was my belief that such concepts have already received ample examination in the work of many analysts, myself included.[1] It also seemed to me that the features of our present institutional geography could best be grasped if viewed in isolation from the rest of the intellectual scene. There appeared to be a real danger that the less familiar institutional analysis presented here might be lost in the discussion of the far more familiar aspects of this generation's intellectual currents. Still, a common thread connects all the intellectual fads of our present society. The ideas and attitudes producing institutional enmassment, like the other dominant ideas of our time, depend upon their own special view of morality, a morality deriving from certain "modern" assumptions concerning human nature.

The past decade alone has seen publication of such best sellers as Robert Ardrey's *African Genesis* and *The Territorial Imperative*, Desmond Morris' *The Naked Ape* and *The Human Zoo*, and Konrad Lorenz' *On Aggression*. These books have had wide intellectual appeal, and their underlying message is a denial of free will, an insistence upon biological determinism, and a consequent, though usually implicit, denial of more traditional views of human nature and morality. Thus these books and many others of similar nature are an expression of the thinking which produced in our society what Richard Weaver has termed "a felt loss of center." As I have said before in these pages, we are no longer so sure of who we are and what we are expected to do with our lives.

It is astounding that man, the instigator, inventor and vehicle of all these developments, the originator of all judgments and decisions and the planner of the future, must make himself such a *quantité négligeable*. The contradiction, the paradoxical evaluation of humanity by man himself, is in truth a matter for wonder, and one can only explain it as springing from an extraordinary uncertainty of judgment — in other words, man is an enigma to himself.[2]

The result of that "extraordinary uncertainty of judgment" has been the most complete secularization of culture the world has ever known. In the

---

[1]George C. Roche III, *Legacy of Freedom* (New Rochelle, N. Y.: Arlington House, 1969).
[2]C. G. Jung, *The Undiscovered Self* (New York: New American Library, 1964), p. 55.

absence of inner spiritual values and responsibilities for the individual —
the traditional moral framework — we have substituted a modernist faith
in externals and social "rights," to be guaranteed by the collectivity. Modern politics is the natural result of that transition in moral values.

Now, that political structure which promised to be all things to all men
is beginning to disintegrate. What the planners of political heaven-on-earth
failed to take into account is that lasting political cohesion demands common moral beliefs and attitudes, and such are impossible in a social order
which denies the validity of all fixed values. The political regime which
cannot discover a universal definition of justice cannot govern justly — and
soon cannot govern at all.

Institutional Religion

As the political structure fails in the absence of moral direction, it would
seem natural to turn to organized religion for leadership. Unfortunately, the
direction of most modern institutional religion is decidedly secular. The
institutional enmassment which has attacked so many aspects of our lives
has not spared the churches. Today they are among the institutions most
oriented to unviable political schemes and least concerned with the inner
spiritual dignity of the individual. The honorable exceptions are so exceptional as to prove the rule. Traditionally, the role of the Church was to
confront a failing world with God. Today the struggle of a remnant within
the various denominations is to confront a failing church with God.

> There is small expectancy, then, that those who belong to the Church
> will be able to set this reeling civilization of ours right side up and then
> steady it. The Church and its people too largely conform, unconscious
> that they do conform, uncritically conform, almost automatically
> conform, to the compulsions of current culture. They seem largely to
> have forgotten that witness to a divine moral law in the face of a
> worldly secularist human society which has always constituted, and
> still constitutes, religion's right to claim social pertinence. The world,
> hurtling on toward political, economic, psychic catastrophe, is not
> going to be saved, if it is saved at all, by the Church if the Church
> remains an uncommitted host of politely respectable people, willing
> to be led by professional ecclesiastics whose methods of promotion
> and administration are just about as worldly as those of the sick
> society they say they wish to reform but which, as a matter of fact,
> deforms them almost as easily as it deforms everybody else. If the
> Church is to help in restoring the world to moral sanity, there must
> first be revolt and recovery of moral sanity within the Church.[3]

[3]Bernard Iddings Bell, *Crowd Culture* (Chicago: Regnery [Gateway Edition], 1956), p. 67.

In Christopher Dawson's monumental *Religion and Culture*, the case is developed at some length that the institutional Church has historically been strongest when it exercised moral leadership by refusing to come to terms with the social order in which it found itself. Conversely, the Church has provided the least moral leadership in periods when it has identified itself most closely with the cultural synthesis of its society. Today the identification of organized religion and our contemporary cultural synthesis is almost complete — with the predictable result that the moral leadership coming from the Church is at a new low.

Individuals seeking spiritual guidance and moral instruction often find themselves cast in the role of reactionaries within their churches. Often such individuals are far more outspoken in defense of religious and moral values than many of the contemporary clergy. In today's institutional religious world, more and more people are finding that they must look elsewhere for their moral leadership.

Alternative Sources of Moral Leadership

Some sociologists of religion are predicting the end of institutional religion in its present form before the year 2000. Whether or not the changes are so sudden and sweeping as such a prediction would indicate, it does appear that change is underway. The "underground church" is a common phenomenon in all denominations, as people cast about for the religious and moral leadership which many of the churches fail to supply. The underground church is a fine example of the evolution which is possible from enmassed institutions which are not responsive to individual needs, to new patterns of social cooperation among those members of the leadership elite who are capable of developing a new institutional framework. The result in many cases is a new religious vitality, often more reminiscent of the early Christians, meeting in tiny but dedicated groups, than the meaningless social religion of many nominal Christian churches of today.

As such religiously committed individuals provide moral leadership for themselves and their children, the institutional churches sniff at such radical departures from the trite formulas of social religion. But whether the moral leaders I describe work inside or outside the present institutional structure, the issue is drawn more clearly each year:

> Whoever argues for a restoration of values is sooner or later met with the objection that one cannot return, or as the phrase is likely to be, "you can't turn the clock back." By thus assuming that we are prisoners of the moment, the objection well reveals the philosophic position of modernism. The believer in truth, on the other hand, is bound to maintain that the things of highest value are not affected by the passage of time; otherwise the very concept of truth becomes impossi-

ble. In declaring that we wish to recover lost ideals and values, we are looking toward an ontological realm which is timeless. Only the sheerest relativism insists that passing time renders unattainable one ideal while forcing upon us another.[4]

The timeless nature of moral values has its appeal for the common man concerned with the proper upbringing of his children, as well as for the literary leadership elite who can contribute so much to everyone's understanding. Among the intellectuals deeply attracted to religious values have been some of the finest minds of our time: T. S. Eliot, Evelyn Waugh, C. S. Lewis, and many more. The late Dorothy Sayers predicted a religious revival of greater intensity than anything in the past two centuries, and the revival now under way among laymen and a dedicated minority of the clergy may yet fulfill her prediction. Such individuals understand the real meaning of Scottish philosopher George MacDonald's assertion: "There is no massing of men with God. When he speaks of gathered men, it is as a spiritual *body,* not as a *mass.*"

The Responsible Individual

Those who are willing to assume the task of providing their own moral leadership are likely to display large amounts of humility and responsibility. George Washington Carver loved to describe a dream he once had, in which he conversed with God. He respectfully asked that the Lord might explain to him the riddle of the universe.

"No, George, that knowledge is reserved to me alone."

"Then, Lord, can you explain to me the riddle of the peanut?"

"Yes, George, I can let you learn about that, for that is more your size."

Such displays of humility are all too uncommon in a world which is likely to emphasize neither the individual nor God. Such humility should cause us to suspect that good ends are nothing without good means, that enmassed institutions, presumably designed to serve people, can hardly perform that task when they refuse to treat those people as individuals. The individual moral leaders who can guide us from the wilderness will be those who first recognize that we are *all* responsible when we participate in an institutional process which imposes itself on other peoples' lives. So long as we are willing to lend our support to such processes, in the mistaken belief that good ends can come from such bad means, the level of moral understanding among us will guarantee more of the same failures we have already incurred.

Granted that the right way is usually not the easy way, the question

[4]Richard M. Weaver, *Ideas Have Consequences* (Chicago: University of Chicago Press, 1948), p. 52.

remains: Is it possible for such morally responsible individual leadership to redirect our present society?

> . . . people, I am certain, greatly underestimate the power of men to achieve their real choices. But the choices must be real and primary, not secondary, ones. Men will often say that they want such and such a thing, and true, they do want such and such a thing, but it turns out that they want something else more. It is what they want most that they will be most active, ingenious, imaginative, and tireless in seeking. When a person decides that he really wants something, he finds he can surpass himself; he can change circumstances and attain to a goal that in his duller hours seemed unattainable. As an old teacher of mine used to say, "When you have done your utmost, something will be given to you." But first must come the honest desire.[5]

With that honest desire, the job can be done. Certainly those who effect great revolutions are always small in number. Such people need not wait to become a majority. No one else can do the job except those who understand what needs to be done.

The price of such individual action is likely to be high. In Emerson's words: "God offers to every mind its choice between truth and repose. Take which you please — you can never have both." Never was that choice more clearly presented to the individual than in the America of the 1970s.

If the individual is to search for truth as a means of discovering his own reason for living, the first step in that search is a sense of God in one's life:

> "I want to know why," one of the most native of our voices [Sherwood Anderson] asked in a line that rises out of all else he did and said because it sums up all the rest. I want to know why. It is for this we seek a little height. . . . Happy is he who finds any height, however lowly.[6]

Men finally can find true freedom in neither society nor nature, but only within themselves. A man can free no tiny portion of the world until he himself is free. Such freedom is not handed to us ready-made by any social or institutional system. Each of us has to make it for himself, by bearing witness to a moral level which the collectivity can never grasp:

[5]Richard M. Weaver, *Life Without Prejudice* (Chicago: Regnery, 1965), p. 119.
[6]Whittaker Chambers, *Cold Friday*, p. 85.

To those for whom the intellect alone has force, such a witness has little or no force. It bewilders and exasperates them. It challenges them to suppose that there is something greater about man than his ability to add and subtract. It submits that that something is the soul. Plain men understood the witness easily. It speaks directly to their condition. For it is peculiarly the Christian witness. They still hear in it, whenever it truly reaches their ears, the ring of those glad tidings that once stirred mankind with an immense hope. For it frees them from the trap of irreversible Fate at the point at which it whispers to them that each soul is individually responsible to God, that it has only to assert that responsibility, and out of man's weakness will come strength, out of his corruption incorruption, out of his evil good, and out of what is false invulnerable truth.[7]

It takes such faith to believe that free men will prevail. At a time when all the world seems to sanction the denial of individual responsibility, it takes faith to understand that no determinism has ever offered sufficient compensation for the loss of self, for the loss of the chance to be a real person. Such a faith comes only from the recognition of God within each of us. Such a faith promises, in the words of Robert Frost:

> Back out of all this now too much for us . . .
> Here are your waters and your watering place.
> Drink and be whole again beyond confusion.

[7]Whittaker Chambers, *Witness* (Chicago: Regnery, 1952), pp. 762–763.

EPILOGUE

A Reason for Living

As long as we are thinking only of natural values we must say that the sun looks down on nothing half so good as a household laughing together over a meal, or two friends talking over a pint of beer, or a man alone reading a book that interests him; and that all economics, politics, law, armies, and institutions, save insofar as they prolong and multiply such scenes, are a mere ploughing the sand and sowing the ocean, a meaningless vanity and vexation of spirit. Collective activities are, of course, necessary; but this is the end to which they are necessary.

> C. S. Lewis,
> *An Address to the Society of St. Alban and St. Sergius*

Admittedly, this book is a strange mixture of puffs and pans. Americans and their institutions are simultaneously criticized and praised. The criticism is directed toward an advanced stage of institutional decay that confronts us on every hand. The praise is for the courage, zest, energy, and moral sense that still abound among us despite every politicalized, enmassed attempt to kill such individual values.

It has been my thesis that the institutional enmassment which afflicts us has come about because of our failure to defend our values from the right premise. *We give away the case* when we limit ourselves to the materialistic and the collective, rather than the spiritual and the individual. Such a distinction is often attacked by Right and Left as a "nostalgic yearning for a simpler world," before the discovery of the Cold War or the War on Poverty or some other cause presumably making spiritual and individual values hopelessly old-fashioned. The resultant materialism and enmassment which pervades so much of the thinking on both Right and Left is the number one enemy of individual personality.

What solutions do I propose? No nine-point programs for social reform are likely to solve our problems. People must understand that they can look only to themselves for their salvation. The farmer may have only one cow, but let it be *his* cow, not the "public cow," not one of the cow's belonging to "the cow industry." Each of us must husband his own resources, material and spiritual, and in the process must find his own "reason to be." Anything less makes too little of each of us. When we have our own place, our own

responsibility as an extension of our personality, we can find a real reason
for "free enterprise." No amount of cliché or hypocritical, self-serving
double-talk from those who profit through government-induced bigness can
fill the vital need in the life of the individual.

We must learn that anyone who promises to care for us through the
substitution of institutional bigness in place of our own efforts is either
stupid or out to take us.

The rewards to the individual for taking such a stand are likely to be high.
He will know who he is and what he can do. He will know the meaning
of dignity, self-respect, pride, responsibility and those other terms which
serve to identify the whole man. He will emphasize *freedom*, not "adjustment."

Such goals will be attained through a fusion which could happen only in
America — a combination of libertarian and conservative attitudes. Men
left free to pursue their own goals are most likely to adopt sound, traditional
values and responsibilities, most likely to preserve a viable social order and
the healthy institutions it requires. Who is more likely to value freedom
and order than the self-responsible man?

In Christopher Dawson's phrase, "Behind every civilization there is a
vision," a vision providing form to that civilization. What better vision for
our civilization than "elbow room," room for the individual to discover and
pursue his own goals?

What are the alternatives? Electronic Man? Economic Man? Technological Man? Collective Man? How about less talk concerning MAN, and more
emphasis upon men, peculiarly unique, marvelously different men?

Throughout this concluding section of the book, I have suggested various
means of reemphasizing the individual's place in the sun, offering certain
values which would go far toward restoration of an institutional framework
suited to individual human beings. Don't politicalize the lives of men; leave
them free to make their own choices; allow the individual's innate sense of
community to reassert itself; emphasize the real over the contrived, the
natural over the unnatural; above all, emphasize the spiritual over the
material. These changes become possible only as individuals take a different
and more elevated view of themselves. Then and only then will our institutions, our society and our politics be on a humane scale. Before a social
order can have any reason for continued existence, each man within that
society must first discover his own reason for living.

Whittaker Chambers once insisted that the proper question was not,
"Will the West be saved?" but "Should the West be saved?" My answer to
both questions is yes — the West *will* be saved, because it *should* be saved.
But the salvation will not come from more polemics of Right and Left. It
will come from a poetic, figurative analysis that touches the wellsprings of
the earth and of men's hearts. Life *is* worth living, despite the terrible things

we do to one another. The pressing necessity of finding "a life worth living" is nearly inexpressible. Most expressions of such a concept are likely to be trite and meaningless. That is why I suggested earlier that only fiction of a highly artistic order could carry such an enormous emotional and symbolic load without being crushed. But it can be done. We need men *and* values of mythic and heroic proportion. Americans once had such a myth — such a dream, such a vision of themselves — with men and values to match. We can recapture the dream — and the decision is in our hands.

Acknowledgments

Any author who stops for a moment to consider the process which produced a book suddenly discovers that he has had far less to do with that process than he might have expected. In every stage of development—the formation of ideas, the actual writing, the editing —many influences take a hand in producing the final result. Prefaces are written in recognition of that fact.

In my case, special thanks are due to several people whose influence and assistance were especially important in the writing of this book: Mr. Al Purdue, in whose company the idea of *The Bewildered Society* first took form; Dr. Paul Poirot, whose common sense and editorial advice made such an important contribution; Miss Vern Crawford, who did her customarily fine job of indexing; and particularly Mrs. Muriel Brown, whose patience, dedication and integrity were present at every stage of the book's development, making the entire project possible.

To these, and others too numerous to mention, I owe a vote of thanks and *The Bewildered Society* owes its existence.

GEORGE C. ROCHE III

INDEX*

References to chapters and parts of chapters under the appropriate subject classification are hyphenated. The number in each other instance generally refers to the *first* page of a discussion. The letter "n" following a number indicates a footnote.

Prepared by Vernelia A. Crawford